NEWS, NEWSPAPERS, AND SOCIETY IN EARLY MODERN BRITAIN

BOOKS OF RELATED INTEREST

THE EMERGENCE OF QUAKER WRITING
Dissenting Literature in Seventeenth-Century England
Edited by Thomas N. Corns and David Loewenstein

TELLING PEOPLE WHAT TO THINK
Early Eighteenth-Century Periodicals from *The Review* to *The Rambler*
Edited by J.A. Downie and Thomas N. Corns

PAMPHLET WARS
Prose in the English Revolution
Edited by James Holstun

AUTOBIOGRAPHY AND QUESTIONS OF GENDER
Edited by Shirley Neuman

EDWARD CARPENTER AND LATE VICTORIAN RADICALISM
Edited by Tony Brown

COLERIDGE AND THE ARMOURY OF THE HUMAN MIND
Essays on his Prose Writing
Edited by Peter J. Kitson and Thomas N. Corns

News, Newspapers, and Society in Early Modern Britain

edited by

JOAD RAYMOND

FRANK CASS
LONDON • PORTLAND, OR

First published in 1999 in Great Britain by
FRANK CASS AND COMPANY LIMITED
Newbury House, 900 Eastern Avenue, London IG2 7HH, England

and in the United States of America by
FRANK CASS
International Specialized Book Services, Inc.
5804 N.E. Hassalo Street, Portland, Oregon 97213-3644

Copyright © 1999 Frank Cass & Co. Ltd

British Library Cataloguing in Publication Data

News, newspapers, and society in early modern Britain
   1. Newspapers - Great Britain - History - 17th century
   2. Newspapers - Great Britain - History - 18th century
   3. Press - Great Britain - Influence - History - 17th century
   4. Press - Great Britain - Influence - History - 18th century
   5. Newspapers - Social aspects - Great Britain
   I. Raymond, Joad
   070.1'7'0941'09032

ISBN 0 7146 4944 9 (h/back)
ISBN 0 7146 8003 6 (p/back)

Library of Congress Cataloging-in-Publication Data

News, newspapers, and society in early modern Britain / edited by
   Joad Raymond
      p. cm.
   Includes index.
   ISBN 0-7146-4944-9. — ISBN 0-7146-8003-6 (pbk.)
   1. Press - Great Britain - History - 17th century.
   2. Press - Great Britain - History - 18th century.
   3. Journalism - Social aspects - Great Britain.
   I. Raymond, Joad.
   PN5115.N49   1999
   072'.09'032 - dc21   98-45230
                                   CIP

This group of studies first appeared in a Special Issue of *Prose Studies*, Vol.21, No.2
(August 1998), [News, Newspapers, and Society in Early Modern Britain].

Contents

Acknowledgements

This volume began life during 1994 and 1995 as a seminar at Magdalen College funded by News International plc; I should like to express my gratitude both to News International and the President and Fellows of Magdalen for their support. This translated into a one-day conference at the Centre for English Studies, London, entitled "The News, 1600–1800," on 10 May 1997. I should like to thank the Centre for English Studies for its accommodation, administration, and financial generosity, and particularly Warren Chernaik for his characteristic helpfulness. Those who participated in the seminars and conference created a dialogue that left its mark on this volume in several ways, and I give them my thanks. I should like to single out Nigel Smith and Luc Borot, both lively interlocutors who had hoped to contribute but were unable to do so. Finally, I offer my appreciation to the contributors for their patience, cooperation, and their work.

JR
Cambridge, December 1998

Introduction: Newspapers, Forgeries, and Histories

JOAD RAYMOND

Scholarly study of the newspaper and its history arrived with a forgery, which frustrated the endeavour to write the story of periodical news even before the significance of that story had been recognized. In the 1740s Philip Yorke, second Earl of Hardwicke, wrote, as part of a literary game with a circle of friends, five issues of a periodical newspaper, entitled *The English Mercurie*. He gave them the date 1588, a credible date for a pamphlet, but precocious for a numbered periodical. Three of these fabrications were then printed, with imperfect attention to old spelling and typography.[1] In 1766, the historian Thomas Birch, a collaborator in Hardwicke's literary circle, bequeathed, among his other papers, both manuscript and printed copies of *The English Mercurie* to the British Museum. He left no comment on their nature or provenance. The potential of this contrivance to deceive lay dormant until a Scottish antiquary named George Chalmers stumbled across the forgeries in the 1790s. Chalmers, who was conducting research for a biography of Thomas Ruddiman, seized upon the supposed early newspapers as evidence of England's prodigious contribution to the craft of news.

Chalmers' *The Life of Thomas Ruddiman* (1794) is a curious mixture of biography and cultural history, combining a sensitivity to the relationship between a life, scholarship and political change with a Jacobite's resistance to the transformations in ideology and intellectual debate that occurred in the mid-eighteenth century.[2] Ruddiman, a scholar and keeper of the library of the Faculty of Advocates at Edinburgh, had worked for some years as a printer then proprietor of the *Caledonian Mercury*, an Edinburgh newspaper founded in 1720 and regarded by Chalmers with some pride as an emblem of Scottish civilization. His versatility gave Chalmers the opportunity for numerous digressions of a philological and antiquarian bent, none more impressive and surprising than a discussion of early newspapers:

> The origin of news-papers, those pleasant vehicles of instruction, those entertaining companions of our mornings, has not yet been

Joad Raymond, University of Aberdeen

investigated with the precision, which is undoubtedly due to what has been emphatically called one of the safeguards of our privileges. We are still unacquainted with the name of our first news-paper, and we are still ignorant of the epoch of its original publication.[3]

Chalmers offers a narrative account of the emergence of newspapers in England and Scotland; and he appends a series of substantial bibliographies of English and Scottish newspapers of the seventeenth and eighteenth centuries.[4] Using bibliographical evidence alongside literary satire, he traces the development of periodicity as the defining characteristic of the newspaper and sketches the parallel growth in the rest of the world with sensitivity to the distinction between printed and manuscript news. Thus he comments that while Venice had entertained "Gazetta" since 1536, these were not printed, as "a jealous Government did not allow a *printed* news-paper."[5] He notes the appearance of *Mercurius Gallobelgicus* (which he dates incorrectly to 1605, rather than 1594), and claims that it is not a newspaper as it is both too large and too infrequent. And the 1588 *English Mercurie* enables him to speak with pride:

> After inquiring, in various countries, for the origin of news-papers, I had the satisfaction to find what I sought for in England. It may gratify our national pride to be told, that mankind are indebted to the wisdom of Elizabeth, and the prudence of Burleigh, for the first news-paper. ...
>
> Yet, we are told, that posts gave rise to weekly news-papers, *which are likewise a French invention* ... the *English Mercurie* will remain an incontestible proof of the existence of a printed news-paper in England, in an epoch, when no other nation can boast a vehicle of news of a similar kind.[6]

Chalmers paradoxically acknowledges that his 1588 newspaper is occasional rather than fully periodical, published when the Elizabethan Secretary of State "wished, either to inform, or to terrify the people."[7] Yet for him it is proof that the English invented the first printed newspaper, the guardian of the people's democratic liberties.

Like many eighteenth-century Scottish authors, Chalmers is a cultural amphibian, moving freely (if not without discomfort) between habitats left divided by the 1707 Act of Union.[8] He feels qualified pride in English accomplishments, and qualified embarrassment at Scottish under-achievement: "It is a remarkable fact, which history was either too idle to ascertain, or much too ashamed to relate, that the arms of Cromwell communicated to Scotland, with other benefits, the first news-paper, which had ever illuminated the gloom, or dispelled the fanaticism, of the North"

(117). Yet Scotland shares the triumph of England's international precedence in the newspaper, and the foundation of the *Edinburgh Gazette* in 1699 is part of the same narrative. Notwithstanding – or perhaps because of – the contradictory impulses of Chalmers' account, and the turmoil of his politics, nationalism, and philology, it is a remarkable performance. It offered what may be the first serious and scholarly account of the origins of the newspaper in Britain, engaged with bibliographical characteristics and the thorny issues of periodicity, precedence, and origins. Before Chalmers there were of course notes on early newspapers and their forerunners (including the discussion of the Roman *Acta Diurna* in the *Gentleman's Magazine* in 1740, which may have been written by Samuel Johnson[9]), annotations in literary texts, and historical reflections on the power of the press, but no attempt to synthesize a history, and to offer definitions; for newspaper history to come into being, such scattered comments had to be systematized. Many of Chalmer's concerns are our concerns, and the thread of his narrative was soon translated into *Britannica* and other encyclopaedias and into foreign lexicons.[10] A revised version of John Nichols' *Literary Anecdotes of the Eighteenth Century* (1812–16) reported Chalmers' discovery, and an expanded edition of Isaac D'Israeli's *The Curiosities of Literature* (1817) shared in the excitement of "these patriarchal newspapers, covered by the dust of two centuries."[11]

The connection between newspapers, democracy and national self-esteem (already present in Macaulay's designation of the news press as "The Fourth Estate") was to be further elaborated in nineteenth-century newspaper historiography. Unfortunately, the claim to precedence had to be conceded to others. Chalmers' own discovery, and the basis for his pride, was soon debunked. A glance at the typography, orthography, paper, and the hand in which the manuscripts were written was enough to suggest to a librarian at the British Museum that these documents were not as venerable as they claimed. In *A letter to Antonio Panizzi ... on the reputed earliest printed newspaper: the English Mercurie 1588* (1839), Thomas Watts demonstrated with considerable care that the *Mercurie* was an eighteenth-century creation. He subsequently laid the crime at Lord Hardwicke's door. News of the imposture rapidly spread, and D'Israeli renounced Chalmers' work in a later edition, though others continued to repeat the mistake. Surprisingly, one of the forgeries was silently reprinted in the nineteenth century.[12]

Within a few decades Victorian writers had begun to think of the newspaper as something that merited a scholarly history; and the mercurial fraud troubled their conscience. They worried at the dangers of error and ruminated on the immorality of deceiving posterity. The cozening of Chalmers became the founding moment of their scholarship.[13] James Grant found the bait censurable, even if committed as a *jeu d'esprit*, and he criticized Birch for not indicating the inauthenticity of the papers. If it were not for Watts, Grant wrote, "an important historical mis-statement might have been everywhere, and by everybody, implicitly believed till the end of time. The detection of historical errors like this has a very painful and injurious effect when reading the annals of any age or country."[14] It inspired readers, he suggested, with distrust. Perhaps he was unduly pessimistic, however, as the forgery led to epistemological anxiety, which led to laborious rummaging in archives and the painstaking detailing of the story of the periodical press. Nor did the deception deter scholars entirely from negotiating tendentious evidence: one of the characteristics of Victorian histories of the early newspaper is the extensive deployment of literary evidence, including explicitly hostile sources. They recognized that Jonson's satirical presentation of a news office in *The Staple of Newes* (performed 1626, published 1631) offered real insights into the commercial distribution of news in the early seventeenth century. They measured such fictional evidence against hard bibliographical facts. From meticulous navigating of the mounds of dusty evidence, works such as Frederick Knight Hunt's *The Fourth Estate* (1850), Alexander Andrews' *The History of British Journalism* (1859), Henry Richard Fox Bourne's *English Newspapers* (1887) and, later, J.G. Muddiman's *A History of English Journalism* (1908, written under the pseudonym J.B. Williams) established the narratives that dazzle us today, both underpinning modern scholarship, and suggesting its lines of inquiry.

Another driving factor in nineteenth-century histories of newspapers was a belief in democracy. When John Milton figures in these works, it is not through his connections to *Mercurius Politicus* in the 1650s, but as a defender of liberty, especially that of the press. The newspaper emerges pitted in a mortal fight against censorship: Hunt, for example, offers an extended account of the trials and punishments of Henry Burton, John Bastwicke, William Prynne and John Lilburne, victims of Star Chamber in the 1630s. Like Milton, he describes press controls as Roman in origin and nature; they are somehow un-English in character.[15] The anonymous author of *The Periodical Press of Great Britain and Ireland: Or An Inquiry into the State of the Public Journals, Chiefly as Regards their Moral and Political Influence* (1824) expressed the idealism succinctly:

> The Periodical Press of Great Britain is justly the boast of Englishmen, and the envy and admiration of foreigners. It is the most powerful moral machine in the world, and exercises a greater influence over the manners and opinions of civilized society than the united eloquence of the bar, the senate and the pulpit. Like the Steam

Engine, however, it may be said to be in its infancy, for those advantages which it is capable of conferring on the human race, appear to be designed, principally, for future generations. The Press has undoubtedly within itself the seeds of indestructibility; but it is, nevertheless, difficult to determine how arduous and protracted may be the contest which it has yet to wage with the prejudiced and despotic rulers of the Continent of Europe, before its powers or its liberty be recognized.[16]

Though its presumption makes it vulnerable to satire, this statement needs to be remembered as much as it needs to be refined. Utopianism is a powerful force in these narratives; the authors sense the unlimited possibilities of the periodical form. With a more sceptical, ambivalent voice, Thomas Carlyle suggested the extent to which the newspaper had penetrated civil life: "the Journalists are now the true Kings and Clergy: henceforth Historians, unless they are fools, must write not of Bourbon Dynasties, and Tudors and Hapsburgs, but of the Broad-sheet Dynasties, and quite new successive names, according as this Able Editor, or Combination of Able Editors, gains the world's ear."[17]

Of course, such idealism was not born with the Victorians, nor did it die with them. Thomas Jefferson wrote in January 1786 that "Our liberty depends on the freedom of the press, and that cannot be limited without being lost." A year later he elaborated:

The basis of our governments being the opinion of the people, the very first object should be to keep that right; and were it left to me to decide whether we should have a government without newspapers or newspapers without a government, I should not hesitate a moment to prefer the latter. But I should mean that every man should receive these papers and be capable of reading them.[18]

The connection between democracy and a (relatively) free press has been frequently taken as self-evident through much of the twentieth century. For Winston Churchill, freedom of the press was "the unsleeping Guardian of every other right that free men prize," a sentiment endorsed in most histories of the newspaper written in the early twentieth century.[19] Marshall McLuhan, who probably did more than any twentieth-century commentator to insist on radical re-perception of the news media, their inner logic and potentials, assumed a connection between the press and democracy.[20] For McLuhan, the newspaper press was a participatory form, responsive to readers; sensitive to readers' reaction, or "feedback" as it is called in communication studies.[21] A startling evocation of the Utopian dream of the newspaper was offered by the journalist and historian of newspapers Harold

Herd in *The Newspaper of To-morrow* (1930). His subject is the impending emancipation of women:

> Once they have freed themselves from man-made ideas, women will no doubt evolve original newspaper and magazine forms. They will probably use colour liberally, and may print their journals on papers of delicate hues. ... Women will use their newspapers to get better houses, and probably insist on a generous minimum of land for each house, in order to encourage the cultivation of beautiful gardens as one of the most natural and healthy recreations for the masses.[22]

A notable dissenting voice was that of the socialist Norman Angel in *The Press and the Organisation of Society* (1922), which suggested that this former ally in the struggle for political democracy "has become one of the worst obstacles to the development of *a capacity for real self-government*, perhaps the worst of all the menaces to modern democracy."[23] The general connection between freedom as political rights and newspapers was probably most effectively severed by the Frankfurt School, whose dark, post-war vision of Enlightenment and reason challenged optimistic perspectives on the media. It was in reaction to their view of the periodical press as an instrument of ideology, and therefore a constraint upon life, that Habermas developed his account of *The Structural Transformation of the Public Sphere* (1962; English translation 1989). Here Habermas deploys a strategic optimism alongside a highly sophisticated understanding of the relationships between reason, ideology, and commerce. In English studies this remains one of the most influential – if not the most influential – accounts of early newspaper history.[24] Its vision of public critical debate being crushed by the very technology that created it has gained particular currency. It is a deep irony that only a few decades ago, according to McLuhan, secondary school students "could not for a moment accept the suggestion that the press or any other public means of communication could be used with base intent"; whereas now it is difficult to impress the opinion that they can be used for any other intent.[25]

While literary critics (and observers of the media) have been most inspired by theoretical issues, and have allowed their perspectives upon early modern newspapers to be driven largely by present concerns rather than the massive bibliographical developments of the twentieth century (including catalogues of early newspapers), historians have been exercised by the approaches known as revisionism and post-revisionism. The archive-driven works of these schools – if they may be so designated – frequently attend to the means by which information was transmitted, in manuscript and print, and to the extent of the dissemination of news. In the arguments over, for example, the causes or origins of the Wars of the Three Kingdoms in the mid-seventeenth century, news media can play a significant role, as thermometers of public opinion, evidence of political tension, indicators of the shifting language of politics.[26] Yet the part that newsletters and newspapers play is usually a walk-on one; they infrequently occupy centre-stage. Revisionists and their successors rightly had little interest in separating the history of newspapers and other news media from the political narratives they had in hand. As a consequence, we have few studies focused on newspapers which acknowledge the methodological resources and analytical sophistication that have been fruitfully encouraged in early modern historiography in general.[27] High expectations might attend another trend in historiography: the history of reading, which has followed from the increased attention to the history of culture in its broadest sense.[28] Older histories of newspapers tended either to take readers for granted, or to infer readership and the relationship between readers and texts from the newspapers themselves. This is a wholly unsatisfactory procedure, and newspaper history will be substantially modified as more attention is paid to real readers and their experiences, as revealed by diaries, commonplace books, and marginalia.[29]

Viewed from the exclusive perspective of newspaper history, then, the trajectory looks something like this: early modern comments on the press are generally satiric and frequently semi-fictitious; they comment on news pamphlets and newsbooks as innovations, but take it for granted that their readers know what these media are. The late seventeenth and eighteenth centuries see serious philological notes, and a notorious forgery that thwarts such research; then, at the turn of the century, Chalmers offers a sustained narrative based on bibliographic research. Victorian accounts build on Chalmers' narrative, using its analytic elements: they establish at the centre of their investigations questions regarding the relationship between news periodicals and occasional pamphlets; they chart the emergence of periodicity; they acknowledge the international context by noting continental parallels; they consider the emergence of advertising, and the typographical developments that give newspapers their characteristic form; they dwell on censorship, the diversity of readers and their purported thirst for news; and they reflect on the political significance both of individual periodicals and of the press in society. The narrative is unabashedly teleological, which gives imaginative power to the story they tell. The same story is told in modern, popular accounts of the newspaper.[30] The early twentieth century witnessed much bibliographical activity, notably the work of Stanley Morison and Folke Dahl, and, more recently, the magnificent *British Newspapers and Periodicals: A Short Title Catalogue, 1641–1700* (1987) compiled by Carolyn Nelson and Matthew Seccombe. A handful of mid-twentieth century historians began more systematically to incorporate this wealth of material into their political narratives, some offering an account of political history viewed from the pages of one or more newspapers.[31] Such scholarship, both bibliographical and historical, has revealed the extensive resources which the historian of newspapers must confront with patience and not infrequent boredom. It has shown that the history of newspapers has to be written from the archives. The later twentieth century has seen monographs which broaden or enhance the story, focusing on particular kinds of newspapers and confined periods.[32] The commitment to narrative remains, while the ambition to write universal histories has been abandoned in the face of the superabundance of materials.[33] The story of newspapers is being implicitly revised in studies which address politics and public opinion; such accounts recognize the thoroughly permeable boundaries between newspapers and other cultural forms.[34] But no revised narrative has been written. We stand, then, at a juncture which invites post-revisionist narratives of the newspaper combining scholarship and sensitivity to the problems of narrative history with the sustained and integrating vision the Victorians brought to bear on the subject.[35]

Newspapers have been our weekly or daily companions for between three hundred and four hundred years, depending on how they are defined, and we will continue to negotiate with them – as their readers and historians – for as long as they survive. We can see this, for instance, as internet news influences struggles in oppressive regimes in the far east, once again raising the questions of whether freedom of the press is an intrinsically liberating force, or whether it will merely become subject to the laws of capital concentration. *The English Mercurie* may have troubled the scholars of the eighteenth century, but they were well prepared to weigh the persuasive force of fiction against the solidity of bibliographical fact, as their accounts of newspapers drawn from poetic satire and representations of news on the Jacobean stage suggest. It is in part the confidence with which they pare away fiction and history that makes their stories so readable.

Having been our daily companion for so long, it is easy for the contemporary newspaper to mould our perception of the early modern press. Current attitudes are deftly summarized by Jeremy Paxman, who has suggested that, when confronted with a politician in the news media, the immediate response of the reader or viewer is to ask: "Why is this lying bastard lying to me?" The point is not just that all politicians lie, but that the politician is by definition a "lying bastard." His or her speech-act is always under suspicion, will always be perceived from a perspective of its sincerity rather than its manifest or communicative content. The very way we read activities in the public, political sphere is conditioned in this way by the press. There is, in other words, a cycle of tautology by which the viewer's or reader's expectations are produced and satisfied.

The same point is made in another fiction, *Primary Colors* (1996), a *roman a clef* about Bill Clinton's 1991 campaign to become the democratic candidate for the presidency. The narrator, Henry Burton, is a spin doctor in Clinton's team, who finds himself operating in a new reality governed by a morass of tabloids, with their stereotypical and alliterative modes of representation. A telling moment occurs when the journalists bear down on Burton and quiz him about how the campaign team will be able to get its message out with the press interested only in rumours of the candidate's womanizing: "They weren't scumbag gossip reporters, they were media analysts ... the press was reporting about how the candidate would deal with how the press would report about the story."[36] The same dynamic was created in late 1998, when reporters asked Clinton how he could continue to perform as a leader when overwhelmed with reports of the Monica Lewinsky scandal.

The histories dealt with in this volume precede the evolution of this dystopian and tautological relationship between press and politics. News is not a set of events with shared characteristics, nor a set of institutions with shared procedures, but a basis for verbal (and partly visual) exchange. It is a footing for intercourse, a conversation beginning "what news?" Yet we have grown so accustomed to such media saturation that it seems inevitable; this is just as blinkered a vision as Herd's dream of pink, feminine journals. The essays in this volume are written by scholars from various fields, including history, literary criticism, the history of medicine, and the history of the book. In addition, many share an interest in the renovating force of multidisciplinary approaches. In this volume – and in the scholarly dialogues from which it grows – they contribute to a new history of the newspaper which aspires to embrace the diversity of recent methodologies and to rebuild the story from the archives.

NOTES

1. Thomas Watts, *A letter to Antonio Panizzi ... on the reputed earliest printed newspaper: the English Mercurie 1588* (London: William Pickering, 1839).
2. See Douglas Duncan, *Thomas Ruddiman: A Study in Scottish Scholarship of the Early Eighteenth Century* (Edinburgh and London: Oliver & Boyd, 1965), 6–9.
3. George Chalmers, *The Life of Thomas Ruddiman* (London: John Stockdale; Edinburgh: William Laing, 1794), 102; I am grateful to Hamish Mathison for discussions of this work and of eighteenth-century Scottish newspapers.
4. Ibid., 102–25, 404–42.
5. Ibid., 105.
6. Ibid., 106, 108.
7. Ibid., 107.
8. See Robert Crawford, *Devolving English Literature* (Oxford: Oxford University Press, 1992); I am indebted to George Rousseau for discussions of this subject.

9. F. Knight Hunt, *The Fourth Estate: Contributions Towards a History of Newspapers, and of the Liberty of the Press*, 2 vols. (1850; repr. London: Routledge/Thoemmes Press, 1998), 1: 289–92.
10. Watts, *A letter to Antonio Panizzi*; Hunt, *The Fourth Estate*, 1: 292–302; Alexander Andrews, *The History of British Journalism, from the foundation of the newspaper press in England, to the repeal of the Stamp act in 1855*, 2 vols. (1859; repr. London: Routledge/Thoemmes Press, 1998), 1: 19–20.
11. Isaac D'Israeli, *The Curiosities of Literature* (Newry: Alexander Wilkinson, 1817), 184.
12. There is a copy of this in Cambridge University Library: 8540.b.10.
13. See, for example, Hunt, *The Fourth Estate*, 1: 33–5; Andrews, *History of British Journalism*, 1: 19–22; James Grant, *The Newspaper Press: Its Origin–Progress–and Present Position*, 3 vols. (London: Tinsley Brothers, 1871), 1: 9–15.
14. Grant, *The Newspaper Press*, 1: 15.
15. Hunt, *The Fourth Estate*, 1: 37–8, 58–90.
16. *The Periodical Press of Great Britain and Ireland* (London: Hurst, Robinson, & Co., 1824), 1–2.
17. Quoted in H.R. Fox Bourne's *English Newspapers: Chapters in the History of Journalism*, 2 vols. (1887; repr. London: Routledge/Thoemmes Press, 1998), 2: 389–90.
18. *The Papers of Thomas Jefferson*, 26 vols. (Princeton, NJ: Princeton University Press, 1950–95), 9: 239, 11: 49.
19. Churchill quoted by T.C. Bray, *A Newspaper's Role in Modern Society* (St Lucia: University of Queensland Press, 1965), 26–7. For examples, see William M. Clyde, *The Struggle for the Freedom of the Press from Caxton to Cromwell* (London: St Andrews University/Humphrey Milford, 1934); Harold Herd, *The Newspaper of Tomorrow* (London: George Allen & Unwin, 1930), *passim*; David Keir, *Newspapers* (London: Edward Arnold, 1948); Leon Nelson Flint, *The Conscience of the Newspaper: A Case Book in the Principles and Problems of Journalism* (New York: D. Appleton, 1925), 8; K. Gibbard, *Citizenship Through the Newspaper* (London: J.M. Dent, 1939); Gerald W. Johnson, *What is News? A Tentative Outline* (New York: Alfred A. Knopf, 1926); Wilson Harris, *The Daily Press* (Cambridge: Cambridge University Press, 1943).
20. See, for example, Marshall McLuhan, *Understanding Media: The Extensions of Man* (London: Routledge and Kegan Paul, 1964).
21. John Fiske, *Introduction to Communication Studies* (1982; London: Routledge, 1990), 21.
22. Herd, *The Newspaper of Tomorrow*, 45.
23. Norman Angel, *The Press and the Organisation of Society* (London: Labour Publishing Company, 1922), 16; see also H.A. Inglis, *The Press: A Neglected Factor in the Economic History of the Twentieth Century* (London: Oxford University Press, 1949).
24. For Habermas, see my article in this volume.
25. McLuhan, *Understanding Media*, 209.
26. Richard Cust and Ann Hughes (eds.), *Conflict in Early Stuart England: Studies in Religion and Politics, 1603–1642* (London: Longman, 1989); Anthony Fletcher, *The Outbreak of the English Civil War* (London: Edward Arnold, 1981); John Morrill, *The Nature of the English Revolution* (London: Longman, 1993); Alastair Bellany, "'Rayling Rymes and Vaunting Verse': Libellous Politics in Early Stuart England, 1603–1628," in Kevin Sharpe and Peter Lake (eds.), *Culture and Politics in Early Stuart England* (London: Macmillan, 1994), 285–310; Alastair Bellany, "Mistress Turner's Deadly Sins: Sartorial Transgression, Court Scandal, and Politics in Early Stuart England," *Huntington Library Quarterly* 58 (1996): 179–210.
27. Though see Richard Cust, "News and Politics in Early Seventeenth-Century England," *Past and Present* 112 (1986): 60–90; Tom Cogswell, "The Politics of Propaganda: Charles I and the People in the 1620s," *Journal of British Studies* 29 (1990): 187–215; Kevin Sharpe, *The Personal Rule of Charles I* (New Haven, CT, and London: Yale University Press, 1992), ch. 17; Michael Colin Frearson, "The English Corantos of the 1620s" (Cambridge University Ph.D. thesis, 1993); Christine Gerrard, *The Patriot Opposition to Walpole: Politics, Poetry, and National Myth, 1725–1742* (Oxford: Clarendon Press, 1994); Joad Raymond, *The Invention of the Newspaper: English Newsbooks, 1641–1649* (Oxford: Clarendon Press,

1996); and the article by Ian Atherton in this volume.

28. Lisa Jardine and Anthony Grafton, "'Studied for Action': How Gabriel Harvey Read his Livy," *Past and Present* 129 (1990): 30–78; Robert Darnton, "History of Reading," in Peter Burke (ed.), *New Perspectives on Historical Writing* (Cambridge: Polity Press, 1991), 140–67; James Raven, Helen Small and Naomi Tadmor (eds.), *The Practice and Representation of Reading in England* (Cambridge: Cambridge University Press, 1996); Anthony Grafton, "Is the History of Reading a Marginal Enterprise? Guillaume Budé and His Books," *Papers of the Bibliographical Society of America* 91 (1997): 139–57.

29. Raymond, *Invention of the Newspaper*, esp. ch. 5.

30. For example, Harold Herd, *The March of Journalism: The Story of the British Press from 1622 to the Present Day* (London: Allen and Unwin, 1952); Stanley Morison, *Origins of the Newspaper: Some Account of the Physical Development of Journals printed in London between 1622 and the present day* (London: The Times, 1954); Jim Allee Hart, *Views on the News: The Developing Editorial Syndrome, 1500–1800* (Carbondale and Edwardsville, IL: Southern Illinois University Press, 1970); Keith Williams, *The English Newspaper: An Illustrated History to 1900* (London: Springwood Books, 1977); George Boyce, James Curran and Pauline Wingate (eds.), *Newspaper History: From the Seventeenth Century to the Present Day* (London: Acton Society, 1978); Geoffrey A. Cranfield, *The Press & Society: From Caxton to Northcliffe* (London: Longman, 1978); Anthony Smith, *The Newspaper: An International History* (London: Thames and Hudson, 1979); Mitchell Stephens, *A History of News: From the Drum to the Satellite* (New York: Viking, 1988).

31. Robert L. Haig, *The Gazeteer, 1735–1797: A Study in the Eighteenth-Century English Newspaper* (Carbondale, IL: Southern Illinois University Press, 1960); Robert R. Rea, *The English Press in Politics, 1760–1774* (Lincoln, NB: University of Nebraska Press, 1963); Lucyle Werkmeister, *The London Daily Press, 1772–1792* (Lincoln, NB: University of Nebraska Press, 1963), and *A Newspaper History of England 1792–1793* (Lincoln, NB: University of Nebraska Press, 1967).

32. To name a few examples among many: Joseph Frank, *The Beginnings of the English Newspaper, 1620–1660* (Cambridge, MA: Harvard University Press, 1961); Geoffrey A. Cranfield, *The Development of the Provincial Newspaper, 1700–1760* (Oxford: Clarendon Press, 1962); R.M. Wiles, *Freshest Advices: Early Provincial Newspapers in England* (Columbus, OH: Ohio State University Press, 1965); Robert Munter, *The History of the Irish Newspaper, 1685–1760* (Cambridge: Cambridge University Press, 1967); James Sutherland, *The Restoration Newspaper and its Development* (Cambridge: Cambridge University Press, 1986); Charles E. Clark, *The Public Prints: The Newspaper in Anglo-American Culture, 1665–1740* (New York and Oxford: Oxford University Press, 1994).

33. Except perhaps C. John Sommerville, *The News Revolution in England: Cultural Dynamics of Daily Information* (New York and Oxford: Oxford University Press, 1997), which does not address primary sources in any detail but instead offers a sweeping and pessimistic narrative.

34. See, for example, the references on Restoration public opinion in my article in this volume.

35. There is not space here for me to discuss the relationship between these developments in the history of newspapers and those in other areas of early modern historiography, but for some stimulating perspectives, see J.S.A. Adamson, "Eminent Victorian, S.R. Gardiner and the Liberal Hero", *Historical Journal* 33 (1990): 641–57; Peter Lake, "Retrospective: Wentworth's Political World in Revisionist and Post-Revisionist Perspective", in J.F. Merritt (ed.), *The Political World of Thomas Wentworth, Earl of Strafford, 1621–1641* (Cambridge: Cambridge University Press, 1996), 252–83.

36. Anonymous, *Primary Colors* (New York and London: Chatto and Windus, 1996), 116–17.

The Decorum of News

FRITZ LEVY

On 24 December 1620, with a new Parliament approaching, King James I issued a proclamation against excesses of lavish and licentious speech in political affairs. The King pointed out that he had been more than generous in allowing "a greater opennesse, and libertie of discourse" than his predecessors, even in matters of state which, he argued, "are no Theames, or subjects fit for vulgar persons, or common meetings." He had cause for alarm. Foreign policy engaged the popular attention, for fighting had begun on the Continent, and the King's son-in-law had done more than his share in igniting it. Hatred of Spain continued unabated. The swirl of commentary was such that even the French Ambassador wrote home about the "free speaking, cartoons, defamatory libels" he saw about him, and wondered whether these had now turned into "the ordinary precursors of civil war." In order to quiet this verbal tumult, the proclamation told the King's subjects to "take heede, how they intermeddle by Penne, or Speech, with causes of State, and secrets of Empire, either at home, or abroad" and ordered them instead to limit themselves to matters not above their reach or calling. However, by insisting that no one might presume to plead extenuation by citing the multitude and generality of offenders, the authors of the proclamation seem to have had some doubts about its likely efficacy.[1]

The doubts were amply justified. Little more than half a year later, a new proclamation had to be issued, very similar to the old. That insatiable gossip, John Chamberlain, was probably right when he wrote that the common people had no idea of how to understand it, nor did they comprehend "how far matter of state may stretch or extend," with the predictable result that "they continue to take no notice of yt."[2] In any event, men and women were too much enthralled with talk of news to abandon it. Simonds D'Ewes, the future parliamentarian and historian of Parliament, now still a student at Cambridge, tells how in May 1620 rumours ran through the university that the Elector Palatine, husband of King James's daughter, Elizabeth, had suffered heavy defeats; the rumours proved false then, but presaged the later truth. By the time Frederick was decisively defeated at the Battle of the White Mountain, D'Ewes had moved to the

Fritz Levy, University of Washington

Middle Temple in London, and thus was able to partake of what he described as "the best intelligence the town afforded"; nevertheless, he tells us, the results of the battle were described diversely, with rumour attributing victory first to one side, then to the other, and though D'Ewes inquired after the results daily, it was many weeks before he knew the truth.[3] Like so many others, D'Ewes felt compelled to talk over so great a Protestant loss, and found a ready ear in his minister, Mr Masters. That the two men soon fell to talking about "divers matters concerning our King and government," praying that he might give over his timorousness at home and abroad, was, of course, precisely what the government feared and had hoped by its proclamations to prevent.[4] Yet it might be argued that the King and his ministers were responsible for their own discomfiture. James was right when he admitted that he had been more generous than his predecessors in allowing news to get about. In addition, his own vanity played a part: when at last he dismissed the 1621 Parliament, the King justified his action by way of a proclamation that was issued not only in the usual "posting" version but also in the form of a news pamphlet. By publishing an account of his action in this form, he virtually admitted that the repressive policy of the proclamations had failed, and that it made more sense to control the news than to suppress it.

But there is more to the story than James' change of mind. Some of the justifications the King used for controlling talk about the news, and particularly those depending on social hierarchy, themselves represented older attitudes that were gradually being abandoned; others, like his interpretation of the prerogative, soon became the subject of contestation. A look at sumptuary legislation, perhaps the most blatant of all efforts to enforce social markers, will help explain the situation.

II

For generations, the men and women of England had been taught that the peace and harmony of the realm depended on preserving the social hierarchy, itself a subset of the "Great Chain of Being." Each stratum of society had rights and duties *vis-à-vis* those above and below.[5] The preamble to the Act of 1533, passed at Henry VIII's insistence but itself repeating earlier statutes, informed the King's subjects that the increasing and excessive wear of sumptuous and costly clothing had reached the point of causing such notable effects as "the great, manifest and notorious detriment of the common weal, the subversion of good and politic order in knowledge and distinction of people according to their estates, pre-eminences, dignities and degrees."[6] The Act noted as well that such overdressing was the result of pride, a sin that soon led to poverty. Further reenactments, scattered through the remainder of the century, generally made the same point about social order, though the practical justifications ranged from considerations of preserving home industries from expensive foreign competition to preserving resources during times of agricultural distress. Strict legal enforcement was plainly difficult, though on occasion a serious effort was made to help officials by delineating, in great detail, exactly what was permissible to each order of society. Some arrests even ensued.[7] Nevertheless, the quantities of proclamations, homilies, and sermons suggest that the government's principal weapon was moral suasion together with a bit of embarrassment and, as the emphasis on the sin of pride suggests, the preachers found this more to their taste than ordinary men or women. Additionally, in an age of great social mobility, the mercantile community came increasingly to dislike the laws. Some of them, of course, wanted to show off their success by wearing the new clothes; others wanted the freedom to sell to any of the numerous *nouveaux-riches* prepared to buy. Elizabeth's Act of 1597, passed just at the end of a period of famine, seems to have been the last of them; by 1604, with James newly on the throne, most of the legislation was gone and other social markers would have to be found.

The same system of restrictions might apply to reading and religion. When the vernacular Bible was first published under Henry VIII, there were no restrictions about who could read it, with the inevitable result that the populace at large began publicly to discuss its meaning without clerical assistance. Such uninformed and unrestrained reading, especially when conducted in public, might undermine authority. An Act of 1543 attempted to prevent this by permitting only noblemen, gentlemen, and merchant householders to read Scripture in their private quarters, and noblewomen and gentlewomen to read it to themselves, while prohibiting other women, artisans, apprentices, and the like from reading Scripture either privately or openly.[8] Such social differentiation might prevent fractiousness but did little to promote the spread of Protestantism. Fifteen years later, after the turmoil of the reigns of Edward VI and Mary, the new Elizabethan government tried to reset the bounds. After ordering each parish to provide both an English Bible and a copy of Erasmus' *Paraphrases*, the Queen's proclamation went on to say that the clergy should discourage no one from reading any part of the Bible but instead "shall rather exhort every person to read the same with great humility and reverence ... whereby they may the better know their duties to God, to their sovereign lady the Queen, and their neighbor, ever gently and charitably exhorting them, and in her majesty's name straightly charging and commanding them, that in their reading thereof no man to reason or contend but quietly to hear the reader."[9] Thus, despite the effort to enforce obedience to ecclesiastical authority, and to restrict argument, reading and discussion by ordinary parishioners came to be permitted.

Traditional ideas of decorum were also beginning to break down among the literary genres. George Puttenham, the theorist of the socio-politics of poetry, remained insistent that "it is comely that euery estate and vocation should be knowen by the differences of their habit: a clarke from a lay man: a gentleman from a yeoman: a souldier from a citizen, and the chiefe of euery degree fro[m] their inferiours," because, he believed, "in confusion and disorder there is no manner of decencie." For Puttenham, decorum of clothing was intimately linked to decorum of style. The "highest" subjects for literature were the religious; next to them were "the noble gests and great fortunes of Princes, and the notable accide[n]ts of time, as the greatest affaires of war & peace."[10] Traditionally, such political matters were worked up into tragedy, written by men of elevated rank to whom the high style was natural, and whose place in life ensured their proper understanding of such great affairs. The same was to be true of the audience. Thus Fulke Greville, politician and gentleman, insisted that his tragedies were written for the politically experienced, excluding those "on whose feet the black ox had not already trod."[11] Yet Greville could enforce his vision of tragedy only by writing closet drama, played – if at all – in the theatre of the mind. Meanwhile, men of lower birth, like Marlowe, Kyd, and Shakespeare, were presenting political tragedies to the eyes of the masses. The same argument applies as well to that other political genre, history writing. Francis Bacon contended that ordinary men might be allowed to collect the materials of history, but they were no fit guides to its interpretation. "It is for ministers and great officers to judge of these things, and those who have handled the helm of government, and been acquainted with the difficulties and mysteries of state business."[12] Yet even as Bacon wrote, the playwrights presented their analytical histories upon the stage, opening the secrets of governance to the eyes of the multitude. History, it was commonly believed, was not only past politics but commentary on the present. Sir John Holles, instructing his son in the arts of politics, wrote "all is but a play, yet for us of these tyms more instruction is to be had at the starr-chamber, then at the globe," thus essentially equating the political and theatrical.[13] Well before King James wrote, matters which he was convinced "are no Theames, or subjects fit for vulgar persons, or common meetings" had already become so.

As James clearly recognized, all this had political implications in the present. The King – any King – had need of good counsel. The question before the King then became: what was good counsel, who was to give it to him, and how much of it did he need to accept. Thomas More, years before, had argued that good counsel meant moral counsel. Such advice had once been given by the King's "natural" advisors, the great nobles, who – in the absence of a meeting of Parliament – also served as links between the monarch and his people. With the growing complexity of politics, especially international politics, in the sixteenth century, good counsel came increasingly to be identified with information and its interpretation. The great lords, who once had had a near-monopoly on mobilizing military force, now had to give way to men of lesser status who had a clearer grasp of how to raise and control the new mass armies, as well as to those who understood the even more important question of how to finance them. In an era of rapidly shifting alliances, men who had seen the Continent and comprehended how the governments of France, Spain, and the Low Countries actually worked had a clear advantage. Each would return home with the equipment necessary to offer informed political advice. The new men, trained in the arts of rhetoric and with a humanist education giving them access to all European culture, forced the ancient nobility to make room at the council table. Sir Henry Sidney had this in mind when he sent his son, Philip, on the sixteenth-century version of the Grand Tour; the same might be said of Sir Nicholas Bacon, who "apprenticed" young Francis to the English Ambassador in Paris. When royal employment failed to materialize for them, both Francis Bacon and his brother, Anthony, were to discover that even the great lords needed to take on specialist advisors: the Earl of Essex, once he received a place on the council, soon found that rank and military prowess were not enough, and that he needed a constant supply of information, and thus found places for both the brothers in his secretariat.

The careers of Philip Sidney, and of Francis and Anthony Bacon, were no more than symptomatic of a wider trend. A humanist education, meaning some knowledge of the classics imbibed along with the conviction that a gentleman's duty was to serve the common wealth, together with a knowledge of the political world abroad and at home, soon became the hallmark of anyone wishing to make a career in the royal service. Those who failed to find a place continued to drift around London, parading their expertise: they became common enough to be called "malcontents." John Donne, himself in search of preferment, recalls meeting one such: "This thing has travail'd, and saith, speakes all tongues, / And only know'th what to all States belongs." But a knowledge of foreign news alone was insufficient. Domestic news – or was it gossip? – too was required, and Donne's interlocutor spoke

> ... like a privileg'd spie, whom nothing can
> Discredit, Libells now 'gainst each great man.
> He names a price for every office paid;
> He saith, our warres thrive ill, because delai'd;
> That offices are entail'd, and that there are
> Perpetuities of them, lasting as farre
> As the last day; And that great officers,
> Doe with the Pirates share ...[14]

Because they were the failed representatives of a much larger segment of society, such unemployed place-seekers were figures of fun, principal objects of the thriving industry of late Elizabethan satire. Some, like John Chamberlain, were *flaneurs,* haunting the precincts of St Paul's. Others, their ambitions blocked, took out their frustrations by joining Essex in rebellion. What all had in common was the pursuit of news, for news had become their stock-in-trade. Claiming inside knowledge was the way to be noticed; indeed, for many of them, news replaced (or at least supplemented) clothes as the new social marker, the way of distinguishing themselves from the hordes pressing on them from below.[15] These men became the market for news, whether passed on by gossip, letter, or print.

A shrewd monarch, especially one with a theoretical bent like James I, came to recognize the dangers in all this. The King's ability to rule depended on control of what was coming to be called the *arcana imperii*, by which was meant not merely the sleights of government, the tricks by which kings kept control, but access to the sources of information underlying the whole structure. James, like Elizabeth before him, was prepared to share information with advisors he chose himself; now, as such information spread downwards through the ranks of society, the pressure from below mounted, and control of foreign policy – long an acknowledged part of the royal prerogative – increasingly became a matter of public debate.[16]

III

The general area of what may for convenience be called "news" had already become a field of contestation well before the end of the sixteenth century. Further analysis, however, will depend on making some distinctions within the category. Contemporaries (including the censors) certainly saw a great difference between domestic news and foreign news. Similarly, they drew a line between domestic news concerning the great ones of the kingdom (up to and including the activities of the monarch and the government), and that involving the doings and sufferings of lesser men. Murders, witchcraft, and other criminal acts were regularly the subject of pamphlets and broadside ballads; so too were "accidents" like earthquakes or fires. On the other hand, while the death of some great lord might safely be lamented in verse, excess or mistimed praise for those at the centre of politics could lead to trouble. Permissible news, however, did include a variety of pamphlets embodying royal decrees, battles, even propaganda from whatever country was currently of interest. The adventures of the Huguenots in France or of the Protestant rebels in the Low Countries engendered a wide variety of tracts. Some, like *The French King's Edict ... for the Pacification of his Realm* (1581), were hardly more than translations of government documents, while others, like *News from Antwerp* (1580), consisted of a series of "intercepted" letters intended to prove that peace with Spain was impossible. Sandwiched between the revolts and the edicts were pamphlets and ballads describing the wonders of God's providence, and deciphering their meaning. *An example of Gods iudgement shew[n] vpon two Children borne in high* Dutch La[nd] *in the Citie of* Lutssolof, *the first day of* Iulie. *and translated out of Dutche into English the 6. Nouuember last* celebrated the implications of the birth of two deformed children, while *A Most Strange and wonderfull Herring, taken on the 26. day of Nouember 1597, neere vnto Drenton* [in Norway] was unusual for *Hauing on the one side the picture of two armed men fighting, and on the other most strange Characters, as in the picture is here expressed.* This tract was first issued in Rotterdam, but was soon printed in English by John Wolfe, with the subhead, "Repent, for the kingdome of God is at hand." Wolfe, it should be noted, was the leading publisher of news pamphlets concerning the war in France and the Low Countries, and the format of *A Most Strange and wonderfull Herring* differed from his more mundane productions only in having an illustration.

News of this sort was entirely *ad hoc,* missing any hint of periodicity. This was inevitably true of any news spread by way of personal letters – and this long remained the most common means of dissemination – but it was even more true of news in its printed form.[17] Looking back at the records, we can see "bulges" of news around the time of the Henrician Reformation, most of it published by the King's propagandists. Similarly, there is suddenly a group of at least a dozen tracts published in 1562, when an English expeditionary force, intended to help the Huguenots, crossed the Channel. As these pamphlets tended to justify English intervention by including graphic accounts of events like the massacre of Vassy, when the Duke of Guise's men murdered a group of Protestants at worship, it is probably safe to conclude that Elizabeth's government had a hand in encouraging their production, a conclusion bolstered by noting that, in the following year, the numbers dropped off abruptly. The size and format of these pamphlets suggests that the intended audience was the literate upper strata of society; two broadside ballads, however, presumably aimed lower down the social scale.[18] In 1569, during the revolt of the northern earls, the situation was reversed, and broadside ballads predominated. On this occasion, the number of ballads was great enough for their readers and auditors to track the movements of the rebels, their defeat, and their ultimate trial and execution.[19] For the government to permit the publication of so much domestic news, aimed at the commons, was enough contrary to custom to raise questions. One answer may lie in the specifically local, northern nature of the revolt: ballads, published in London, must always have circulated more widely in the south and, on this occasion, may well have been intended to reassure the population below York that everything was under control. Another possible reason – suggested by the publication of *A newe Ballade, intituled, Agaynst Rebellious and false rumours* – may have involved the government's fear of rumour, which tended to increase dramatically during any crisis. As it turned out, by the time the ballad appeared, in 1570, the emergency was over, and it was possible to take a tone more amused than angry:

> For euery one doth talke,
> There tongues contrary walke,
> And semes to meddell of this and that,
> There babling tongues so large doth chatte,...
> And euery one doth besie him still
> About the thing he hath no skill.[20]

Everything changed once the war with Spain became open. From 1585, the desire for news and, correspondingly, the number of news pamphlets, increased rapidly. So, too, did the pressure of censorship. In this process, the role of the Stationers' Company was crucial. Nothing was to be published without first being entered in the Company's register, and the entries required licences from the appropriate officials. In the wake of the 1569 revolt, the Company had been ordered to "suffer neither booke ballett nor any other matter to be published in print whatsoever the argument thereof shalbe until the same be first seene and allowed either by us of her M^tes pryvie cownsell or by thee Commissioners for cawses ecclesyasticall there at London"; in 1586, the system was regularized and tightened by a Star Chamber decree.[21] Theatrical productions also gradually came under control, in this case that of the Master of the Revels. The tightened censorship meant, for example, that the "foolish idle headed ballade maker" who caused pictures of the Earl of Essex, then out of favour, to be printed, along with a list of all his titles of honour, all his services and "exceeding praise for wisdom, honour, worth," found that his production was quickly called in.[22] Reports concerning foreign affairs were generally restricted, because there was too much danger of insulting a fellow monarch, thus leading to ambassadorial complaints. Setting any of the great on the stage was generally forbidden as detrimental to respect. The Earl of Essex, not always averse to publicity, nevertheless loathed the idea that "they print me and make me speak to the world, and shortly they will play me in what forms they list upon the stage," and asked for protection.[23] Yet Sir Robert Sidney's London agent was gleeful in writing to his master, then stationed with the English army in the Netherlands, that "Two daies agon, the overthrow of Turnholt was acted upon a stage, and all your names used that were at yt; especially Sir Francis Veres, and he that plaid that part gott a beard resembling his, and a watchet satten doublett, with hose trimd with silver lace."[24] But this episode was exceptional, for the battle of Turnhout was seen as a great victory in which English forces played a notable part, and so was celebrated in pamphlets and ballads as well.

Faced with such restrictions, those wishing to receive news and in a position to do so turned increasingly to private correspondence. Gabriel Harvey, former Cambridge don and would-be politician, provides a useful example, not least because of his habit of naked self-revelation. In the first of *Foure Letters*, Harvey's friend Christopher Bird writes to introduce him to the Dutch merchant and historian, Emmanuel van Meteren, for Harvey wishes "for some conference touching the state of forraine countries: as your leisure may conueniently serue." Van Meteren, it should be noted, was well known as a conduit of information from the Protestant Low Countries, and Bird duly thanks him "for your two letters of forreine newes, receiued the last weeke." Now settled into a network of newsletters, Harvey in his turn offers to pass them on to Bird: "The next weeke, you may happily haue a letter of such French occurrences, and other intelligences, as the credible relation of inquisitiue frendes, or imployed straungers shall acquaint me withall."[25] As Harvey regularly stayed in London with John Wolfe, in those days the principal publisher of news pamphlets, his boast of access to such treasures must (for once) be taken seriously.[26]

There is, of course, plenty of evidence for news being transmitted by letter. Some was provided by professional newswriters like Peter Proby.[27] Wise politicians who found themselves abroad for extended periods of time encouraged friends or servants to keep them informed. Rowland Whyte, as we have seen, performed this chore for Sir Robert Sidney, on the Queen's business in the Low Countries at Flushing; John Chamberlain did the same for Dudley Carleton. During times of particularly great tension, the business might verge on the dangerous. "Burn my letters," said Whyte, "else I shall be afraid to write. Be careful about what you write here, or what you say where you are. Now are letters intercepted and stayed."[28] And even Whyte, commonly a very blunt critic of events, found some things to be outside his range, "for *Arcana principis* are not to be medled in."[29] Fortunately, most writers of news never came close enough to the flame to risk singeing. Philip Gawdy, whose family in Norfolk constantly clamoured for news, usually sent little more than one-liners, and many of those concerned the adventures of friends and acquaintances from the same district. Only occasionally did he venture further afield. When his father was particularly insistent, Gawdy felt he had to comply: "The only newes w[ch] shaddoweth and as it wer darkneth all the rest is of the ffrenche mens commyng ouer, w[ch] allthoughe it be as common with yow, as with vs yet it is not so certeyne there as it is here."[30] Confirming the common rumour was the most he could do. Yet one suspects most news did circulate by letter, a point reinforced by the number of printed news tracts authenticating themselves by purporting to be "A Copy of a Letter from a Gentleman."

Additionally, however, there were informal means of communication such as conversation, rumour-mongering, and what contemporaries called libels. That last category included placards, manuscript poems circulated among friends or posted in conspicuous places – in other words, informal, unofficial, and highly unregulated publication.[31] All were worrisome to the government, not altogether without reason.[32] The long war with Spain was responsible for much of this. Despite the success of the English against the Armada of 1588, Spanish fleets continued to set sail for Britain, and the slightest hint of an invasion set off a firestorm of rumours. 1599 was particularly bad in this respect, and it is not surprising that a Londoner named G. Coppin, worried that all this might be part of a Spanish conspiracy, felt duty-bound to inform Sir Robert Cecil, the Principal Secretary,

> of the strange rumours and abundance of news spread abroad in the city, and so flying into the country, as there cannot be laid a more dangerous plot to amaze and discourage our people, and to advance the strength and mighty power of the Spaniard, working doubts in the better sort, fear in the poorer sort, and a great distraction in all ...

and then went on to spell out in detail the stories spreading through the city. Not least among the dangers was the well-meaning preacher who, picking up on the rumour that the King of Spain had come to a settlement with James VI of Scotland, "in his prayer before his sermon, prayed to be delivered from the mighty forces of the Spaniard, the Scots and the Danes."[33] The well-meaning might be as troublesome as the ill-intentioned, as a group of Norfolk gentlemen discovered when their request for a fast to pray for God's help against the enemies of the kingdom ran into the objection that "the subiectes therby may be further terified, & brought into expectac[i]on of greater daunger then is to be feared."[34]

Infectious fear of invasion was not the only result of the long war with Spain. There was a good deal of economic dislocation, disturbing the fragile agricultural sector as well the urban workshop.[35] In addition, there was concern about repatriated veterans, men with some military training but no obvious means of employment, who might at any time join, or even help organize, disturbances. Added to that, the mid-1590s saw one of the worst agrarian crises on record: by the end of four years of terrible harvests, prices had reached extraordinary heights, hunger was rampant and outright starvation not unheard of. Food riots occurred in Oxfordshire, Gloucestershire, and, more dangerous still, in London itself, which had to be put under martial law.[36] Any grain moving about the country might spark trouble, yet grain had constantly to be sent to feed the cities as well as English armies in Ireland, the Low Countries, and France. Furthermore, the various political battles Joel Hurstfield called "the succession struggle in late Elizabeth England" became more and more heated.[37] In the absence of a standing army or any sort of national police force, the Queen and her advisors coped with the crises by resisting even the slightest challenges. Rioters who ordinarily faced a fine or a whipping were executed. Letters were opened. The censorship was tightened, most notably in 1599, when the bishops banned not only a group of satires that called attention to the current uneasiness, but also some pamphlets of personal invective that might lead men to take sides even in debates of no discernible political importance.[38] The Lord Keeper's public speeches in the Star Chamber warned the "gentlemen that leave hospitalitie and housekeping and hide themselves in Cities and Borough-townes," instructing them to return to their country seats, where they were needed to help keep order – though some suspected that the authorities also wished to keep them from talking to each other. There was a renewed interest in enforcing the sumptuary laws, especially "the vanitie and excesse of women apparell" – decorum in dress was an outward sign of order. Most of all, "discoursers and medlers in Princes matters," together with libellers, were to be stopped.[39] Any of these might serve to undermine public order. The extraordinary meeting at Star Chamber in November 1599, at the height of the Irish crisis, with the former commander of the Queen's troops, the Earl of Essex, in prison, showed how fearful the government was. One after another, members of the Privy Council stood to denounce those who played preacher; who talked politics at ordinaries, where they have hardly money to pay for a meal; who scattered libels about London and the Court itself, not hesitating to tax even the Queen with not providing for the troubled state of Ireland. The Lord Treasurer believed the libellers were worse than traitors and so should, by rights, be executed. The Lord Chief Justice worried that the libellers intended "to scandalize the Queen, censure Councillors, and write against all authority; and the purpose is to disgrace those in authority, and cause disobedience and sedition, and bring all to confusion."[40] Always there was the fear that the lower orders would succumb to sedition if the gentlemen did not do their part. That included even members of the House of Commons, who had to be warned not to allow it that "Parliament matters are ordinary talk in the Street," for if "Sovereignty were converted into Popularity, ... the World is apt to slander most especially the Ministers of Government."[41]

However, it must soon have become evident that public opinion might better be influenced by putting the right materials into circulation. The basic idea was not new: we have seen it operating in 1562 and, in a different way, in 1569–70. What *was* new, in the years after 1585, was the scale and continuity of the endeavour. The central figure in this activity was John Wolfe, a printer and publisher distinguished from his fellows by considerable continental experience. Although he began his career conventionally enough, as an apprentice to the stationer, John Day, in 1576 his name appeared in the colophons of two books printed in Italy. How – or why – Wolfe reached Italy remains a mystery. What is clear is that he continued printing in Italian after his return to England, and that among the works he printed there, though with a false Italian address in the imprint, were Machiavelli's *History of Florence* and *Discourses*, plus the banned, and thus no doubt desirable, *Prince*. Because of Machiavelli's notoriety, these would sell well on the Continent as well as in England, so it is usually supposed that Wolfe also intended them for distribution abroad.[42] Wolfe's ability to print books in foreign languages, and to market them on the Continent, came to the attention of the Queen's Principal Minister, Sir William Cecil, Lord Burghley, who used Wolfe to print an Italian translation of his propaganda piece, *The Execution of Justice in England* (1584), a defence of the trial and hanging of the Jesuit, Thomas Campion.[43] Four years later, Wolfe also printed the Italian version of Burghley's *The copie of a letter sent out of England to Don Bernardin de Mendoza*, trumpeting the defeat of the Armada. By this time, Wolfe was also printing English translations of French pamphlets, notably those of the Protestant Henry of Navarre's great supporter, Michel Hurault.[44] After the assassination, in 1589, of the French King Henry III, Henry of Navarre claimed the throne, and both Spain and England sent troops to intervene in the ensuing civil war. France was now added to the Low Countries as a matter of consuming interest, and Wolfe was ready to fuel the flames of patriotism with his publications. For many of these, the translator was Edward Aggas, who also published similar pamphlets on his own account.

In addition to producing pamphlets focused on a single subject, Wolfe and his friends introduced into England the first "corantos," small booklets including news from abroad from a variety of sources (and often several countries). *Credible Reportes from France, and Flanders. In the moneth of May. 1590.* was printed by Wolfe for the bookseller, William Wright.[45] The opening paragraph imparted an atmosphere of immediacy: "A Weeke since, came from Diepe a certaine Bark the which arrived at Plymmouth which reported ... ," and then followed news of Dieppe itself and of various Protestant victories in France. Then the focus shifted to Flanders: the letter quoted, very much in the style of "we" (Protestants) and "they" (Catholics), had a dateline of Bergen-op-Zoom, 15 May 1590. By the next page, attention returned once more to "the late newes from France." The last couple of pages contained general news, some of it from Spain. The whole occupied one sheet of paper, folded twice: eight pages, with the news crammed into six of them. Another of these, again sold by Wright (and possibly printed by Wolfe), has a somewhat more informative title page: *Newes from Rome, Spaine, Palermo, Geneuae, and France. With the miserable state of the Citty of Paris, and the late yeelding vppe of sundrie Towns of great strength, vnto the King* (1590). Despite the seeming objectivity, and the statement that the news had been translated out of Italian and French into English, this pamphlet – of two sheets rather than one – might more properly have been entitled "The progress of Henry IV and of Protestant forces throughout Europe." Often the news was validated by reference to the social distinction of its recipients: "Truely translated out of the French and Italian Copies, as they were sent to right Honourable persons."[46] Some of these tracts were more focused. As the title suggests, *The Chiefe Occurrences of both the Armies, from the Eight of Aprill, till the seuenteenth of the same month. With other intelligences giuen by credible letters* (1592), concentrates on a single event, the fighting between Henry IV and the Prince of Parma; interest here was so intense that two further pamphlets continued the story. Not every work concerned the struggles of the Protestants. *Newes from Rome, Venice, and Vienna* (1595) instead described the see-saw battles between Turks and Christians; unlike most of Wolfe's pamphlets, this one (printed by John Danter for Thomas Gosson) opens by drawing a moral. It manages as well to stretch to three sheets by including the confessions of a captured Tartar horseman, as well as a petition from "some afflicted Christians in those parts" that allows a return to the moral with which it all began.

When the English were directly involved, notes of epic heroism edged their way into the account. *The True Reporte of the seruice in Britanie. Performed lately by the Honorable Knight Sir John Norreys ...* (1591) began by affirming the importance of fame for the military man, and then moved on to the real news, the successful assault on a small Breton town by a combined Anglo-French force, in which the English, by a throw of the dice, won the right to lead the charge. Rather more than most of Wolfe's productions, the subject of this one would have suited Gabriel Harvey, who thought that, in these matters, "gallant wits, and braue pennes may honorably bethinke themselues: and euen ambitiouslye frame their stile to a noble emulation of Liuy, Homer, and the diuinest spirits of all ages."[47] Fortunately, the tract's author did not share his enthusiasm, and most readers, one suspects, preferred to read *The Battaile fought betweene Count Maurice of Nassaw, and Albertus Arch-duke of Austria, nere Newport in*

Flaunders, the xxij of Iune 1600... Written by a Gentleman imploied in the said seruice, and so slog with Sir Francis Vere and his troops through the sand dunes, and learn the names of those killed, injured, or taken prisoner.

Who the readers of these early collections of news might have been is almost impossible to determine precisely. Unfortunately, I know of no bookseller's inventories during the critical years between the later 1580s and the end of the reign, and the inventories of private libraries are not very helpful. The little information that survives is fragmentary in the extreme. In 1585, the bookseller, Thomas Marshe, sued his customer, Edward Wingfield of Kimbolton Castle, for £8. The bill included such serious works as Virgil in Latin and English, Ovid's *Metamorphoses* in English, Cicero's *De officiis* in Latin and English, Homer in English, a variety of dictionaries and medical books, plus a history of the Saracens and John Stow's *Chronicle*. It also included some romances, together with "Newes from the Turk" and "The headles beare," either or both of which might be called newsbooks.[48] An inventory of the Earl of Bedford's library in 1584 contained a number of tracts on events in the Low Countries and a pair on recent events in France, as well as Thomas Churchyard's *A scourge for rebels*, an account of the troubles in Ireland published that same year.[49] There is no indication where Bedford purchased his books – he might have bought them, or had them bought, in London, or he might have found them on the shelves of some provincial bookseller. Thomas Chard, some of whose bills of 1583–84 sent to Cambridge stationers survive as binding fragments, listed seven copies of a book called "Assalt of ye Prince," most likely *A briefe discourse of the assault, committed vpon the person of the most noble prince, the lord William Prince of Orange, Earle of Nassau, Marques de la vere &c. By Iohn Iauregui Spanierd* (Imprinted in London: at the three Cranes in the Vintree by Thomas Dawson for T. C[hard] and W. B[roome], 1582), a book that might be found in Bedford's collection.[50] A later bill, also for books sent to Cambridge and datable to 1588–90, lists twelve copies of "Kinge of navarr," probably a broadside to be sold for a penny.[51] Roger Ward's Shrewsbury stock, inventoried in 1585, contained a good many second-hand books, a fact making it more problematic even than usual to identify the items from the brief titles supplied. Only a few are clear enough: a copy of the discourse of the assault on Orange was here too, along with an account of the entertainment of the Duke of Alençon, which might have been either a pamphlet or a broadside. Yet the appearance at the end of the list of a box for ballads indicates that Ward was not above selling at the less expensive and more ephemeral end of the trade.[52]

Other evidence about the identity of the readers is still more indirect. The destruction by fire of the town of Beccles, Suffolk, in 1586, produced two ballads, both quite detailed in their accounts of the destruction, and both printed for Nicholas Colman, a Norwich bookseller. One was written by Thomas Deloney, a professional author of broadsides, who minutely spells out the losses; the other is rather more moralistic. The sheer quantity of detail suggests both might well have had considerable distribution in East Anglia among the middling sort. When East Dereham, also in East Anglia, similarly suffered disastrous losses through fire, Arthur Gurney published an account intended to correct the broadside ballad – now lost – that had provided the first news of the tragedy. Gurney, an eye-witness to the event, writing a sober tract fully equipped with a dedication as well as a discussion of God's providence, obviously had read the ballad, and acts as if his readers had as well. In these two instances, at least, it seems unwise to assume that news ballads appealed only to those at the bottom end of society. Somewhat later, and certainly by the early 1620s, broadside ballads might conclude with an advertisement for a more complete news pamphlet, telling the reader, "you shall see the full Relation at large in the Booke newly printed."[53] Pamphlets of news, denser in text and more expensive, were aimed directly at those higher up the social scale – though they, of course, might well have shared the information contained in them with their less fortunate neighbours, especially when the event in question was of major national importance and interest was high. The execution of the Earl of Essex, only recently a popular military hero, caused the government to issue a defence of its actions. Margaret Hill, writing a letter full of news from London, told the story to Richard Carnsew and appears to have enclosed a newsbook. "I think there is scarse any of them in the contray," she said, adding "I receiued it but yesterday." She might have sent Barlow's sermon on the Earl's death as well, "but ther be many of them abrode," and she would not do so unless asked.[54] These pamphlets, with their English importance, were much sought after, and appear to have spread throughout the countryside with great rapidity.

The situation at the end of Elizabeth's reign, then, was this: a tight censorship continued to forbid the publication of any domestic news, with the exception of natural calamities and miraculous wonders, murders, instances of witchcraft, government-inspired justifications for trials and executions, plus the occasional story of some English heroism abroad. Accounts of actions in London and Westminster spread by letter, libel, and word of mouth, with the latter – in the form of rumour – often inaccurate and occasionally dangerous, and with both correspondence and speech subject to governmental interference. Foreign news was simply sporadic. At moments when English forces were heavily involved, as in France in the early 1590s, the flow of foreign news suddenly increased; Dutch news, always a bit more problematic because the Queen in essence disapproved of the Dutch rebels, flowed in a continuous if thin trickle. The activities of the army in Ireland appear to have been excluded from any sort of printed news reports until the Spanish actually landed at Kinsale in 1601.[55] Commentary on the news had, perforce, to be indirect, with historical analogy the form most often used. Yet there is every indication that interest in such news was high. Words like "pasquil" – the Italian for comic libel – came into common usage, and more than one humorous pamphlet inserted the word in its title. As all of them had to pass the censor, it is hardly surprising that the content of these pasquils was innocuous, but it is telling that the word was thought to have marketing value. Similarly, John Wolfe and his friends had come to realize that publishing news pamphlets in a series was good business; that practice, now only occasional, would become much more common in the next reign.

IV

The accession of James I in 1603 did not immediately lead to any change of policy. There was no sudden rise in the usual quantity of news pamphlets or broadside ballads, and the few blips in the even tenor of publications were the result of "special" events like the arrival of the King of Denmark and its attendant entertainments or, across the Channel, the murder of King Henry IV. Samuel Daniel, Ben Jonson, and George Chapman, together with the companies for which they wrote, tested the waters by presenting plays dealing tangentially with the overheated politics of the later 1590s; all three ran into difficulties with the Privy Council, though none suffered more than pecuniary loss, and none stopped writing. On the other hand, there is certainly more surviving evidence of an interest in news. One of the examples of what has been called a "news-diary," that of Walter Yonge, begins in 1604, and is interesting precisely because so much of the news it records is second-hand, thus providing evidence of the circulation of materials from London to the provinces and then within circles of provincial gentry. Yonge was well aware of the possibility that the information would be deformed in its passage from hand to hand, and took extraordinary trouble to verify what he heard.[56] With Yonge and others like him clamouring for news, paid writers of manuscript newsletters increased in number, and their connections at court improved. There is also evidence of a greater traffic in foreign newsbooks and newsletters (corantos), some of them sent in by merchants and by officials like Sir Dudley Carleton, the Ambassador to the Low Countries, who provided them to his friend John Chamberlain, no doubt in exchange for Chamberlain's assiduous collections of English news. As their printing in England was still prohibited, entrepreneurs in London copied them in manuscript and forwarded them to whoever was ready to pay. At the same time, a growing trade in "separates" circulated not only copies of speeches in the House of Commons (whose dissemination outside the walls of Parliament was entirely illegal) but also other documents of contemporary interest. One of the great scandals of the age, the murder of Sir Thomas Overbury by a cast of characters including the King's favourite, the Earl of Somerset, provided the writers of separates with a wonderful opportunity: manuscript copies of these documents are remarkably widespread, and there is some evidence that they were recopied as they passed from hand to hand in the countryside.[57] At the same time, the beginnings of a new war on the Continent, in which Britain had no choice but to become involved, piqued curiosity enough for the number of news publications to rise sharply. By 1619 or 1620, the potential market appeared lucrative enough for Dutch printers to produce corantos in English for illegal shipment to London and beyond.[58]

This situation of high demand and inadequate supply led John Pory, one of the writers of manuscript newsletters, to use his connections at Court to try to establish a monopoly of *printed* news. Pory's justifications included the observation that in other countries "the ploughman and artisan can talk of thes matters" to the general benefit, while in England such talk was prohibited; however, Pory added, the interests of the nation were best served if the news were doled out in carefully controlled doses. A news monopoly would serve "to establish a speedy and reddy way wherby to disperse into the veynes of the whole body of a state such matter as may best temper it, & be most agreeable to the disposition of the head & the principale members."[59] Nothing came of this venture, though the idea was revived after the Restoration.

Instead of seizing control of the entire news "industry," the King and his councillors limited their efforts to occasional repression. Censorship was, of course, part of this strategy, as were the continuing (if sporadic) attempts to curb the spread of rumour by letter or speech. However, on at least one occasion, that of the trial and execution of Johan van Oldenbarnevelt, the Advocate of Holland, intervention was assertive rather than restrictive. Not only did the censor allow the publication of a number of news tracts and a broadside ballad, but the whole episode was almost immediately made into a play, John Fletcher and Philip Massinger's *Sir John Van Olden Barnavelt*. Barnavelt – as the play consistently refers to him – had for long been one of the leading figures in the revolt of the Dutch provinces against the Spanish; as the chief politician in Holland, the largest and wealthiest of the Dutch provinces, he had supplied the money and forged the alliances that bolstered independence. His pride in "the labourinthes of pollicie, I haue trod / to find the clew of saffetie for my Cuntrie"[60] was by no means unjustified. Nevertheless, over the years, Barnavelt had come into increasing conflict with the United Provinces' chief military commander, Maurice, Prince of

Orange, a conflict now exacerbated by differences over religion. When Barnavelt tried to oust his rival by setting up his own army, Maurice accused the old man of conspiracy, and had him tried and executed. That execution took place on 3 May 1619, and the English Ambassador, Sir Dudley Carleton, wrote of the event to King James on the same day. On 8 May Carleton's London correspondent, John Chamberlain, wrote "We heard here on Thursday" – that is, on 6 May – "of Barnevelts defeat by some that were eye-witnesses, but there were few or no letters come of any particulers."[61] The first of the newsbook publications on the subject – largely translations of Dutch documents – was registered on 17 May; a vitriolic broadside ballad, undated and unregistered, must have appeared at the same time. Less than three months later, Thomas Locke informed Carleton: "The Players heere were bringing of Barnavelt vpon the stage, & had bestowed a great deale of mony to prepare all things for the purpose," and then added that "at th'instant were prohibited by my Lo: of London," that is, by Bishop John King. Two weeks thereafter, the Bishop's objections had been overcome, and the "players haue fownd the meanes to goe through wth the play of Barnevelt & it hath had many spectators."[62]

The story has its puzzles, of which the greatest was the fact that the play was performed at all. As a staged newsbook dealing with strictly contemporary events abroad, *Sir John Van Olden Barnavelt* is unusual in the long history of Elizabethan drama. Other examples, such as the lost *Battle of Turnholt*, were records of English victories, intended no doubt to set the groundlings cheering, but no danger to the conduct of England's continental affairs. Christopher Marlowe's *Massacre at Paris* (1593), on the other hand, did generate a protest from the French Ambassador, probably because it put on the stage men like the new French King, Henry IV, who remained very much alive. Another ambassadorial protest greeted George Chapman's *Biron* plays, though the case there is rather more complicated because of the none too oblique parallels with the death of the Earl of Essex. Doubly motivated, the government ordered a temporary closure of the theatres and a large fine for the players; additionally, the players were forced to agree "no longer to perform any modern histories nor speak of contemporary affairs on pain of death."[63]

Considering that recent decision, it is odd that the censor even agreed to look at the play. Not only did he do so, but his surviving excisions and deletions indicate that he edited the play to bring it into closer alignment with the royal point of view. Fletcher and Massinger's original text depicted Barnavelt as a schemer, ready to turn Arminian, stir up sedition, even turn against his country for the sake of ambition. Sir George Buc left that rather tendentious portrait alone, deleting only a passage in which Barnavelt compared himself to Cato and so justified his actions by calling Prince

Maurice a tyrant. Such anti-monarchical rhetoric had been dangerous in the 1590s, and remained so. What survived Buc's ministrations was a play even closer to King James's Netherlands policy than Fletcher and Massinger's original. James, we know, disliked the Low Countries' form of government and hated Arminianism, along with Barnavelt's defence of the doctrine. However, while the King was no doubt delighted to see the old man gone, not all Englishmen agreed. John Chamberlain believed "that divers of good judgement thincke he had hard measure, considering that no cleere matter of conspiracie with the ennemies of the state appeares, or can be proved, so that yt seemes to be meere matter of faction and opposition rather then infidelitie or treacherie."[64] Chamberlain hinted that he had, for a time, himself shared that view, but had changed his mind because he had read the sentence against Barnavelt – that is, the tract printing a translation of the Dutch court judgment, one of the many such newsbooks issued, in London, in the wake of the execution. It is worth noting that printing pamphlets of this sort required the censor's permission, and that, in other cases, the government had had no inhibitions about preventing such publication, and had done so in the aftermath of Henry IV's assassination.[65] If Chamberlain is the ideal reader at whom the barrage of news was aimed, then the pamphlets had done their work well. And I would argue that it is no mere coincidence that the play, in a scene that is almost intrusively long, rehearses in detail all the charges against Barnavelt.

The prohibition of news plays, enacted in the wake of the uproar over Chapman's *Biron*, plainly did not apply in this instance. The authors flouted the prohibition, as did the King's Men in putting it on. Moreover, as we have already noted, they added to their risk by bestowing a great deal of money on the production. In addition, as Trevor Howard-Hill has pointed out, the whole operation was conducted with remarkable speed: three months, he argues, is about as rapidly as it could have been done.[66] That the company would rush into and persist with such a risky and expensive production leads to the conclusion that the authors and players had been promised protection, if not outright encouragement, by someone in a position of considerable authority, most likely by a member of the Privy Council. The play still had to make its way through Buc's censorship, but, as we have seen, that served mainly to make it hew more closely to the official line. The remaining puzzle is Bishop King's interference. This author is inclined to agree with Richard Dutton's suggestion that the bishop wished to make sure that a play intended to allay political controversies did not arouse religious ones.[67] Once Bishop King was satisfied, performances began. The point here is simply that the censors would not have found it difficult to suppress the play altogether. They did not choose to do so. Moreover, the very fact of the bishop's intervention, and its temporary nature, lends credence to the argument that the whole business was officially inspired, for Bishop King was a member of the Privy Council and can hardly have helped being aware of what was going on.

The story of the production of *Sir John Van Olden Barnavelt* reflects the situation of news in the years immediately preceding the arrival of corantos on the English scene. A man as well placed as John Chamberlain had no discernible trouble in getting access either to the story or to the Dutch documents in the case – and this would have been true whether or not King James's government licensed their publication. Indeed, Chamberlain's reputation in London depended precisely on his access to such news. From him, and others like him, the story of Barnavelt would have spread to other members of the "political nation," either by word of mouth or by the distribution of separates. All of this would, of course, have taken time. By permitting publication of the tracts, James shortened the time required for his preferred interpretation to take root; by allowing the play to go forward, James also allowed discussion of the issues by those whom, under other circumstances, he would have preferred to keep in ignorance. The "greater opennesse, and libertie of discourse" of which he complained only a year later was in part the result of his own actions and, as war approached ever nearer, the need to "draw in the vulgar," the need to replace one kind of decorum with another, gradually pushed the government into allowing the open distribution of foreign news. Extending the same permission to domestic news had to wait until the era of civil war.

V

In writing about the corantos of the early 1620s, D.C. Collins, the editor of a still very useful bibliography of the newsbooks of 1590–1610, states that "Except for the greater frequency of their publishing and the variety of news offered under one cover, they show little, if any, advance in essentials on the Elizabethan news pamphlets."[68] Nor is Collins the only writer who treats the newsbooks as filling simply the role of forerunners. Indeed, if one looks at pamphlets such as Wolfe's *Credible Reportes from France, and Flanders. In the moneth of May 1590*, there appears to be a good deal of truth in the statement. Yet Wolfe's little booklet is exceptional. Most of the newsbooks of the 1590s more closely resembled the *Battle of Nieuport*, the very text Collins was editing, in relating to a single event and appearing only on that occasion. By treating the newsbooks as forerunners rather than by examining them in the context of their own time, Collins and those who follow him seem to miss the point; indeed, the two exceptions he notes, periodicity and variety, serve to define the crucial differences, not only between the two types of publication but also between the atmosphere for news in the 1590s and the 1620s.

Public affairs must always have been the subject of rumour, and private letters on public subjects also have a venerable history. Yet, in England, at least, the situation began to alter in the 1590s. What seems to be occurring is an increase in both the velocity and quantity of news. If the evidence of the libels is to be believed, rumour – news passed on orally – propagated rapidly despite governmental efforts at repression. Series of letters containing news also proliferated, notwithstanding the fear expressed by their writers. Professional newsletter writers appeared. Even the amount of printed news – the material most susceptible to the activities of the censor – began to grow, because the government itself on some occasions seems to have found it useful. Underlying all this as a cause for the apparent rise in speed was the extraordinary growth of London, not only in terms of population, but as a centre for government, for conspicuous consumption, even for a national marriage market.[69] London was the centre of fashion, the place where well-connected young men spent the later years of their adolescence as students at the Inns of Court, where they became accustomed to parading their finery at the Queen's Court and up and down the centre aisle of Paul's. London was the market-place for all sorts of commodities, including the intellectual. Books perforce were printed in the city; even those whose subject matter was regional had to be sent up to London for printing before being returned to the country. London was the place to search out old books, or unusual books imported from the Continent, or maps, or prints. Preeminently, London was the place to exchange news, and the Inns, the Royal Court, and Paul's were the three places where the exchange most often took place. Old-timers like John Chamberlain haunted these precincts. Aspirants, the younger men, marked their status by the richness of their clothes and the quality of their inside information – as they later did by way of their knowledge of the arts and of science. Only thus could the new men stay ahead of those still newer.

Most such men would not remain in London forever. Family responsibilities called them back to the shires; royal proclamations ordered them home to perform their duty of keeping the peace in the localities. Many found occasion to return to London, for meetings of Parliament, for pursuing a law case, for consulting all sorts of specialists ranging from architects to jewellers to portraitists. When they came back to the city, they went to the theatres and renewed their contacts with the booksellers, many of whom also arranged for newsletters and acted as general agents for their clients. Books and newsletters followed the gentlemen back to the countryside and, increasingly, these were shared with their friends. Thus news, and much else, spread outward from the metropolis, and downward through the social scale.

That news was part of a market-place of fashion did not prevent its accuracy from becoming a matter of concern. Wonders had to be attested by lists of witnesses. The Reverend Joseph Mead ran around Cambridge to authenticate some of the stories sent him from London.[70] News diarists like Yonge and John Rous checked the accuracy of the rumours they heard – Rous on occasion walked to the neighbouring town to consult proclamations or to ask acquaintances. Richard Shanne seized on refugees from the burning of Cork to question them whether the story of the battle of the starlings reported in a newsbook and a broadside was really true.[71] And the growing habit of linking broadsides to newsbooks suggests that it was becoming more common for women and men to pursue a story in ever greater detail. The wondrous and the prurient, of course, continued to abound, but a disposition to check, to examine information rationally, had taken root.

To what extent do these activities construct what has come to be called the "public sphere"? In a recent book, Alexandra Halasz has argued that the existence of a market-place of print, stabilized by the Stationers' Company's regime of copyright, and regulating the relations between author, textual property, and a reading audience has fulfilled one of the necessary conditions for constituting a public sphere. Unlike Jürgen Habermas, whose conception of the public sphere, despite its abstractness and resemblance to a Weberian ideal type, nevertheless retains some air of physicality in positing actual meeting places, Halasz places her public sphere entirely within the realm of discourse. Such discourse is an abstract entity, a limitless source on which capital draws in order to produce textual property, a property then commodified by being put into as wide a circulation as possible to maximize profits. Such circulation is not free of constraints: the state, the church, the market, even an intimate private sphere all try to control the flow of textual property for their own ends. Instead of lying in an intermediary position between the sphere of the state and the private sphere, this "public sphere is [not only] inseparable from state, market, and 'intimate sphere,' it is the medium of their interweaving."[72] Douglas Bruster, in briefer compass, also argues that we must move away from the physicality of Habermas' "conversations" toward constituting the public sphere as a matter of language. For both, the pamphleteering of the late 1580s and 1590s, from the Marprelate tracts onward, served to expand the limits of print and, more especially, the sort of language permissible in print. By attacking the bishops in language hitherto used only for the personal, Martin Marprelate decoupled the decorum of language from the decorum of subject; and Thomas Nashe, by defending the *status quo* in similar language, only widened the gap further. Thus, "the private had been made public through the medium of print" by individuals who came from the middle orders of society, and who expected to be read by their social equals.[73]

That the creation of a new discourse by members of society hitherto largely silent, and distributed through a relatively open market-place, would ultimately have an affect in the political sphere seems to me undeniable. Nevertheless, the creation of a new discourse alone is not enough to constitute a public sphere. In the period running from the late 1580s to the early 1620s, such discourse was still occasional and often constrained by governmental intervention. As Habermas himself remarked, "There was as yet [in the seventeenth century] no publication of commercially distributed news; the irregularly published reports of recent events were not comparable to the routine production of news."[74] Perhaps more important still, the constituent members of a still nascent public sphere had to find ways of "conversing" on a regular basis – sporadic mutterings in London or at Quarter-Sessions hardly seem sufficient. There needed to be a chain of distribution running outward from London to the hinterland and downward from the most politically aware and well-connected to those not so blessed, and it was necessary that such a chain be used on a regular basis. That was far from the case at the end of the sixteenth century. Once the era of severe repression ended with the death of Elizabeth, the distribution of political news began to increase; once England was caught up in the beginnings of the Thirty Years' War, the demand for such news exploded, the number of newsbooks multiplied, and Dutch printers found it profitable to translate their corantos into English and send them to London. English printers responded to the challenge, and began to publish corantos on their own. Thomas Archer, the first of them, "was laid by the heels for making, or adding to his corrantos, as they say. But now there is another that hath got license to print them and sell them, honestly translated out of the Dutch."[75] The licence was issued within two months of James's proclamation against licentious speech in matters of state, and its issuance effectively marked a shift in policy. For whatever reason, the King changed his mind. Once he did so, and the news began to flow more freely, the possibility of the constitution of a real public sphere, in being for an extended period, becomes imaginable.

NOTES

1. James F. Larkin and Paul L. Hughes (eds.), *Stuart Royal Proclamations*, vol. I, James I (Oxford, 1973), No.208, pp.495–6. The quotation from the French Ambassador is on p.496n.
2. Norman Egbert McClure (ed.), *The Letters of John Chamberlain*, 2 vols. (Philadelphia, 1939), II, 396. John Chamberlain to Sir Dudley Carleton (London, 4 Aug. 1621).

3. James Orchard Halliwell (ed.), *The Autobiography and Correspondence of Sir Simonds D'Ewes, Bart.,* 2 vols. (London, 1845), I: 143, 154.

4. Elisabeth Bourcier (ed.), *The Diary of Sir Simonds D'Ewes (1622–1624)* (Paris, 1974), 59, 85.

5. T. McAlindon, *Shakespeare and Decorum* (New York, 1973), 1–18, has a useful discussion of the ramifications of the idea of decorum.

6. Alan Hunt, *Governance of the Consuming Passions. A History of Sumptuary Law* (Basingstoke: Macmillan Press Ltd., 1996), 310–11. For details of the legislation, Frances Elizabeth Baldwin, *Sumptuary Legislation and Personal Regulation in England,* Johns Hopkins University Studies in Historical and Political Science, series XLIV, No.1 (Baltimore, MD: The Johns Hopkins Press, 1926), and Wilfrid Hooper, "The Tudor Sumptuary Laws," *English Historical Review,* 30 (1915): 433–49.

7. Frederic A. Youngs, Jr., *The Proclamations of the Tudor Queens* (Cambridge, 1976), 161–70.

8. J.R. Tanner (ed.), *Tudor Constitutional Documents* (Cambridge, 2nd edn. 1930), 94.

9. Paul L. Hughes and James F. Larkin (eds.), *Tudor Royal Proclamations,* 3 vols. (New Haven, CT, and London, 1964–69), II: 119.

10. George Puttenham, *The Arte of English Poesie* (London: Richard Field, 1589), 237, 127.

11. Fulke Greville, "A Dedication to Sir Philip Sidney," in *The Prose Works of Fulke Greville, Lord Brooke,* ed. John Gouws (Oxford, 1986), 134.

12. Francis Bacon, "On the Fortunate Memory of Elizabeth, Queen of England," in F.J. Levy (ed.), *The History of the Reign of King Henry the Seventh* (Indianapolis, IN, 1972), 266.

13. *Letters of John Holles, 1587–1637,* ed. P.R. Seddon, 3 vols., Thoroton Society, Record Series, XXXI, XXXV, XXXVI (Nottingham, 1975–86), II: 222. To his loving son, John Holles, esq. [at London, 26 Jan. 1619].

14. John Donne, *The Satires, Epigrams and Verse Letters,* ed. W. Milgate (Oxford, 1967), 15, 18.

15. On this point, Andrew Mousley, "Self, State, and Seventeenth Century News," *The Seventeenth Century,* 6 (1991): 150–52.

16. An analysis of the political theory behind all this, in terms of the intersection of ascending and descending authority, is in J.G.A. Pocock, *The Machiavellian Moment* (Princeton, NJ, 1975), 353.

17. On the early period, C.A.J. Armstrong, "Some Examples of the Distribution and Speed of News in England at the Time of the Wars of the Roses," in R.W. Hunt, W.A. Pantin, and R.W. Southern (eds.), *Studies in Medieval History Presented to Frederick Maurice Powicke* (Oxford: Clarendon Press, 1948), 429–54.

18. There is some discussion of these materials in Matthias A. Shaaber, *Some Forerunners of the Newspaper in England, 1476–1622* (Philadelphia, PA, 1929), 177–9.

19. James K. Lowers, *Mirrors for Rebels,* University of California English Studies, 6 (Berkeley and Los Angeles, CA, 1953), provides a list and studies them as reflections of the Elizabethan world order; there is another list in Shaaber, *Some Forerunners of the Newspaper,* 114–16.

20. Joseph Lilly (ed.), *A Collection of Seventy-nine Black-Letter Ballads and Broadsides* (London: Joseph Lilly, 1867), 239–40.

21. Edward Arber (ed.), *A Transcript of the Registers of the Company of Stationers of London,* 5 vols. (London and Birmingham, 1875–94), V: lxxvi. Order of Privy Council requiring all Books to be licensed before Publication.

22. H[istorical]M[anuscripts]C[ommission] De L'Isle & Dudley, II, 435. 2 Feb. 1599/1600.

23. Walter Bourchier Devereux, *Lives and Letters of the Devereux, Earls of Essex,* 2 vols. (London, 1853), II: 99. 12 May 1599.

24. HMC De L'Isle & Dudley, II: 404. 26 Oct. 1599.

25. Gabriel Harvey, *Foure Letters and Certeine Sonnets... 1592,* ed. G.B. Harrison, The Bodley Head Quartos (London: John Lane, 1922), 10, 25.

26. Clifford Chalmers Huffman, *Elizabethan Impressions. John Wolfe and His Press* (New York, 1988), 99–121.

27. Lawrence Stone, *The Crisis of the Aristocracy 1558–1641* (Oxford, 1965), 388.

28. HMC De L'Isle and Dudley, II: 397. John Harington, on duty in Ireland with the Earl of Essex, received much the same advice.

29. Ibid., II: 420.
30. *Letters of Philip Gawdy*, ed. I.H. Jeayes, Roxburghe Club (London, 1906), 5.
31. On libels, Pauline Croft, "Libels, Popular Literacy and Public Opinion in Early Modern England," *Historical Research*, 68 (1995), 266–85, and her earlier "The Reputation of Robert Cecil: Libels, Political Opinion and Popular Awareness in the Early Seventeenth Century," *Transactions of the Royal Historical Society*, 6th ser., 1 (1991), 43–69; and Thomas Cogswell, "Underground Verse and the Transformation of Early Stuart Political Culture," in Susan D. Amussen and Mark A. Kishlansky (eds.), *Political Culture and Cultural Politics in Early Modern England* (Manchester and New York, 1995), 277–300; Alastair Bellany, "'Raylinge Rymes and Vaunting Verse': Libellous Politics in Early Stuart England, 1603–1628," in Kevin Sharpe and Peter Lake (eds.), *Culture and Politics in Early Stuart England* (Stanford, 1993), 285–310 is slightly less relevant to my theme.
32. Looking back over this whole period, the very shrewd John Selden remarked that these "light" writings best served to show which way the wind was blowing: "More solid Things do not show the Complexion of the times so well as Ballads and Libels." *Table Talk* in James Thornton (ed.), *Table Talk from Ben Jonson to Leigh Hunt*, Everyman's Library (London: J.M. Dent & Sons, 1934), 62.
33. HMC Salisbury, 9 (1599), I:282.
34. British Library, Add. MS. 38,492, f. 100.
35. Thomas Dekker's play, *The Shoemaker's Holiday* provides a good picture of the latter, but only by setting the story in the fifteenth century.
36. At the height of the London disturbances, libels were scattered about London: BL Lansdowne MS.78, f. 159, John Spencer, Lord Mayor of London, to Burghley, 29 Aug. 1595; f. 161, same to same. 23 July 1596.
37. Joel Hurstfield, "The Succession Struggle in late Elizabethan England," in his *Freedom, Corruption and Government in Elizabethan England* (London, 1973), 104–34.
38. See the sensible discussion of the ban in Cyndia Susan Clegg, *Press Censorship in Elizabethan England* (Cambridge, 1997), 198ff. Clegg argues that the censorship was related to the particular events of 1599 rather than to such general considerations as the genre of satire.
39. *The Letters of John Chamberlain*, I: 97.
40. *Calendar of State Papers, Domestic, 1598–1601*, 350.
41. Simonds d'Ewes, *The Journals of all the Parliaments during the Reign of Queen Elizabeth* (London, 1682), 653.
42. Peter S. Donaldson, *Machiavelli and Mystery of State* (Cambridge, 1988), 103–4, argues that Wolfe's reasons for publishing Machiavelli were republican; that is, Wolfe followed the line of Alberico Gentili in believing that Machiavelli revealed the secrets of princes and especially tyrants, and so publishing him was an anti-tyrannical move. Denis B. Woodfield, *Surreptitious Printing in England 1550–1640* (New York, 1973), 21, believes Wolfe's motives were largely commercial.
43. Woodfield, *Surreptitious Printing*, 24–5. The French translation was published by Thomas Vautrollier.
44. Huffman, *Elizabethan Impressions*, 84ff., discusses the importance of Hurault.
45. William Wright often collaborated with Wolfe – though, like Aggas, he too sometimes worked alone.
46. *Newes Lately come on the last day of Februarie 1591* (London: John Wolfe, 1591).
47. Harvey, *Foure Letters and Certeine Sonnets*, 26.
48. Henry R. Plomer, "Some Elizabethan Book Sales," *The Library*, 3rd ser., 7 (1916): 318–29.
49. M. St. Clare Byrne and Gladys Scott Thomson, "'My Lord's Books': The Library of Francis, Second Earl of Bedford, in 1584," *Review of English Studies*, 7 (1931): 385–405. The inventory of Richard Stonley's books contains one or two titles that may represent books of news; the large number of bundles of pamphlets may conceal more. See Leslie Hotson, "The Library of Elizabeth's Embezzling Teller," *Studies in Bibliography* 2 (1949–50), 49–61.
50. Robert Jahn, "Letters and Booklists of Thomas Chard (or Chare) of London, 1583–4," *The Library*, 4th ser., 4 (1924): 219–37.

51. Donald Paige, "An Additional Letter and Booklist of Thomas Chard, Stationer of London," *The Library*, 4th ser., 21 (1940): 28, 30.

52. Alexander Rodger, "Roger Ward's Shrewsbury Stock: an Inventory of 1585," *The Library*, 5th ser., 13 (1958): 247–68.

53. Hyder E. Rollins, *A Pepysian Garland* (Cambridge, 1922), 160.

54. P[ublic]R[ecord]O[ffice], SP 46/71, f. 224. 10 May 1601.

55. D.C. Collins, *A Handlist of News Pamphlets, 1590–1610* (London: Southwest-West Essex Technical College, 1943) lists one pamphlet about the landing, with two more (plus a ballad) about the defeat of the Spanish forces. One of the latter opens "In my last of the 19th of December," suggesting that another tract once existed. It is possible, of course, that one manuscript letter of a series fell into the hands of the printers, who then set it up without alteration.

56. *Diary of Walter Yonge, Esq.*, ed. George Roberts, Camden Society (London, 1848), 24, for an example. Yonge's diary is discussed in Richard Cust, "News and Politics in Early Seventeenth-Century England," *Past & Present*, 112 (1986): 79–87, and in Mousley, "Self, State, and Seventeenth Century News," 161–6.

57. J.S. Morrill, "William Davenport and the 'Silent Majority' of Early Stuart England," *Journal of the Chester Archaeological Society*, 58 (1975): 115–29. At least one Elizabethan document could also be found in numerous collections: the exchange of letters between Lord Keeper Egerton and the Earl of Essex on the limits of obedience in a monarchy. That subject was of general interest for a very long time, and so there is no way of determining whether the copies were created contemporaneous with the event, or years (perhaps decades) later.

58. William Barlow, writing from Amsterdam in 1620, complained that the trade had already got ahead of the amateurs: "If I should send you ouer the Relations both in Latin, Dutch, and French, which come to this Towne concerning the variety of Newes about the troubles of Europe, I should weary you with the multiplicity of Bookes and myselfe with the cunning of transportation: Besides, I am sure to be preuented in sending you Newes, because it will bee stale ere it come to your handes by my meanes." The quotation is from Laurence Hanson, "English Newsbooks, 1620–1641," *The Library*, 4th ser., 18 (1938): 355–84, at 379.

59. William S. Powell, *John Pory, 1572–1636* (Chapel Hill, 1977), 52–3, citing *Calendar of State Papers Domestic*, 1619–23, 330; the petition is undated, and has commonly been assigned to 1621. I suspect it may be a year or two earlier.

60. John Fletcher and Philip Massinger, *Sir John Van Olden Barnavelt*, ed. T.H. Howard-Hill, The Malone Society Reprints (1980 for 1979), 2.

61. *The Letters of John Chamberlain*, II: 236. Chamberlain to Carleton [London, 8 May 1619].

62. T.H. Howard-Hill, "Buc and the Censorship of *Sir John Van Olden Barnavelt* in 1619," *Review of English Studies*, n.s. 39 (1988): 39–63, at 42.

63. Richard Dutton, *Mastering the Revels* (London, 1991), 183; see also A.R. Braunmuller (ed.), *A Seventeenth-Century Letter-Book* (Newark, DE, 1983), 435–7.

64. *The Letters of John Chamberlain*, II: 239. Chamberlain to Carleton [London, 31 May 1619].

65. Janet Clare, *"Art made tongue-tied by authority"* (Manchester, 1990), 153.

66. T.H. Howard-Hill, "Crane's 'Promptbook' of *Barnavelt* and Theatrical Processes," *Modern Philology*, 86 (1988–89): 146–70.

67. Dutton, *Mastering the Revels*, 207, 217.

68. *Battle of Nieuport 1600*, ed. D.C. Collins, Shakespeare Association Facsimiles no. 9 (London: Humphrey Milford, 1935), v.

69. F.J. Fisher, "The Development of London as a Centre of Conspicuous Consumption in the Sixteenth and Seventeenth Centuries," in E.M. Carus-Wilson (ed.), *Essays in Economic History*, 3 vols. (New York, 1962), II: 197–207; Lawrence Manley, *Literature and Culture in Early Modern London* (Cambridge, 1995).

70. On checking accuracy, see above, plus my "How Information Spread among the Gentry," *Journal of British Studies*, 21 (1982): 11–34, and Michael Frearson, "The Distribution and Readership of London Corantos in the 1620s," in Robin Myers and Michael Harris (eds.), *Serials and their Readers* (Winchester and New Castle, DE, 1993): 1–25.

71. Hyder E. Rollins, *A Pepysian Garland* (Cambridge: Cambridge University Press, 1922), 156.

72. Alexandra Halasz, *The Marketplace of Print. Pamphlets and the Public Sphere in Early Modern England* (Cambridge: Cambridge University Press, 1997), 163, 169.
73. Douglas Bruster, "The Structural Transformation of Print in Late Elizabethan England," typescript kindly sent to me by the author, 17.
74. Jürgen Habermas, *The Structural Transformation of the Public Sphere,* trans. Thomas Burger with the assistance of Frederick Lawrence (Cambridge, MA: The MIT Press, 1991), 17.
75. Joseph Mead to Sir Martin Stuteville, 22 Sept. 1621, quoted in Folke Dahl, *A Bibliography of English Corantos and Periodical Newsbooks 1620–1642* (London: The Bibliographical Society, 1952), 49.

The Itch Grown a Disease:
Manuscript Transmission of News in the
Seventeenth Century

IAN ATHERTON

"You cannot imagine to what a disease the itch of news is grown," exclaimed John Cooper in 1667. The medical analogy was a common one: Sir George Fletcher diagnosed himself as "infected" with "the love of news"; the *London Courant* in 1688 described the "curiosity after News" as an "itch" and a "humour."[1] From the 1620s, anecdotal evidence suggests that English folk of all degrees were hungry for news. They greeted one another with "What news?" – the more learned asking *"Quelles nouvelles?"* or *"Quid novi."*[2] Even imprisonment in a foreign land could not dull the appetite for news: English prisoners-of-war in 1666 had the *London Gazette* smuggled into their Rotterdam gaol as beer-bottle stoppers.[3]

Contemporary comment emphasized that the volume of political news was increasing throughout the seventeenth century. Two proclamations in 1620–21 noted that news did "dayly more and more increase."[4] Particularly at times of national and European crisis, such as the Thirty Years' War and the Second Anglo-Dutch War, the country was awash with news. In 1632, Sir Henry Herbert described the London Exchange as a place "wher they minte more news then siluer at the Tower"; in a version of the "coals to Newcastle" aphorism, Thomas Bradford claimed in 1665 that to send news to Norwich was "to throw water into the sea."[5]

Analyzing the transmission of news in the seventeenth century is not, however, straightforward. Most news spread by word of mouth. Most of the entries copied into the news diaries of John Rous in Suffolk and Walter Yonge in Devon are unattributed, but where the origin is given it is usually common rumour or oral news: "it is said," *"ut dicitur,"* even "country intelligence" and "a secret whispering."[6] All forms of written news – newsbooks and newspapers, pamphlets, newsletters, sermons, plays, and ballads – depended heavily upon spoken transmission, and the last four lay across the permeable interface between the oral and the written. Too clear a distinction should not be drawn between oral news and newsletters. Written

Ian Atherton, Keele University

news derived from oral sources and vice versa: Thomas Gainsford wrote of "Nuncupatorie, or Letters of Newes." Newsletters conveyed common rumour and, once received, their contents were divulged to others by word of mouth and by further letters.[7]

Brief glimpses apart, oral transmission of the news is largely lost to us. Historians are forced to pursue the written. With this limitation in mind, we shall turn to the manuscript, rather than the printed, and to newsletters especially. Here, again, the boundary between the written and the printed was blurred. Manuscript and printed transmission of the news went hand-in-hand. Newsmongers often sent out newspapers with their newsletters. The *Flying Post* in the early eighteenth century was printed on one side of the paper only "for the convenience of any person's writing what they please with it into the country."[8] The seventeenth century employed a variety of synonyms for manuscript letters conveying items of news: "newsletters"; "letters of news"; "advertisements"; "occurrences"; "advices"; "intelligences"; "written news"; "papers of news"; and even "newspapers."[9] Most were also used as titles of printed newsbooks and newspapers.

Manuscript was the more important form of written news until the early eighteenth century: it was more plentiful than printed news; it was more accurate, less censored, and regarded as more authoritative; it preceded the regular printing of news; and, for historians, it usually makes a better form of historical evidence. Manuscript news had a number of advantages over its printed sibling. Restrictions on manuscript news were lighter than those on the printed. Except for the period 1641–60, parliamentary proceedings could not be printed, but reports of Parliament circulated relatively freely in manuscript. Between 1666 and 1679 there was only one English newspaper, the *London Gazette*, and this was a rather bland journal, the more interesting news reserved for manuscript newsletters.[10] Late news was more readily accommodated in manuscript than in print: a scribe could add an item more easily than a typesetter. The very form of the printed news emphasized its secondary role. Newsbooks were often little more than printed compendia of newsletters, beginning their reports with the form "By letters from ..." or similar.[11]

Of all the genres of manuscript news, newsletters are particularly suitable for analysis for three reasons. First, they survive in relatively large numbers (whereas few manuscript news diaries are extant). Second, they are datable, whereas manuscript separates or "pocket Manuscripts" – transcripts of treaties, trials, parliamentary proceedings and such like – often circulated many years after they were first written.[12] Finally, most newsletters were signed and addressed, allowing us to study some of the interactions and relationships between writer and reader.

What is a "newsletter"? Richard Cust has distinguished between the "unformalized newsletter," "consisting simply of news items sandwiched between personal and business correspondence in letters to friends or relations", and the "'pure newsletter', given over wholly to news."[13] This attractive division is too simple to encompass the wide range of letters that carried news. Most newsletters, even those written by professional newsmongers, carried some personal details. John Pory's efficient, weekly news service sometimes conveyed personal messages to and from his recipients, assuring Viscount Scudamore that all his friends at Warwick House were well, for example, or exchanging greetings between Sir William Beecher and Scudamore.[14] No clear distinction can be made between the "pure" and the "unformalized." The correspondence from Sir Henry Herbert to Viscount Scudamore between 1624 and 1669 varied from friendly letters mentioning the odd item of news to three or four pages of occurrences with hardly a personal line in them.[15] Only a broad definition, from professionally written newsletters to ordinary correspondence that refers in passing to an item of news, can convey the wide range of manuscript sources of news in the seventeenth century.

The point can be illustrated by examining the newsletter collection of Viscount Scudamore (1601–71), a Herefordshire justice, deputy lieutenant and MP, and, between 1635 and 1639, Charles I's Ambassador in Paris. Among his surviving papers this author has counted over one thousand letters conveying news, sent from at least forty-three correspondents. Most date from the 1620s and 1630s. The collection is by no means complete: Scudamore received newsletters from a Mr Tucker in the 1620s and from Joseph Williamson in the 1660s, but none survives among his papers.[16] In addition, he amassed a large collection of news separates.[17] Over 600 of these newsletters were received by Scudamore as part of his official diplomatic duties. The remainder he chose to receive. The writers of these 400 newsletters can be divided into three rough categories: professional writers; government officials and those connected by office with the Court; and friends and relatives.[18]

Four of Scudamore's correspondents were professional newsmongers: John Flower, John Pory, Edward Rossingham, and Ralph Starkey. All wrote weekly, at not inconsiderable expense. Ralph Starkey had a sliding scale of charges for separates ranging from twenty shillings a quire for parliamentary proceedings to ten pounds for a copy of the Black Book of the Order of the Garter.[19] John Pory charged the viscount £20 for a year's worth of weekly newsletters in 1632.[20]

Regular newsletters, weekly or fortnightly, were received by Scudamore from several government officials or those connected by office with the court. Amerigo Salvetti, the Tuscan resident in London, wrote newsletters in the 1620s. Georg Rudolf Weckherlin, Latin secretary, German interpreter and secretary to Sir John Coke (one of the principal secretaries of state), sent weekly abstracts out of foreign letters in the mid-1630s. Scudamore received Saturday's newsletter from Joseph Williamson, Under-Secretary of State, in the 1660s.

Most of those who sent news to Scudamore were already known to him by ties of family or friendship. He received detailed newsletters from his life-long friend, Sir Henry Herbert, military news from his younger brothers, James and Barnaby, and Spanish news from his former chaplain; news of the war in the Netherlands was sent by a family friend; news came from a "poor kinsman" and via several neighbours; his neighbour, cousin, and brother-in-law, John Scudamore of Ballingham, reported from his travels in France and Italy; printed news pamphlets were sent by another of the Ballingham Scudamores, newsbooks by one of the viscount's servants. Hardly a friend or a neighbour can have left Herefordshire without a charge to write back with whatever news and gossip came to hand.

Most news writers conveyed a changing mixture of home and foreign news, though some specialized in one type. Salvetti sent Scudamore a weekly or fortnightly "gazetta" of mainly foreign news "not daringe uenture of home ones, because I do knowe you are sufficientlie fed by others, that understand them, at this tyme, better than my selfe." Through him Scudamore procured someone to write "Italian occorrences," while Sir Henry Herbert endeavoured to find someone who would send French news.[21]

Most of the news conveyed was foreign; in the 1620s and 1630s it was illegal to *print* domestic news in England.[22] Censorship of manuscript news was lighter, but sufficient to control the expression of discussion, channelling it into certain areas such as private conversation and news diaries. While censorship of manuscripts was real enough for much of the seventeenth century – Charles I's government not infrequently seized private papers, those of the republic and restored monarchy regularly intercepted the mail – the fear of the censor was even greater, despite Kevin Sharpe's recent claims to the contrary.[23] Much of the news was written under this Damoclean sword,[24] but censorship alone does not account for the slanting of manuscript news to the Continent.[25] There are three further reasons why most written news concerned foreign parts. First, home news circulated more easily than foreign by word of mouth and so was less likely to be copied in newsletters. Pory, for one, considered it a "crambe" (a distasteful repetition) to write of what his correspondents already knew.[26] Second, it was usually foreign news that proved the more interesting. At least until the outbreak of the civil wars, the more exciting events – and certainly the more blood-curdling – were abroad. Only with the outbreak of the Bishops' Wars did the balance in Rossingham's newsletters shift to concentrate on British news.[27] Finally, for those who saw the unfolding of events in eschatological terms, it was in the Continental theatre that the final battles against the forces of the Antichrist were being played out, battles that might determine the future of the whole world.

Indeed, it was such struggles against Spain that had first stimulated the English appetite for news in the 1580s and 1590s.[28] A new vocabulary of news terms entered the English language around the turn of the sixteenth century.[29] John Chamberlain, the most famous Jacobethan intelligence writer, probably began his news gathering in 1588.[30] Thereafter, the volume of news in circulation seems to have increased markedly with each new conflict, particularly the Thirty Years' War.[31]

II

As is so often the case with novel developments, one of the strongest and quickest reactions to this growth, judging by literary sources, was ridicule. The news writer, the news reader and the newsletter became stock targets of wits and dramatists in the early seventeenth century. Starting with Joseph Hall's *Characters of Vertues and Vices* (1608), few character books were complete without satirizing the news.[32] The common theme of this mockery was that the written news was untrustworthy: intelligencers were inconstant, peddling lies, and the truth was no concern of theirs.

The news, then, was accorded a low status in contemporary literature. It is, therefore, worth considering how the news was read by others, those "infected with the love of news." First of all, however, it must be remembered that for most people it was a case of hearing, not reading the news. The masses had little opportunity but to hear whatever news they could, asking a passing carrier "What news at London?"[33] For the elite, by contrast, reading the news meant a complex chain of choices. What form should news reports take: oral, manuscript, or printed news? Where to hear or read the news: the Exchange and Paul's Walk for Londoners, the inn or the coffeehouse, the privacy of one's own home? The French had the additional choices of meeting in the bookshop to discuss the news or renting a *Gazette* for a few minutes' browse in the street outside.[34] Few Englishmen can have been as unwise as William Coe, who decided to read the *Northampton Mercury* on horseback: unable to see where he was going, he fell off.[35] Such choices concerning reading the news were largely a matter of what one proposed to do with the news and how much discussion and reflection was intended.

After reading the news, there was the question of what to do with the information: how much to share, how much to preserve, and how to understand and interpret events. Much news was for sharing, but it was a mark of discernment to know how much to divulge to whom and in what form. In extreme cases arrest and imprisonment could be the rewards for the incautious newsmonger.[36] In Bristol, coffee-house keepers were complained of for receiving newsletters and were bound over not to allow the reading or discussing of scandalous news in their establishments; one lost her licence "For publishing & exposing to publick view ... false scandalous seditious libells."[37]

Sensitive to accusations of rumour-mongering, some readers and writers sought to control the conditions under which their news might be divulged. "Burn this letter" was a frequent postscript, frequently ignored. John Drake read a sensitive newsletter to his friend Walter Yonge, rather than giving him the letter itself; Yonge then wrote up parts in his news diary, using Anglo-Saxon characters to disguise the controversial news (about Catholics at Court).[38] When, throwing caution to the wind, Thomas Cotton decided to read aloud his weekly London newsletter every market day at Colchester "as people [do] where Ballads are sunge," he was complained of to Archbishop Laud.[39]

Under varying controls, newsletters were recopied in whole or part, or passed around among groups of friends. Sir Thomas Puckering and Sir Thomas Lucy shared Pory's newsletter and split the cost of buying separates.[40] An enterprising Oxfordshire alehouse keeper sold news stories to his customers, a halfpenny a time.[41] News was constantly recirculated, a perpetual motion of news by word of mouth and in fresh newsletters. The writing of newsletters was an accomplishment the gentry were expected to possess: a gentleman's handbook of 1616 included advice on the composition of "Letters of Newes."[42] The educated knew how to read and to write a newsletter and were engaged in both processes. On 22 June 1626 Scudamore penned a newsletter to his great-uncle Rowland. Two-thirds of this letter were copied straight from the newsletter he had just received from James Palmer dated 16 June. He changed one detail with information from Salvetti's newsletter of 17 June and added a few other lines from another source which it has not been possible to identify. Even the (rare) lines of comment in Palmer's letter, decrying the dissolution of Parliament and the attacks on Buckingham, were copied out by Scudamore, with the plea to his great-uncle to burn the letter.[43]

A little more about the reading and writing of newsletters can be gleaned from the activities of diplomatic staff, for whom collecting, sifting, and recirculating news was a positive duty. In this capacity they acted very like London news factors such as Chamberlain or Pory. The intelligence, gossip, and newsletters received at the Embassy were processed and then summarized in a weekly "advice." These abstracts were circulated to the secretaries of state and others in London. Here they were often endorsed with a summary of their contents, read at the foreign committee, and filed. Such abbreviation of newsletters was a duty of the secretaries of state often delegated to their own personal secretaries, so much so that the Earl of Shrewsbury, Secretary of State in the 1690s, admitted, "I never read or write a letter," leaving it to his under-secretary to summarize all the correspondence.[44]

Newsletters had to be read *extensively*. A large volume of news was demanded by the discerning and wise because it was recognized that even the best reports might be uncertain, temporary judgements in need of later confirmation or denial. Scudamore prefixed his newsletter to his great-uncle thus: "Because I presume you to desire to know the certainty of things in these vncertaine and most perilous times, I am bold to impart to you such occurrences as come from good hands, that by comparing these with other intelligence & reports, truth may shew it self sooner to you."[45] Pory was most insistent that Scudamore should read corantos (the earliest newsbooks), "for the wisest men that ever I was acquainted with both here & beyond the sea would doe so," but extensive reading was needed:

> a man that reads those toyes every week as they come forth is like one that stands in a fielde of Archers, where though hee sees not the marke, but observing how the arrowes fall, some short, some gone, some on the right and some on the lefte hand, he hath a near guesse where about the marke is; so that hee that reads those bable for a year or however will be able very handsomely to conjecture at the general state of Christendome.[46]

In other words, "truth will out," but only by constant attention to the news.

That truth had two parts, the "Glory of God" and "the Instruction of Men."[47] For many, the main way to read the news was to seek the divine hand that lay behind human actions. The news could be read as an expression of the workings of God's providence, the playing out of divine intervention in the wider world just as many "experimental Calvinists" and others read their own lives as a series of providences and punishments. This was how the Puritan artisan Nehemiah Wallington read the news.[48] Recalling the Biblical plagues of Egypt, Yonge recorded what he called "the Plagues of England" in his news diary: not only bad weather and disease, but the Spanish match, moves towards greater toleration of Roman Catholics and the extra-parliamentary benevolence of 1622.[49]

It was a seventeenth-century commonplace that history could teach useful lessons. In offering Scudamore a commonplace book of various separates (including news items such as diplomatic instructions and orders for the Council of the North), Starkey advised that "you may make severall

vsses of them for presidente and Story."[50] The seventeenth century was the
great age of both the precedent and the commonplace book. The educated
and the not so educated copied down and read precedents, history, sermons,
the sayings of the great and the good and the dead in the hope of
understanding their world and their lives. Gentlemen were advised to study
history for delight and profit.[51] Civil or political history was considered to
be none other than an accurate report of past and present facts and events.[52]
Reading contemporary history – the news – could, therefore, be as
profitable as reading ancient history. Moreover, the news could be read for
its style as well as its content. Henry Peacham advised gentlemen to procure
parliamentary speeches and pleadings in Star Chamber "and other publique
Courts" (all of which circulated widely in the manuscript news) as means to
"better your speech, [and] enrich your vnderstanding."[53] The study of
rhetoric was one of the main reasons for the compilation of so many
parliamentary diaries in the 1620s.[54]

The news, dismissed with disdain and distaste by wits and dramatists,
was seen as worthy of preservation. Newsletters were not merely ephemeral
collections of lies; they could, wrote James Howell in 1645 (publishing an
edition of his own newsletters) "treasure up, and transmit Matters of State
to Posterity" and be "safe Repositories of Truth."[55] Rous and Yonge, lacking
newsletters of their own (to judge from the sources they recorded),
compiled news diaries, preserving the news from oral, manuscript, and
printed sources. One way of reading the news was to write it down, for
preservation. Jamie, one of the characters in a 1641 pamphlet entitled *Vox
Borealis*, relates how he had a "good store of News in my pocket Book."[56]
Similar were the compilers of city annals, who commenced their histories
of cities with the first medieval charter, but continued into the present noting
the news as they chronicled each year.[57] Separates were also to be kept. Sir
Richard Grosvenor insisted that his collection of manuscript separates was
inalienable, to be passed with the rest of his library from generation to
generation.[58] John Rushworth hoped that his *Historical Collections*, itself a
type of printed collection of separates with a connecting narrative, would be
a means "to separate Truth from Falshood, things real from things fictitious
or imaginary," enabling "After Ages to ground a true history."[59]

The news was read with an eye to discovering the truth. Yonge, for
example, went over the entries in his news diary noting which later proved
false and, occasionally, which true.[60] There was, in other words, a tension
between the writing of news which, as the wags joked about novelty, news
and the new, was an ephemeral, daily activity, and the reading of news,
where things more constant – truth, the divine will – might be sought.

In their reading of news, contemporaries recognized a scale of reliability,
hierarchies of source and genre. Bottom of the scale, usually the least

reliable source, were oral reports – rumour. Almost all of the attributed entries which Yonge later erased from his diary as untrue were originally spread by word of mouth; only one had come from a letter. Printed news was usually considered more reliable than speech: according to the printer in Ben Jonson's *Newes from the New World* there were "a great many" who would "beleeve nothing but what's in Print"; in his news dairy Rous occasionally confirmed an oral report with a printed account.[61] Nonetheless, printed news was only a rung above rumour on the ladder of credibility. Corantos were held to be notoriously unreliable. "Currantes many tymes publish currant lies" punned one correspondent in 1626; "now euery one can say, its euen as true as a Currantoe, meaning that it's all false," quipped Donald Lupton in 1632. Even Pory, associated with the production of corantos, recognized that they were not wholly reliable.[62] Newsbooks as a whole (there were, of course, important differences between individual titles which some could recognize) were also regarded as an untrustworthy genre. Howell, who a year later was to praise (his own) newsletters as "authentick Registers," castigated newsbooks as "those Ephemeran creatures ... that are borne in the morning, grow up till noon, and perish the same night."[63]

Widely held to be the most authoritative, and as such regularly copied into commonplace books, was the separate. When Scudamore accused one of Starkey's scribes of inaccuracy, Starkey promised to rectify any faults immediately and to be more careful in checking items in the future.[64] Newsletters lay between trustworthy separates and untrustworthy newsbooks on this scale of reliability.[65] As an ambassador, Viscount Scudamore was charged with informing Charles I's government by newsletter – "weekely advertisements" – which had to be "faithfull discoueries," "not collected from Gazettes or vulgar rumors."[66]

Aware of widespread criticism, and wishing to emulate the reputation of the separates (many of which they also produced), newsletter writers were always at pains to stress the reliability of their information. They regularly prefixed items with their sources and were careful to point out which stories were likely to prove less reliable. John Flower, for example, mentioned "divers stragling reports" of the Duke of Bavaria and Wallenstein, "but because I perceive noe creditt is given to them, I will forbear the writing of them, seing it is likelie that before it be longe more certaine advertisements will come of all occurrents there."[67] Accuracy was the goal, and any authorial interjections or editorial comment would be likely to detract from that end.

The final way of reading that we can recover concerns the evaluation and discussion of the news. Judgements and opinions had to be read into the news. Until the heated party atmosphere of the Popish Plot and Exclusion Crisis, most newsletters make no comment on the news (apart from judging the reliability of sources), they merely purport to report it. Newsletters were not the place for opinion or comment on the news: as James Palmer closed one of his, "... and thes beinge the text the observations is left to your iudgment."[68] Ambassadorial weekly advices rarely commented on the news they conveyed; the opinions of the Ambassador were saved for the covering letters to the secretaries of state.[69]

III

News was a problematic form of knowledge in the seventeenth century, causing problems of writing and problems of audience, and raising conservative fears of "licentious discourse." We shall begin with the problems of writing the news.

As we have seen, the affinity between truth and falsehood in the news was a complex one, and the news was often held to be unreliable. "False News follows true at the Heels, and oftentimes outstrips it," explained Thomas Lushington, adding that the news was "variously and contrarily related, till the false controuls the true."[70] Nigel Smith has described news writing as existing "in the margin between fact and fiction."[71] The relationship between fact and fiction was a central literary problem of the seventeenth century, and the development of English newspapers has been placed in the context of the breaking down of the epistemological barrier between knowledge and opinion.[72] The early seventeenth century sought to contain these problems raised by the news in two ways which shaped the writing and transmission of manuscript news. The first was to fit the news to the degree of the reader, the second was to bind writer and reader in a close and clearly understood relationship.

Newsletters were written with the audience in mind, but it was the fitness of the news for the audience as a whole and vice versa rather than the ideological stance of the individual reader that shaped the writing. There were different sorts of news for different people. Jonson wrote mockingly of "Barbers newes / And Taylors Newes, Porters, and Watermens newes," but there was a division of news by degree, a hierarchy of readers just as there were hierarchies of sources and hierarchies of news genres.[73]

Printed news was for everyone, even those who could not afford to buy it. In 1625 Abraham Holland complained of corantos that "euerie week besmeare / Each publike post, and Church dore" and bemoaned "the wals / Butter'd with weekly Newes compos'd in Pauls." Moreover, as Pory wrote, corantos were "toyes" for the vulgar (even if it was important for "men of quality" to read them also).[74] Newsletters, by comparison, were for the elite, their very cost putting them out of the reach of the masses. The most extreme example of this is the government newsletter service of the

1660s and 1670s, whose recipients were carefully and punctually regulated, hand-picked by Williamson and Lord Arlington, Secretary of State. Williamson's control of this newsletter and censorship of the *Gazette* were exercises in information management.[75] News readers as well as news writers recognized the distinctions inherent in the system, even if much "select" news eventually leaked out into public discourse. Scudamore the experienced politician wrote to Williamson in 1666 thanking him for his newsletters and adding: "This is an entertainment which my employment heertofore made mee well acquainted with And therfore, if you please sometime to entrust mee with something that is not comunicated to euery correspondent, you may expect mee capable to apprehend it."[76]

If news could be categorized by the degree of the reader, there are indications that the news could also be differentiated by gender, for there were gender differences in the transmission and readership/listenership of news. Men could draw on a wider range of news sources than women could. The "Paul's walkers" and "Duke Humphrey's diners" who flocked to St Paul's Cathedral in London to exchange news seem, in contemporary descriptions, to have been male: attorneys, courtiers, gentlemen, and merchants.[77] Newsletters were generally procured by men.[78] It is possible that women may have been less interested in the news. Female correspondents very rarely included even a line of news in their letters, where their male counterparts rarely let a letter pass without some mention of the events of the day. Dorothy Osborne wrote to her suitor in 1653 that "I know not how I stumbled upon a new's book this week, and for want of something else to doe read it."[79] Either she had little interest in reading the news, or she felt it necessary to excuse her reading of it; either way, it is significant. All of the sources identified in the news diaries of Walter Yonge and John Rous were male.[80] The private world of the family, not the public world of politics, was seen as the sphere for women. After sending the Earl of Denbigh a letter of *family* news, Ursula Beaumont added, "yov may see I desire to wright suche nuse as consarnes my plase."[81]

Nevertheless, the apparent gender bias may be overemphasized by the tendency to call reports from men "news" and those from women "gossip." In practice there may often have been no difference, yet gossiping was considered a *female* trait, the subject of increased male fears in early modern England.[82] In Sir George Etheredge's 1676 comedy the *Man of Mode, or Sir Fopling Flutter*, the distinction is drawn between gossip, which interests the women, and the news sent to men. The women consider setting up "an office of intelligence" to circulate gossip, libel, and lampoons. This, it is foretold, will "have great dealings with country ladies / More than Muddiman has with their husbands."[83] The distinctions between the consumption of the news by men and women should not be overdrawn.

There were women involved in producing, selling, and distributing printed news as printers, publishers, hawkers, and coffeehouse keepers,[84] and there were women who eagerly devoured what news they could.[85]

It was a commonplace that the news had to be worthy of the recipient. That it was a rule endlessly repeated and as often flouted does not allow it to be dismissed as wholly debased. John Flower was always keen to stress that he sent only news "worthy" of Scudamore's knowledge, in other words, that not only was it not common or base, but also that it was too important, too serious, for lesser men. Sir Richard Wilbraham assured Sir Richard Grosvenor that his locale "affurdeth nothing worthy your knowleg."[86] Such rhetoric attempted to distinguish the recipient's news from the varieties of news so derided in contemporary literature.

The language of worth was part of the discourse of patronage. Here we are upon the second means by which the problematic, novel, and unstable discourse of news might be controlled and regulated. News was often written in the context of patronage and clientage, of providing a service to a great man. The transmission of news was made to fit, a little awkwardly, the familiar world of hierarchy and deference.

Titbits of news were part of the currency of client–patron exchanges. When Henry Rogers sought assistance in getting out of Fleet prison, he was careful to include some home and foreign news with his letter appealing to Scudamore.[87] John Burghe in London sent news to Scudamore in Paris, at least in part in repayment for Scudamore's promise to employ Burghe's son as a page in the Embassy household.[88] The provision of news could also be part of a process of healing rifts. When John Scudamore of Ballingham provoked his family's anger by journeying to the Continent, he endeavoured to patch up the quarrel by sending news to his brother-in-law as he continued his travels.[89] A second example is William Powell's sending of parliament news to Scudamore in 1660. Powell had defeated Scudamore's candidate in the Herefordshire election to the Convention Parliament and the newsletters can be seen as an attempt to mollify the viscount.[90]

Writing and receiving a newsletter placed writer and reader in a close relationship: as Julia Merritt has commented, it "was not like buying a newspaper."[91] Usually the provision of a newsletter was cast in the mould of deference and service. The Earl of Denbigh advised his son, with the army at the siege of Bois-le-Duc in 1629, to send news of the siege "as often as you cann" to Lord Hamilton, "for he will bee your beste brother."[92] Amerigo Salvetti recognized playing the role of news writer placed him under a bond of service and obligation to his reader. Viscount Scudamore declined to swop weekly newsletters with his friend Hugo Grotius (the Swedish Ambassador in Paris) because he recognized that this would place him under obligation to the envoy of another crown.[93]

Since most newsletters were written from inferiors to superiors (and, when they were not, were still couched in the language of service and deference), it was not appropriate to comment on the news or to instruct the reader. Here, in the writer–reader relationship, lies the final reason for the lack of discussion or opinion in newsletters. Those few newsletters which did gloss the news (such as those written by the Earl of Clare) tend to be written to social equals or even inferiors.[94] For a similar reason, most newsbooks and newsletters (except those to the secretaries of state) were not annotated by the reader: such marginalia on texts often circulated among friends would have been to impose one interpretation on all subsequent readers.[95]

Much of the jesting at the expense of news writers suggests a deep unease with the *selling* of news, lest matters of state should become a commodity hawked on the streets to anyone with money – like cherries and strawberries in Ben Jonson's poem "The New Crie." Jonson's news printer in *Newes from the New World* proclaims that he is "all for sale." A countrywoman in *The Staple of Newes* judges news by its cost, seeking "A groatsworth of any newes." Richard Brathwait's coranto writer in his satirical *Whimzies* (1631) only seeks "currant money." Samuel Butler, in his mocking character of an intelligencer, uses the metaphors of buying and selling: bills of exchange, payment, inland trade, and markets.[96] Such jibes underlined some of the fears that the discourse of patronage sought to control. Francis Bacon was paid for providing intelligence to the Earl of Essex, but his material rewards were hidden behind a cloak of indebtedness involving his brother, Anthony, and couched in the coded language of friendship, exchange, and mutual obligations.[97]

Even with the professional news writers, relations were not always strictly monetary or even commercial. Scudamore paid some of his news writers with silk stockings as well as cash.[98] Starkey, in addition to selling Scudamore news, asked for his help in procuring a copy of an old lease whereby an abbot required his tenant "to fynd him a virgine to purge his Raynes at certayne monethes in the yeare."[99] Nor, as this last example suggests, was the traffic all one way. Pory asked his employers Sir Thomas Puckering and Sir Thomas Lucy to send him news of the riots in the Forest of Dean. The tide of news, foreign and domestic, flowed in and out of London and the principal towns, thereby helping to create a sense of the interdependence of the local, national and international.[100]

News writers performed services other than news writing. Professionals like Pory and Flower provided much more than a weekly newsletter. Each week they sent down a package, the full contents of which are only sometimes incidentally mentioned: corantos, proclamations, copies of letters, bills of mortality, verses, banned books, pamphlets, books of

masques, and foreign newspapers were all sent.[101] From 1683 to 1697
Richard Lapthorne sent weekly letters from London to Richard Coffin in
Devon, each filled with news and details of his endeavours in scouring the
London bookshops and auctions to fill Coffin's library at Portledge, and
each accompanied by the *London Gazette* and a newsletter. He also bought
Coffin a periwig.[102] In 1639 John Dillingham supplied Lord Montagu with
news as well as arms and uniforms for Montagu's men in the Bishops' Wars,
a case of the pen accompanying the sword.[103]

Some news writers acted as London agents for their readers, and the
development of news writing must also be set in the context of the evolution
of the agent at court. Close friends of Scudamore, like Sir Henry Herbert
and the Palmer brothers, Roger and James, looked after Scudamore's
interests at Court and tried to procure his preferment from the King as well
as writing political news back to him. Salvetti also acted as an intermediary
in sending money to Scudamore's brother in the Low Countries. Scudamore
discussed his ambassadorial allowance with John Burghe, who sent him
newsletters from London to Paris.[104]

Indeed, just as newsletters were important for the information they
contained, good news writers were useful for the network of contacts they
built up in the pursuit of their trade. Pory was well known to most of the
great men at Court and council and around London.[105] The cultivation of
such writers and their contacts was as important as the reading of their
letters. Weckherlin's newsletters to Scudamore opened a channel of
communication, or reinforced an existing one, through him to Secretary
Coke. The same reasons probably lay behind Scudamore's request to Robert
Reade, Sir Francis Windebank's secretary, to send news.[106]

IV

With the newsletters sent out by the secretaries and assistants of the two
secretaries of state in the 1630s, we have the precursors of the semi-official
newsletter services provided by Henry Muddiman and Joseph Williamson
from the two offices of the secretaries of state after the Restoration. These
differed in many important ways from newsletters before the civil wars.
Harold Love has claimed that the newsletter was a stable genre,[107] but it is
clear that the manuscript newsletter underwent important changes in the
second half of the seventeenth century. For these we must look first to the
development of printed newsbooks during the civil wars and interregnum.

Printed newsbooks were a product of the English Revolution. Beginning
in November 1641, armies of titles stormed from the presses.[108] Four
features of newsbook production were to influence the writing and
circulation of newsletters in the second half of the seventeenth century.

First, newsbook circulation was broad and socially diverse, crossing barriers of social distinction where newsletters had not. Newsbooks were designed to appeal to a much wider audience than the more exclusive newsletter. They were cheap and often carried pictures on their front pages.[109] Second, newsbooks were in the public sphere, whereas the newsletter belonged to the more private world of correspondence. Mass production and sale by booksellers or hawkers cut the more direct relationship between writer and reader of the newsletter. Third, despite the claims for accuracy made by their titles (*Perfect Diurnall, Faithfull Scout, Trve Relation*, and so on) most abandoned any pretence of impartiality or even truth. Many were vitriolic and polemic, taking sides in the struggles of the English Revolution, a far cry from the style of the pre-civil war newsletter. Finally, the regimes after 1640 began the more systematic management of news circulation. Previously, the government's attempts at news management had been extremely tentative, usually preferring to suppress or control tightly the circulation of printed news.[110] Thereafter the regime (or the competing regimes during the civil wars) usually oversaw the publication of a newspaper as the mouthpiece of the government. From 1665 this was the *London Gazette*, which between September 1666 and June 1679 was the only English newspaper.[111]

The gap in the market was largely filled by Henry Muddiman's newsletter, but this was a newsletter that bore the marks of the printed newsbook and Muddiman's own experience of that genre (he produced four newsbooks between 1659 and 1666).[112] A number of characteristics made Muddiman's product distinctively different from the newsletters of Chamberlain, Pory, or Rossingham thirty years before. By no means as openly partisan as the newsbooks of the 1640s, Muddiman's newsletters in the 1660s were more opinionated than the newsletters of the 1620s and 1630s, voicing criticisms of government policy.[113] Muddiman's newsletter was much more widely distributed than pre-civil war newsletters. Rossingham, charging each client around £20 per annum and with an annual income estimated at £500, must have had approximately twenty-five correspondents. Muddiman, however, had a circulation nearer 150.[114] Moreover, his newsletters were purchased by a socially diverse readership, from the elite to the more humble, including the postmasters, parsons, and a bookseller.[115] His newsletters were also distributed like printed newsbooks. In Norwich they circulated on market day, leading the town clerk to comment that "the poor countrymen" went home with "sacks full of news."[116] Perhaps most significant of all, by the 1670s they were available in coffeehouses across England.[117]

Such wide distribution affected the relationship between writer and reader. Newsletters had been circulated around locales before, but all the readers would presumably have been known to the original recipient. With Muddiman's newsletter, writer and reader might be strangers. His newsletters were not signed. This conscious semi-anonymity may have been a deliberate echoing of printed newsbooks, where, it has been suggested, the periodical assumed its own identity, greater than the identity of the author hidden behind it.[118]

While the means of distribution might distance reader and writer, Muddiman's authority as a writer also changed the relationship between newsmonger and news reader, but in a different way. Early Stuart newsmongers had generally been the social equals or inferiors of their readers. Henry Muddiman was the son of a London tradesman, yet the penetration of his newsletter down the social scale meant that many of his readers were more humble than he.[119] Moreover, Muddiman's newsletters had begun as a government project, a quasi-official news agency. In 1660 Muddiman was attached to one of the secretaries of state and his letters passed post-free. He later had a complicated and sometimes more distant relationship with the government, but retained a kind of official status, enshrined in the heading "Whitehall" on each of his newsletters.[120]

Muddiman had, thus, an authority over some of his readers who received his newsletter directly. Receipt of Muddiman's newsletter was seen by some as a privilege, obliging the recipient to return the favour (although they also had to pay for the newsletters), usually by sending him local news and intelligence. This was a reversal of the chains of deference that characterized other newsletter services. It meant that Muddiman could write a wider range and better quality of news. It also had implications for the government's intelligence networks, for Muddiman passed on some of his news to the government.[121]

After the Restoration most newsletters continued as before, an assortment of personal and business correspondence written to friends, family and acquaintances with a range of items of news, from odd lines to several paragraphs, picked up at the London Exchange or the tavern, or culled from other letters.[122] With such newsletters the only substantial difference was the substitution of the coffeehouse for Paul's Walk as a major site for news circulation. Muddiman's newsletter, however, had a great influence on other organized newsletter services. Joseph Williamson tried to take over Muddiman's newsletter. When he failed, he started his own, a rival semi-official service.[123] This differed in one important respect. Whereas Muddiman retained little or no control over the distribution of his newsletter, Williamson's recipients were hand-picked in an attempt by the writer to control the interpretation of his text. This was also a move away from the relatively straightforward deference and obligations of pre-civil war and less official newsletters. Writer (central government) and reader (local governors) were bound by a series of complex and mutual ties, obliging and benefiting both sides. The Crown could ensure that its governors in the localities were kept informed of what they needed to know; the recipients could rest assured that they were getting some of the most reliable news, the product of the government's thick information network; the government could hope that the provision of news to those who needed to know might sweeten them and help keep them happy; the recipients might feel obliged to the government and in some degree bound to it; both sides kept open a channel of communication between the centre and the localities.[124]

The years of the Popish Plot and Exclusion Crisis saw the culmination of two of the developments in manuscript news set in train by Muddiman's newsletter: the overt ideological slanting of manuscript news and its wide distribution. The lapse of press controls allowed a flood of newspapers, with seventeen new titles coming out between 1679 and 1682, many of them violently partisan. Hand-in-hand with these went the production of an increased number of manuscript newsletters, partly to feed an apparently increased appetite for news as the Crisis unfolded, and partly as deliberate Whig propaganda. The distribution of these newsletters within London was greatly facilitated by the establishment in 1680 of a penny post within the City and Westminster, itself partly a product of the appetite for news.[125]

By the 1680s the genres of the newsletter and the newspaper had virtually converged. Newsletters of the Crisis and after, written by Whigs such as Giles Hancock and William Cotton or Tories like John Dyer, were almost as partisan as their printed counterparts.[126] They were relatively cheap: Cotton offered newsletters at only six pence each.[127] The coalescence of the two genres was symbolized by two newspapers around 1700. In 1704, John Campbell's American newsletter made the transition from manuscript to print, becoming the *Boston News-Letter*. Eight years earlier Ichabod Dawks had begun his *News-Letter* using a specially cut script type to resemble italic handwriting. Writing in the *Tatler*, Richard Steele comprehended its significance: *Dawks's News-Letter* was "such as you cannot distinguish whether Print or Manuscript."[128] Nevertheless, the speed with which a manuscript letter could be altered to accommodate late news, and the lighter censorship applied to manuscript news, ensured that the popularity of the manuscript newsletter did not wane until the reign of George I.[129] As late as 1712, Daniel Defoe could predict that the nation was about to be swamped with "an inconceivable Flood of written News-Letters."[130]

Like newspapers, newsletters were freely available in coffee-houses. During the Crisis, various London coffee-house keepers were reported to have paid newsletter writers four or five shillings a week for their wares.[131]

Coffee-houses appear to have been socially very open, patronized by men and women, rich and poor. This meant that in the early 1680s manuscript news was as freely available as its printed cousin to most of the townsfolk of England. Most of England could read all the news. "From the Lord to the fiddler," ran one comment in 1680, "all are grown states-men."[132]

V

Not only was there a problem in writing the news, there was a problem of audience. The circulation of news came in for criticism on two counts in the seventeenth century. The first was that the news had spread to the vulgar. Matters of state, once the *arcana imperii* restricted to those fitted by birth and education to a wise understanding of their intricacies, had become the common discourse of the masses.[133] Shortly before the Restoration, the Earl of Newcastle bemoaned that "Every man now Is becomed a state man" and advised strict limitations on the circulation of the news.[134] The common people were often considered intemperate and inconstant, unable to weigh up the significance of the news but swayed this way and that by each new report. The "vulgar," thought Rous, "judge of all things by events, not by discretion." Ben Jonson characterized their opinions as "a Babel of wild humours"; to the Earl of Arlington they were "licentious discourses."[135]

The second criticism was that the circulation of the news encouraged division and faction. Thomas Lushington complained that "Chronicle-News" was "the Talk of the Factious and Pragmatick"; as people stood "diverse in Religion, so they feign and affect different News. By their News ye may know their Religion, and by their Religion foreknow their News."[136] Ben Jonson's news hack in his 1620 masque, *Newes from the New World*, says: "I have friends of all rancks, and of all Religions, for which I keepe an answering Catalogue of dispatch; wherein I have my Puritan newes, my Protestant newes, and my Pontificial newes."[137]

Such criticisms have recently been taken up by historians in an argument about the role of the circulation of the news (particularly manuscript news) in polarizing political debate in the early seventeenth century. Richard Cust has argued that the news, by emphasizing conflict and presenting politics as a process involving division and struggle, undermined contemporary rhetoric, which stressed harmony and consensus as the normal political modes. In Cust's argument, the discourse of news helped to develop notions of adversarial politics and so contributed to a process of political polarization.[138]

There were certainly great fears in the seventeenth century that the spread of news brought disharmony and faction in its wake and presaged unrest and even sedition. Francis Bacon thought that "Libels and licentious discourses against the state" were "amongst the signs of troubles" and were the preludes of sedition.[139] Government reaction to the news, seeking to prevent or limit its circulation, was predicated on such beliefs. Nevertheless, the extent to which the news tended to support an "oppositionist" or anti-government line has been exaggerated by historians. The manuscript libels and ballads against the Spanish match, and those attacking the Duke of Buckingham or honouring his assassin, John Felton, have begun to be studied by historians, but the verses supporting the Spanish match and castigating Felton await similar detailed treatment.[140]

In their extremely limited comments, many newsletters were as likely to add a moderate pro-court line as criticize the government. Salvetti's newsletters to Scudamore were occasionally broadly sympathetic to the King's need for money and the various financial expedients resorted to. He feared for the "hinderance" of the forced loan and hoped that the collection went on smoothly in Herefordshire; "prepare your purses, for wee neuer had such neede," he advised in January 1627.[141] Herbert, too, used his newsletters to encourage Scudamore's action as a forced loan commissioner, urging him to "Giue freely" to the King, for "this is not to make him out of loue with Parlaments."[142] These examples are, however, rare among the dry factual reporting that characterized most of the newsletters.

If manuscript news was not normally anti-government, what of the fine tuning of the news to the ideological slant of the recipient that some have detected? What of Jonson's jibes against those who wrote "Reformed newes, Protestant newes / And Pontificall newes"?[143] Analysis of newsletter writing suggests that there was little deliberate slanting of the news to suit the ideological stance of the reader. News writers might, if hurrying to catch the post, send material to one recipient which had been written for another. Pory's willingness to send to Scudamore (a close friend and follower of William Laud) the packet made up for the Earl of Newport or a copy of his newsletter written to Lord Rich (the son of the Puritan Earl of Warwick) does not suggest that any of this was politically embarrassing material or tailored to the dogmatic stance of the reader.[144] Comparison of the news Rossingham sent to Viscount Conway, the Earl of Huntingdon and Lord Scudamore, often on the same day, bears this out. What differences there are between the letters should be seen as changes to avoid repeating what the recipient might already know and variations to relieve the scribe's monotony, not the making up of each one to an individual ideological recipe.[145]

Newsletters were not (at least before the later seventeenth century) purveyors of faction. What, then, of the argument that the circulation of the news made the task of government more difficult? Thomas Cogswell, in discussing the 1620s, has written that "the key to all 'opposition' to royal policies was accurate information, and that the Paul's walkers, more likely than not, were able to provide."[146] Yet this is only half of the picture. Accurate information, again supplied by the news, was just as much a key to defence of royal policy. When, in 1633, Viscount Scudamore wanted to convince the subsidymen of Herefordshire to contribute to the repair of St Paul's Cathedral, he used not only Biblical precedents but also the news that the King himself had given generously.[147] In the 1620s, when Scudamore sought to reform the Herefordshire militia and even formed a troop from his own household, his actions may have been informed by details he had received in newsletters from his brother James, serving in the cavalry in the Low Countries: James had also sent advice on military tactics and training.[148] When Scudamore acted as a forced loan commissioner for Herefordshire, he must have been guided by a separate he had obtained from Starkey showing how the Kings of England "have Releeved their estates without parleament." He had certainly been prepared by newsletters from Herbert and Salvetti.[149]

It is noteworthy that those who criticized the spread of news were often also consumers or purveyors of news. In 1682, the Bristol grand jury presented a number of news writers and newspapers for "infamous scandalous & seditious libells" and asked for the newspapers to be burnt; a few months later the jury asked that the city council put an item of news in the *Gazette* "for the just vindicacon of this Court & consequently of this City." At the same time, the Bristol town clerk, who had recently complained of newsletters in a coffee-house, was subscribing to a newsletter service on behalf of the city corporation.[150] James I complained of the circulation of news verses and sought to command their disuse by issuing his own poem. Charles I is usually remembered for banning corantos, but it should not be forgotten that in the 1620s he oversaw the production of a play discussing the news and allowed Buckingham to issue news pamphlets from his flagship off La Rochelle, in the 1630s he considered a government-sponsored newspaper, and in the 1640s he presided over the publication of *Mercurius Aulicus*.[151] Francis Bacon condemned libels and false news as being "to the disadvantage of the state"; nonetheless, he was also involved in securing not only news and intelligence, but also other intelligencers for various clients, including the Queen, the Earl of Essex, Thomas Bodley, and Sir Francis Walsingham.[152] Much of the criticism levelled at the news was directed at false news, not news in general. Presumably Bacon's news was true, not false; or perhaps we should say that he, like the Bristol grand jury and Charles I, wanted to have his cake and eat it.

It is only with the party fighting that began in the late 1670s that newsletters became overtly and consistently polarized and slanted. This was a response to political division, not its midwife. The circulation of manuscript news played a variety of roles in the seventeenth century. As the debates over press censorship and the differing attitude of the government over the news and whether it should be suppressed or managed suggest, there was no consensus as to the political ramifications of the circulation of news. What should not be overlooked, however, is the contribution of manuscript letters of news to political harmony as well as political conflict: in helping the integration of local, national, and international, in aiding governors with royal policies, in maintaining contacts between court and people outside, in their use to heal rifts, and as part of the currency of client–patron exchanges. In all of these ways newsletters helped to smooth the political process. To return to the medical analogy with which we began, for relief of the itch of news many prescribed manuscript newsletters. To Richard Cust, this medicine was an inflammatory powder; it was in fact as likely to prove a soothing balm.

NOTES

1. S.C.A. Pincus, *Protestantism and Patriotism: Ideologies and the Making of English Foreign Policy, 1650–1668* (Cambridge, 1996), 276; J. Sutherland, *The Restoration Newspaper and its Development* (Cambridge, 1986), 23. See also K. Sharpe, *The Personal Rule of Charles I* (New Haven, CT, and London, 1992), 687, and D.F. McKenzie, "*The Staple of News* and the Late Plays," in W. Blissett *et al.* (eds.), *A Celebration of Ben Jonson* (Toronto, 1973), 124. Earlier versions of this paper were given at the History of News seminar in Oxford, the Early Modern seminar at Keele, and the History of News conference in London; I am grateful for the discussions aired there. I am also grateful to Dr Joad Raymond and the Revd Dr Jane Tillier for their helpful comments.
2. M.A.E. Green (ed.), *The Diary of John Rous* (Camden Society, 1st series, 66, 1856), 44; T. Cogswell, *The Blessed Revolution: English Politics and the Coming of War, 1621–1624* (Cambridge, 1989), 22; Bodleian Library, MS Eng. hist. e. 28, p. 481; S.C.A. Pincus, "'Coffee Politicians does Create': Coffeehouses and Restoration Political Culture," *Journal of Modern History*, 67 (1995): 819–20; W. Shakespeare, *As You Like It*, I.ii.94.
3. F.N.L. Poynter (ed.), *The Journal of James Yonge (1647–1721): Plymouth Surgeon* (London, 1963), 94–5.
4. Cogswell, *Blessed Revolution*, 20.
5. P[ublic] R[ecord] O[ffice], C115/N3/8548; Pincus, *Protestantism and Patriotism*, 277.
6. Rous, *Diary*, especially 3, 19, 37, 43, 52, 54–6; G. Roberts (ed.), *Diary of Walter Yonge* (Camden Society, 1st series, 41, 1848), esp. 4–5, 19, 23–5, 48.
7. R. Cust, "News and Politics in Early Seventeenth-Century England," *Past & Present*, 112 (1986): 66; Rous, *Diary*, 31–2; Yonge, *Diary*, 20, 40; T. Gainsford, *The Secretaries Stvdie* (London, 1616), "The Table."
8. Devon Record Office, Z19/40/3–6; H.L. Snyder, "Newsletters in England, 1689–1715, with Special Reference to John Dyer – a Byway in the History of England," in D.H. Bond and W.R. McLeod (eds.), *Newsletters to Newspapers: Eighteenth-Century Journalism* (Morgantown, 1977), 16 n. 7.
9. C[alender of] S[tate] P[apers,] D[omestic], 1686–87, no. 256; B[ritish] L[ibrary], Add. MS

11044, f. 59r; PRO, C115/M13/7268, C115/M37/8455-76, SP78/100, ff. 33, 59, 175; *CSPD, 1672–73*, 505, 585; *CSPD, 1676–77*, 354; F. Bracher (ed.), *Letters of Sir George Etherege* (Berkeley, 1974), 237, 254.

10. J.G. Muddiman, *The King's Journalist, 1659–1689* (London, 1923), 166, 195–6; A. Marshall, *Intelligence and Espionage in the Reign of Charles II, 1660–1685* (Cambridge, 1994), 60. See also Sutherland, *Restoration Newspaper*, 8, 22–3, 156, 226, for some of the advantages of newsletters over printed newspapers.

11. For examples, see J. Raymond, *Making the News: An Anthology of the Newsbooks of Revolutionary England, 1641–1660* (Moreton-in-Marsh, 1993), 68, 71, 87, 95, 257, 261, 272, 277, 290, 317. The newsbook *Mercurius Civicus* opined that "The most unquestionable way to make good intelligence, is to deliver it in the same Letters from which it was received": quoted in J. Raymond, *The Invention of the Newspaper: English Newsbooks, 1641–49* (Oxford, 1996), 131.

12. W. Cecil, *Certaine Precepts* (London, 1617), t.p. In 1626 Ralph Starkey was selling copies of material from the fourteenth century to the 1624 parliament: PRO C115/N4/8575.

13. Cust, "News and Politics," 62.

14. PRO, C115/M35/8386, 8398, 8383. The newsletters of Edward Rossingham and Henry Muddiman carried no personal details whatsoever. For Rossingham see PRO, C115/M36/8426–54, C115/N9/8851–4, BL, Add. MS 11045; for Muddiman see Muddiman, *King's Journalist*. For Scudamore and his newsletters, see I.J. Atherton, "John, 1st Viscount Scudamore (1601–71): A Career at Court and in the Country, 1601–43" (unpublished Cambridge University Ph.D. thesis, 1993), app. II, and I.J. Atherton, *Ambition and Failure in Stuart England* (Manchester, forthcoming).

15. PRO, C115/N3/8536–74, C115/N9/8844, 8882; BL, Add. MS 11043, ff. 80, 93–6.

16. PRO, C115/N1/8484, 8487, SP29/231, ff. 83v–84r, SP29/161, ff. 238–9, SP29/249, ff. 118–19.

17. For example: BL, Add. MSS 11049, ff. 18–66, 74–8, 11051, ff. 124–30, 11055–6, 11690, 45140–41, 45143, 45145, 45147–8; Bodleian Library, MS Lyell empt. 25; Hereford City Library, MS L.C. 949.023 "Dissertation."

18. These are admittedly rather arbitrary categories: Sir Henry Herbert was a life-long friend of Scudamore and also, as master of the revels, a government official.

19. PRO, C115/N4/8575.

20. W.S. Powell, *John Pory, 1572–1636: The Life and Letters of a Man of Many Parts* (Chapel Hill, 1977), 55. We do not know how much Scudamore paid his other correspondents.

21. PRO, C115/N1/8496, 8490, 8495, 8498, C115/N3/8537; Atherton, "Viscount Scudamore," 429–30.

22. Cust, "News and Politics," 62; Raymond, *Making the News*, 3.

23. Sharpe, *Personal Rule*, 655–8, 682–3; Marshall, *Intelligence and Espionage*, 80–87.

24. Brilliana Harley, Sir Edmund Verney, Owen Wynne, and the Earl of Clare all feared that their newsletters might fall into the wrong hands: J. Eales, *Puritans and Roundheads: The Harleys of Brampton Bryan and the Outbreak of the English Civil War* (Cambridge, 1990), 93–4; J. Bruce (ed.), *Letters and Papers of the Verney Family down to the End of the Year 1639* (Camden Society, 1st series, 56, 1853), 228–9, 233–4; R. Cust, *The Forced Loan in English Politics, 1626–1628* (Oxford, 1987), 12. See also H[istorical] M[anuscripts] C[ommission], *Twelfth Report, Appendix, Part IX. The Manuscripts of the Duke of Beaufort* (London, 1891), 76.

25. Compare the situation in Holland in the late sixteenth and early seventeenth centuries, where much of the news in circulation concerned France and England: A.T. van Deursen, *Plain Lives in a Golden Age: Popular Culture, Religion and Society in Seventeenth-Century Holland* (Cambridge, 1991), 140.

26. PRO, C115/M35/8385. Pory did not send newsletters when Scudamore was in London and could more easily pick up the latest news himself.

27. PRO, C115/M36/8426–54, C115/N9/8851–4; BL, Add. MS 11045.

28. F.J. Levy, "How Information Spread among the Gentry, 1550–1640," *Journal of British Studies*, 21 (1982): 20.

29. According to the *Oxford English Dictionary*, 20 vols. (Oxford, 2nd edn. 1989),

"newsmonger," its synonym "intelligencer," "newsmongery," "news-bearer," "news-man," "news-carrier," "news-lover," "news-teller," and "adviso" were all first used between 1581 and 1612.

30. W. Notestein, *Four Worthies* (London, 1956), 30, n. 1.
31. Cust, "News and Politics," 69.
32. J. Hall, *Works*, 12 vols. (Oxford, 1836–39), VI, 105–7; Cogswell, *Blessed Revolution*, 21–2; "Newes from any whence," in T. Overbury, *Miscellaneous Works in Prose and Verse*, ed. E.F. Rimbault (London, 1890), 171–200; J. Earle, *Microcosmography*, ed. H. Osborne (London, 1933, 1st published 1628), 84–5; Raymond, *Making the News*, 12; S. Butler, *Characters*, ed. C.W. Daves (Cleveland and London, 1970), 128–9.
33. M. Frearson, "The Distribution and Readership of London Corantos in the 1620s," in R. Myers and M. Harris (eds.), *Serials and their Readers, 1620–1914* (Winchester, 1993), 17.
34. R. Chartier, *The Cultural Uses of Print in Early Modern France* (Princeton, 1987), 209, 214–15.
35. M. Storey (ed.), *Two East Anglian Diaries, 1641–1729: Isaac Archer and William Coe* (Suffolk Records Society, 36, 1994), 250, 24 May 1721.
36. Several newsletter writers were arrested in the 1670s: Muddiman, *King's Journalist*, 205–7; M. Knights, *Politics and Opinion in Crisis, 1678–81* (Cambridge, 1994), 176–7.
37. Bristol Record Office, MSS 04447(2), f. 224v, 04434(1), ff. 95r, 449r. The grand jury also complained of certain items of printed news: MS 04452(1), 72–5, 89.
38. Yonge, *Diary*, 20.
39. Frearson, "London Corantos," 17. For the reading of newsletters aloud, see H. Love, *Scribal Publication in Seventeenth-Century England* (Oxford, 1993), 206.
40. Atherton, "Viscount Scudamore," 437–8, 440; Powell, *Pory*, 56; PRO, C115/M14/7317; Yonge, *Diary*, 20, 22, 32, 40, 71, 78, 80.
41. Frearson, "London Corantos," 16–17.
42. Gainsford, *Secretaries Stvdie*, 104–24.
43. BL, Add. MS 11044, ff. 11–12; PRO, C115/N5/8631, C115/N1/8491.
44. PRO, SP101/10–12, C115/M37/8455–76; Marshall, *Intelligence and Espionage*, 39, 44, 51, 248; L. Jardine and A. Grafton, "'Studied for Action': How Gabriel Harvey Read his Livy," *Past & Present*, 129 (Nov. 1990): 73.
45. BL, Add. MS 11044, f. 12r.
46. PRO, C115/M35/8396 for a similar argument about reading newsbooks, see C. Barksdale, *Nympha Libethris*, quoted in Raymond, *Invention*, 263–4.
47. J. Rushworth, *Historical Collections, vol. 1: 1618–29* (London, 1659), preface.
48. Raymond, *Invention*, 258; P.S. Seaver, *Wallington's World: A Puritan Artisan in Seventeenth-Century London* (Stanford, 1985), 81, 152–6, 192.
49. Cust, "News and Politics," 86. The "plagues" are not always noted in the printed edition.
50. PRO, C115/N4/8575.
51. H. Peacham, *The Compleat Gentleman* (London, 1622), 42–54.
52. B.J. Shapiro, *Probability and Certainty in Seventeenth-Century England: A Study of the Relationships between Natural Science, Religion, History, Law, and Literature* (Princeton, 1983), 125–41. For the relationship between the reading of newsbooks and the writing of history, see Raymond, *Invention*, 267–313.
53. Peacham, *Compleat Gentleman*, 53.
54. See R. Cust, *The Papers of Sir Richard Grosvenor, 1st Bart. (1585–1645)* (Record Society of Lancashire and Cheshire, 134, 1996), xv.
55. J. Howell, *Epistolae Ho-Elianae*, ed. J. Jacobs, 2 vols. (London, 1890–92; 1st published 1645), dedication, I, 3–4. Many of the newsletters published by Howell were in fact later compositions masquerading as contemporary letters.
56. [R. Overton], *Vox Borealis, or the Northern Discoverie* ([London], 1641), sig. A3r.
57. See, for example, the chronicles of Exeter and York: Devon Record Office, ECA 73/15; York City Archives, YL/Antiquarian Acc. 104 (a reference I owe to the kindness of Rita Freedman, York city archivist).
58. Cust, *Grosvenor*, 43.
59. Shapiro, *Probability and Certainty*, 141; Rushworth, *Historical Collections*, I, sig. b2r.
60. Yonge, *Diary*, 3, 24, 34, 39, 41–3, 53–5, 59, 62, 64, 67–9, 74, 76, 79, 81, 83, 90–2, 94–5,

105, 108–11, 116. For other examples, see Raymond, *Invention*, 267.

61. Jonson, *Newes from the New World*, ll. 62–3; Rous, *Diary*, 43–4.
62. Broughton to Sir Peter Legh, 20 May 1626, John Rylands Library, Manchester, Legh of Lyme MSS, Correspondence of Sir Peter Legh, 1590–1636; D. Lupton, *London and the Covntry Carbonadoed and Quartred* (London, 1632), 142; Powell, *Pory*, 52–3, 56; PRO, C115/M35/8396; F. Dahl, *A Bibliography of English Corantos and Periodical Newsbooks, 1620–1642* (London, 1952), 22–3.
63. Quoted in N. Smith, *Literature and Revolution in England, 1640–1660* (New Haven, CT, and London, 1994), 59. See Howell, *Epistolae*, I, 3–4, and Raymond, *Making the News*, 12–14, 19–20.
64. Cust, "News," 63; PRO, C115/N4/8575.
65. See Yonge, *Diary*, 78, for an example of Yonge noting that an oral report was confirmed by a newsletter he later had sight of.
66. BL, Add. MS 11044, f. 59r.
67. PRO, C115/M30/8092; see also Powell, *Pory*, 56–7.
68. PRO, C115/N5/8628; see also: Sharpe, *Personal Rule*, 685–7; *CSPD, 1675–76*, 253; *CSPD, 1679–80*, 609.
69. See the letters from France, 1636–39, in PRO, SP78/98–107, SP101/10–12.
70. T. Lushington, *A Sermon Preach'd before the University of Oxford, in the Year 1624* (London, 1711), 3.
71. Smith, *Literature and Revolution*, 57; also A. Mousley, "Self, State, and Seventeenth Century News," *Seventeenth Century*, 6 (1991): esp. 149.
72. Shapiro, *Probability and Certainty*, esp. 3–14, 264–5.
73. Jonson, *Staple of Newes*, I.v.9–10.
74. A. H[olland], "A Continved Inqvisition against Paper-Persecutors," in J. D[avies], *A Scovrge for Paper-Persecutors* (London, 1625), 6–7; PRO, C115/M35/8396. On the wide reception of corantos, see Frearson, "London Corantos."
75. Marshall, *Intelligence and Espionage*, 46, 60.
76. PRO, SP29/161/137, f. 238r.
77. Cogswell, *Blessed Revolution*, 22; H.H. Milman, *Annals of St Paul's Cathedral* (London, 1868), 286–7.
78. For comparatively rare cases of newsletters sent to women see: P.R. Seddon (ed.), *Letters of John Holles, 1587–1637*, 3 vols. (Thoroton Society Record Series, 31, 35–6, 1975–86), II, 345–6; Eales, *Puritans and Roundheads*, 7, 94 n. 64; Muddiman, *King's Journalist*, 219; *CSPD, January–June 1683*, 215–16, 351–2; *CSPD, 1685*, nos. 38, 54, 531.
79. D. Osborne, *Letters to Sir William Temple*, ed. K. Parker (Harmondsworth, 1987), 116.
80. Yonge *Diary, passim*; Rous, *Diary, passim*.
81. Warwickshire Record Office, CR2017/C1/195.
82. A. Fletcher, "Men's Dilemma: The Failure of Patriarchy in England 1560–1660," *Transactions of the Royal Historical Society*, 6th series, 4 (1994): 68, 74–7.
83. G. Etherege, *The Man of Mode*, ed. W.B. Carnochan (London, 1967), III.ii, 57–8. As a recipient of Henry Muddiman's newsletter, Etherege had some knowledge of what he satirized: Bracher, *Etherege Letters*, 237, 254. For an analogous dramatic example of a woman seeking intelligence, but only of fashion, see Ben Jonson's *Volpone* (1606), II.i.26–9.
84. Sutherland, *Restoration Newspaper*, 198–207, 223; Raymond, *Making the News*, 138; *CSPD, 1668–69*, 141; *CSPD, 1677–78*, 339; *CSPD, 1682*, 261–2, 280; Bristol Record Office, MS 04434(1), f. 449r: P. McDowell, *The Women of Grub Street: Press, Politics, and Gender in the London Literary Marketplace 1678–1730* (Oxford, 1998).
85. For example, Brilliana Harley and Joyce Jeffries: Eales, *Puritans and Roundheads*, 92–5; BL, Egerton MS 3054, ff. 46r, 50r.
86. PRO, C115/M30/8086, 8092, 8101; Chester City Record Office, CR63/2/691/5. See also the newsletters of the Earl of Bridgewater from 1638 to 1642, Shropshire Record Office, 212/364/17, 19, 22, 28, 39, and those in S. Brigden (ed.), "The Letters of Richard Scudamore to Sir Philip Hoby, September 1549–March 1555," *Camden Miscellany XXX* (Camden Society, 4th series, 39, 1990), 90, 115, 120, 123, 128, 130–1, 133, 135, 137.
87. BL, Add. MS 11043, ff. 67–8.

88. PRO, C115/N4/8606–8, 8610, 8612–26.
89. PRO, C115/M13/7252.
90. PRO, C115/N9/8880; BL, Add. MSS 11043, ff. 109–10, and 11689, f. 55; B.D. Henning (ed.), *The House of Commons, 1660–1690*, 3 vols. (London, 1983), III, 269–70. For anotherexample of the provision of news being used to patch up a quarrel, see PRO, SP78/102, ff. 103–4.
91. J.F. Merritt (ed.), *The Political World of Thomas Wentworth, Earl of Strafford, 1621–1641* (Cambridge, 1996), 121.
92. Warwickshire Record Office, CR2017/C1/1.
93. PRO, C115/N1/8490, 8492; Atherton, "Viscount Scudamore," 252.
94. For Clare, see Seddon, *Holles Letters*, and Cust, *Forced Loan*, 12.
95. For the lack of annotation in newsbooks (but a different explanation) see Raymond, *Invention*, 265–8.
96. B. Jonson, "The New Crie," ll. 1–4; Jonson, *Newes from the New World*, l. 15; Jonson, *Staple of Newes*, I.iv.10–12; Raymond, *Making the News*, 11–12; Butler, *Characters*, 128–9. See also Shakespeare, *As You Like It*, I.ii.93–4.
97. L. Jardine and W. Sherman, "Pragmatic Readers: Knowledge Transactions and Scholarly Services in Late Elizabethan England," in A. Fletcher and P. Roberts (eds.), *Religion, Culture and Society in Early Modern Britain: Essays in Honour of Patrick Collinson* (Cambridge, 1994), 106–11.
98. PRO, C115/N1/8492, C115/M31/8151, C115/M35/8422.
99. PRO, C115/N4/8578.
100. Cust, "News and Politics," 69–71.
101. PRO, C115/M30/8104, 8113, C115/M31/8132, 8153, 8185, 8194, C115/M32/8213. The only known printed copy of the London and Westminster bill of mortality for 13–20 December 1632 (the earliest known printed weekly bill) is C115/M32/8211 among Flower's newsletters. I am grateful to Paul Laxton for correspondence about the bills of mortality. All the packages have been broken up and most of these items included with the letters have become detached or been lost.
102. Devon Record Office, Z19/40/3–6, especially Z19/40/3, 19 May 1688, Z19/40/5, 31 March 1694. The letters are calendared in H.M.C., *Fifth Report* (London, 1876), 378–86.
103. A.N.B. Cotton, "John Dillingham, Journalist of the Middle Group," *English Historical Review*, 93 (1978): 819.
104. Atherton, "Viscount Scudamore," 429–31, 441–2.
105. Powell, *Pory*, 57.
106. Atherton, "Viscount Scudamore," 157.
107. Love, *Scribal Publication*, 12.
108. See Raymond, *Making the News*; Raymond, *Invention*; and Smith, *Literature and Revolution*, and the sources mentioned therein.
109. The twice-weekly Restoration *London Gazette* cost one penny an issue, or about nine shillings a year, compared to £5 a year for Muddiman's newsletter: Muddiman, *King's Journalist*, 179.
110. T. Cogswell, "The Politics of Propaganda: Charles I and the People in the 1620s," *Journal of British Studies*, 29 (1990): 187–215.
111. Sutherland, *Restoration Newspaper*, 250.
112. Muddiman produced the *Parliamentary Intelligencer* (later renamed the *Kingdome's Intelligencer*), *Mercurius Publicus*, the *Current Intelligence* and the first issues of the *Oxford Gazette*: Sutherland, *Restoration Newspaper*, 11, 250.
113. Pincus, *Protestantism and Patriotism*, 278. In the more polarized world of the Exclusion Crisis, Muddiman's letters were much more sympathetic to the court; by the end of 1688 he was pro-Jacobite: Knights, *Politics and Opinion*, 176; Muddiman, *King's Journalist*, 245.
114. Love, *Scribal Publication*, 11–12.
115. Muddiman, *King's Journalist*, 258–63, 283–6; *CSPD, 1667*, 415; H.M.C., *Beaufort*, 77.
116. Pincus, *Protestantism and Patriotism*, 279.
117. Muddiman, *King's Journalist*, 284–5; R. North, *The Life of the Honourable Sir Dudley North ... and of the Honourable and Reverend Dr. John North* (London, 1744), 249; *CSPD,*

1670, 378–9; *CSPD, 1672–73*, 585; *CSPD, 1676–77*, 354, 368.

118. Raymond, *Making the News*, 20–21. The tradition of semi-anonymous newsbooks may have derived from Rossingham's newsletters of the later 1630s which were signed only "E.R.," if at all. However, since his was a service limited to individual subscribers, his recipients would have been able to identify the author. For archival difficulties in identifying Muddiman's newsletters, see Muddiman, *King's Journalist*, 283–6.

119. Muddiman, *King's Journalist*, 85–6. Many of the newsbook writers (Sir John Berkenhead and Roger L'Estrange for example) were considerably more elevated than most of their readers but, as I have argued, there was little relationship between writer and reader of printed news.

120. Muddiman, *King's Journalist*, 145–8, 172–93; Pincus, *Protestantism and Patriotism*, 278.

121. Ibid., 146–7.

122. For example, Roger Acherley's letters to Lord Paget, 1705–7, Staffordshire Record Office, D603/K/3/6.

123. Muddiman, *King's Journalist*, 172–93.

124. Marshall, *Intelligence and Espionage*, 45–6, 60; P. Fraser, *The Intelligence of the Secretaries of State and their Monopoly of the Licensed News, 1660–1688* (Cambridge, 1956).

125. Sutherland, *Restoration Newspaper*, 48, 250–51; T. Harris, *London Crowds in the Reign of Charles II* (Cambridge, 1987), 96–129.

126. *CSPD, 1683–84*, 51–4; Love, *Scribal Publication*, 11–12; Knights, *Politics and Opinion*, 175, 177.

127. Muddiman, *King's Journalist*, 219.

128. C. Nelson, "American Readership of Early British Serials," in Myers and Harris, *Serials and their Readers*, 35; S. Morison, *Ichabod Dawks and His News-Letter* (Cambridge, 1931), 18–25, 31. Dawks's innovation was followed by *Jones's Evening News Letter* in 1716.

129. W.A. Speck, *Tory and Whig: The Struggle in the Constituencies, 1701–1715* (London, 1970), 91–2; Snyder, "Newsletters in England."

130. Quoted in Love, *Scribal Publication*, 3.

131. Muddiman, *King's Journalist*, 219.

132. Pincus, "Restoration Political Culture," 807, 814–17, 833–4; Harris, *London Crowds*, 99.

133. A. Bellany, "'Raylinge Rymes and Vaunting Verse': Libellous Politics in Early Stuart England, 1603–1628," in K. Sharpe and P. Lake (eds.), *Culture and Politics in Early Stuart England* (Basingstoke, 1994), 294.

134. T.P. Slaughter, *Ideology and Politics on the Eve of the Restoration: Newcastle's Advice to Charles II* (Philadelphia, 1984), 56.

135. Rous, *Diary*, 22; Cogswell, *Blessed Revolution*, 24; Pincus, *Protestantism and Patriotism*, 276. See also Mousley, "Seventeenth Century News," 149, 151.

136. Lushington, *Sermon*, 2.

137. Jonson, *Newes from the New World*, ll. 40–43.

138. Cust, "News and Politics"; Cust, *Forced Loan*, 151; compare Sharpe, *Personal Rule*, 683–90.

139. F. Bacon, *The Essays*, ed. S.H. Reynolds (Oxford, 1890), 95.

140. Bellany, "Libellous Politics," 294, 308.

141. PRO, C115/N1/8494–5, 8497–8, 8501, 8503. Harold Love has claimed that manuscript circulation was "inherently adversarial to authority": *Scribal Publication*, 185, 189–91; whatever the case with other categories, his rule does not work for manuscript news.

142. PRO, C115/N3/8539.

143. Jonson, *The Staple of Newes*, I.v.14–15.

144. PRO, C115/M35/8388, C115/N9/8850.

145. Compare Rossingham's newsletters of 30 April 1639 to Conway, PRO, SP16/418/99 (*CSPD, 1639*, 96–99), and to Scudamore, BL, Add. MS 11045, ff. 16–17; of 14 April 1640 to Conway, PRO, SP16/450/88 (*CSPD, 1640*, 31–4), and to Scudamore, BL, Add. MS 11045, ff. 109–10; and of 13 February 1634/5 to Scudamore, PRO, C115/M36/8449, with that to Huntingdon of 14 February 1634/5, H.M.C., *Report on the Manuscripts of the late*

Reginald Rawdon Hastings, 4 vols. (London, 1928–47), II, 76–8.

146. Cogswell, *Blessed Revolution*, 23–4.
147. BL, Add. MS 11044, ff. 247–9.
148. Atherton, "Viscount Scudamore," 91–5, 432–3.
149. Ibid., 113–16; PRO, C115/N4/8576.
150. Bristol Record Office, MSS 04452(1), pp. 72–5, 89, 04447(2), f. 224v, 04026(50), p. 51.
151. Cogswell, "Politics of Propaganda," 199–200, 204–7; Sharpe, *Personal Rule*, 647.
152. Bacon, *Essays*, 95; Jardine and Sherman, "Pragmatic Readers," 106–7; L. Jardine and A. Stewart, *Hostage to Fortune: The Troubled Life of Francis Bacon* (London, 1998), 47–50, 57–9, 87, 101, 130–31.

Pamphlet Plays in the Civil War News Market: Genre, Politics, and "Context"

S.J. WISEMAN

Citizen   … did you not heare of the Guild-hall night worke?
Countryman What was that I pray, do they work in the night?
Citizen   Noe, noe, they playd all night.
Countryman Why, I thought that Plays and playhouses had beene put downe:
Citizen   Yes, so they were in the Suburbes, but they were set up in the City, and Guild-hall is made a Play-house.

That the Citizen and the Countryman debate in a playlet entitled *The Last News in London* (October, 1642) indicates that "news" in the 1640s included many different genres. How did pamphlet playlets, on sale in the news market, imagine their readers? Who were their readers? How did those readers make distinctions between different kinds of pamphlet, and how are contemporary readers to do so? In assessing the way play pamphlets self-consciously represent themselves as both "news" and as politics, *and* imagine a reader, this essay analyses the place of such material as political polemic.

Apart from periodical newspapers, many kinds of texts were sold as news, from sexual satire to political theory. Clearly, the news market included newspapers, playlets, *The Tenure of Kings and Magistrates*, and other material which shaped the political theory of the 1640s. When such a diversity of material was sold as news, how are we to think of "news" in the 1640s? Where, if anywhere, should a line be drawn between politically influential writing and news? It is because of this question that "news" (taken to mean both serialized writing and the pamphlets of the Civil War) is perhaps the most hotly debated category of evidence and interpretation in the study of the English Civil War. Indeed, the way in which a figure like John Rushworth can be seen as an historian, a parliamentary recorder, a maker and broker of news indicates that, from the inception of the wars of the 1640s, items sold in the market of news – apparently a market in serialized news and pamphlets – have been a dominant source used in

S.J. Wiseman, Warwick University

analysis of the war. George Thomason (bookseller, archivist, collector) recognized the key role of this material; he collected everything, not distinguishing by genre or political perspective. Alongside the reprinted memoirs of the 1640s, both suppressed and printed as political exigency dictated, from the Restoration to the present, the pamphlet, marketed as news, has been the primary category for analysis.

Groups of scholars have used this material according to disciplinary boundaries; but as writers on political theory increasingly contextualize debates, the canon of political thought expands and the question of which texts contributed to political debate and political consciousness becomes ever broader. A pamphlet play or scatalogical dialogue might even look like a highly abstract political treatise. Sometimes, indeed, the scatalogical dialogue, like *England at her Easement* (1648), turns out to be participating in, even shaping, political debate. Is Thomas Tany's *The Nations Right in Magna Charta* political theory, and what about the fictions and speculations of Margaret Cavendish or the newspaper *Mercurius Politicus*? The question of which genres constituted the political debate in England 1640–60 and how they were read has become much wider than the question of whether "ranter" texts are "real" or satirical.[1] William Lamont, writing about material sold in a similar market, rightly indicates that texts have genealogies of ideas as well as the "horizontal" coexistence of similar material in a market.[2] However, genre operates simultaneously "vertically" (calling up similar texts from the past) and "horizontally" (looking like other texts coexisting in the same market).[3] And as Alexandra Halasz has argued, pamphlets not only exist in a print market, but when many of the publications in that market are in pamphlet form their presence influences the nature of that market. Pamphlets change the market not only in Habermas' sense of circulating texts which are outside the control of crown, university, or church (though often within the system of the Stationers' Company), but, because of their ease of production, "generic and substantive flexibility," they also speed the opening up of new areas of marketing, generic hybridization, and the making of "market niches."[4] So, in examining the relationship between scurrilous and populist genres and political theory, Arjun Appadurai's comment that there is a "commodity phase of the social life of any thing" and that there exists a "commodity context in which any thing may be placed" is useful in understanding the way the texts to be examined here coexist as ideas, political debates, and commodities which sell, in part, their ability to make contemporary politics into an intelligible (polemical) shape for a reader.[5] The concretization of political debate in print genres such as the pamphlet play invites yet further reconsideration of the boundaries between political theory and scurrilous satire. How did pamphlet-playlets invent themselves as political commodities and how, in that process, do they imagine their reader?

II

A friend of mine to me then did repaire,
Desiring me, to pen this famous Fayr,
Which I have done, and have it here to sell;
Come buy the Fayre of me, and so farewell.[6]

So Richard Overton's pamphlet of 1642, *New Lambeth Fayr* uses personified narration to propose itself as commodity, pleasure, and politics. Overton's pamphlets from 1641–42 are partly dialogues, at times bordering on playtexts. "News" is what they convey, what they have to sell, and their form. These uses are typical of the formation of the genre of the pamplet play in 1641–42.

In *New Lambeth Fayr* Overton calls attention to the mercantile status of the pamphlet, like a "vessell" "Fraught with ... Reliques," bringing wares to the reader "Such as Romes Conclave long hath kept in store" (A1v). The narrator's analogy between mercantile presentation of "wares" and the role of the pamphlet in presenting a cargo of opinion, with himself as a merchandiser, is significant in terms of the manufacturing of political ideas as commodities in the emergent news market. A year earlier, in 1641, Overton had indicated his self-conscious emphasis on the voice controlling the news when, in *Articles of Treason*, he presented a dialogue between Master Papist "a profest Catholike" and Master Newes "A Temporiser." The connotations of news as a "temporiser," mediating between news and public and turning the times to its own advantage, as political opinion and as commodity, is at the core of the way playlets popularized political debate and were also genericized as news in the 1640s. Such texts have been understood as plays manqué," "dramatic but not dramas."[7] However, they make sense in part in relation to the genres of pre-war theatre, but are also symptoms of the changed relationship between politics, print, and theatre in 1640–42.

While some groups in early modern England do seem to have considered theatrical mechanisms of illusion scandalous in themselves, print was scandalous only as it was condemned, before or after the fact.[8] The differential position of plays and print was registered in the distinct mechanisms of regulation and censorship organizing each institution. The Stationers' Company had a large measure of autonomy continuing into the Civil War period, whereas the theatre was overseen by the Master of the Revels, who regulated scripts prior to performance.[9] Separate critical debates exist about print and theatre regulation (with McKenzie, Lambert, Sharpe, Harris, and Raymond discussing print and Butler, Clare, and Burt on theatre). However, the two are often lumped together in discussions of censorship on the eve of the civil war in a way which has obscured the central importance of the *interaction* of the two in establishing the overlap between prose and drama, populist and abstract genres in the emerging news market of 1641–42.[10]

Separately running systems of print and play censorship were brought into a new relation in 1641–42. The fall of the Star Chamber on 5 July 1641 and the closure of the theatres, first for plague in 1641 and then on 2 September 1642, just before the outbreak of war, because "Publike Sports do not well agree with Publike Calamaties, nor Publike Stage-plays with the Seasons of Humiliation," meant that, at a moment when the news market was in the process of being formed, another, different, mode of representation and political commentary, the theatre, was foregrounded as a politicized genre and put under new constraints. Just a little earlier, constraints on publication had lapsed.

The closure of the theatres in 1642 intensified the contrast with print as the fall of the Star Chamber and other factors produced a freedom of printing that threw into relief the relatively successful legislation against the stage. This counterpoint in legislation regarding print and theatre suggests why at the outbreak of civil war the dramatic pamphlet was to the fore in the news market: the contrasting crises in the regulation of print and theatre seem to have precipitated the fusion of their techniques. From 1641 onwards dialogues began to appear, many, like Overton's *Lambeth Fayr*, commenting not only on the current situation, but also in a circular way on the changed conditions of print which made their own production and sale likely. In *The Downefall of Temporizing Poets, unlicenst Printers, Upstart Booksellers, trotting Mercuries, and bawling Hawkers* (1641) the impact of news on street marketing is discussed amongst Suckbottle the Hawker and Lightfoote the Mercury: "the case is altered: the fiddlers go a-begging" (A2r). The short *Times Alteration* (1641) – a dialogue between Lord Finch and Secretary Windebanke "at their meeting in France" – also discusses their own plight and, significantly, how they are reported in the news.[11] Such texts were imultaneously a "play" or playlet and a sub-genre of news, occupying a similar market position to other genres which attempted to influence the political ferment.

Three elements, then, seem to have coalesced to produce play pamphlets as a specific entity in the early 1640s; legislation connected with print, legislation connected with theatre (and the consequent politicization of dramatic genres), the emergence of a sphere of critical commentary and storytelling about politics and the war – the news market. These changes, which included the ordinances against the stage, produced (amongst other things) a highly hybridized and flexible new type of pamphlet, sitting at the borders of print and oral culture, political theory and polemic, plays and news. This kind of pamphlet advertised its hybridity and flexibility as an aspect of its sales pitch.

As Overton's playlets indicate, the news market of the early 1640s was caught up in a circular relation to political ideas; it circulated ideas, and in doing so popularized them and generated further debate and activity in the pamphlet market. In producing a sphere in which political differences between "cavalier" and "roundhead" were both explored and commodified, the news market – not only the periodical news – played a central role in constituting an emerging sense of the citizen, in part a reader and debater of news. This market, the evidence of the pamphlet plays suggests, shaped a sphere in which the commodification of news and politics took place through the making of a position of identification for the reader. In short, rather than the outbreak of the war producing a silencing of plays and drama, in the genealogy and circulation of the pamphlet play it is possible to trace a concentration on the imagined buyer of the pamphlet and the ideas. Commodity status, political polemic, and literary strategies inviting identification coalesce in the way these political playlets attempt to invent (and "sell") their polemic to a reader.

As titles such as *Newes Newly Discovered* and *Mercurius Britanicus* indicate, these dialogues and play pamphlets marketed themselves as dialogues, dramas, and as news. Drawing on the popular form of the Lucianic, in which any figure may talk to any other, they invited audiences to understand them as plays and as news. In this case the dialogue form borders on that of the play, and, foreshortened and compressed like chapbook narratives, they are also marketed as news. As Joad Raymond notes, contemporaries bound such pamphlet playlets and newsbooks together.[12] The pamphlet playlets under discussion, then, have a double generic valency – they are play pamphlets but exist simultaneously as news. Play pamphlets use genre and address both to mimic other kinds of writing and to frame themselves for the purchaser as part of an urgent market. The pamphlet playlets of the 1640s were marketed with signals that they were part of that large market of news and therefore of political debate. Playlets became at this point, like many of the genres discussed by Elizabeth Skerpan as dominant in the 1640s, one of the genres of news.[13]

Produced by and in the news market, such pamphlet playlets, dialogues, and skits were, though not political theory, claiming a place for themselves as polemically intervening in political debate. As the next section suggests, characteristic of the way these texts intervened in a highly politicized news market was a dual emphasis on the active shaping of the reader's views (the making of a carefully imagined place for the the reader's sympathy through an invitation to audience identification) and a highly self-conscious address to their own status as news.

III

The pamphlet playlet's ability to render political debate dramatic and concrete and its potential for self-reference as a commodity in the news market is evident in the *Mistris Parliament* playlets and *The Kentish Fair*, marketed at the end of the second civil war in 1648.

The first example, the semi-dramatic series of *Mistris Parliament* playlets, appeared as negotiations between Charles I and Parliament finally broke down. In 1648, during the bitter war following Royalist risings in Kent, Wales, and Essex, the Royalist "Mercurius Melancholicus" published the *Mistris Parliament* plays between April and May.[14] As their editor, Lois Potter, explains, these pamphlets responded to political debate – in part to the new Ordinance against unlicensed printing from 28 September 1647 – though also, crucially, to the Westminster Assembly's attempt to reform the Church of England service.[15] Where Overton's *Lambeth Fayr* and *The Arraignment of Mr Persecution* dramatized political debate for anti-episcopal and later Leveller ends, attacking both bishops and Presbyterian religion, the *Mistris Parliament* plays dramatize the familial metaphors underpinning Royalist political theory.[16] The first of these plays transforms Parliament into a woman about to give birth to a monstrous child of reformation (or deformation). The second play continues this theme, the third shows Mistris Parliament's gossiping, and the fourth her pact with London and the Militia.[17]

The first play leads the reader to a climax using the interconnections between political metaphor and the form of popular prodigies in a monstrous birth. Mistris Parliament, pregnant with "her first borne (Being a Precious Babe of Grace)," is attended by "Mrs Synod, *an old dry Nurse*," associated, as Lois Potter tells us, with the Westminster Assembly who were attempting to formulate religious policy (A1r). Rather than marry the king "she hath imprisoned her Husband, and prostituted her body to a very *Eunuch*, that had nothing to help himself withall" (A2r) – the parliamentarian general Manchester.

Manchester's appearance as a procreative eunuch indicates the shifting relationship between political metaphor and less systematic abusive discourses. Throughout, the possibility that Parliament might die points towards the crisis of 1648. The fusion of prodigious discourse of monstrous birth and political metaphor is made clear in the monstrous birth at the end of the first pamphlet. The pamphlet playlet enables the metaphor to be extended and staged by building on the link between political and religious theory and populist imagery:

> the room was strangely overcome with darkness, the candles went out of themselves, and there was smelt noysome smells, and heard terrible

thunderings, intermix'd with wawling of Catts. ... at the same time Mrs. *Parliament*, was miraculously delivered of a *Monster* of a deformed shape, without a head, great goggle eyes, bloody hands growing out of both sides of its devouring paunch, under the belly hung a large baggage, and the feet are like the feet of a Beare; if you purpose to see it, you must make haste; for it is now ready to adjourn to a new *Plantation. God save the King.* (A4v)

This is a meta-monster: the new liturgy, but also the reformed state metaphoricized as a deformed version of "the body of the state." The offspring which the adulterous parliament produces after "7 Yeers Teeming" (A1r) is deformation not reformation, something which draws on the wealth of theories about the shaping (and mis-shaping) of the child in the womb according to the mother's state of mind.[18] It is also, of course, a monster-in-language in that it is assembled indecorously of inappropriate elements and mixed discourses. Mistris Parliament as a rebellious part of the family of the state (in which the King ought to stand for the father) gives birth to the organic metaphor massively deformed. Thus, the birth of the organic metaphor is couched in the popular discourse of marvels: the portents – "wawling of Catts" – serve to demonize Parliament; the playlet limits the parameters of the debate to, as it were, the world *within* the metaphor. The status of the family as political metaphor is held as implicit, rather than explicit, in the attack whilst the ramifications of wifely disobedience and adultery are very thoroughly explored within, as it were, the familial vocabulary of the metaphor.

Parliament is degraded in a movement which might be read as carnivalesque inversion, but without any trace of Mikhail Bakhtin's Utopian idea of shared laughter.[19] The very violence of the images and the violence with which the texts abject these figures from the social body marks the depth of the crisis in imagining the body politic in its antithetical, whole, state. The structure, combining play and narrative and using the most emotive metaphors in the arsenal of Royalist propoganda, clearly signals the position the reader is invited to take.

In the political debates of the later 1640s, as Gordon Schochet has argued, the connections and differences between familial and political power was central to both Royalist and populist political theory. Whilst Charles Herle argued against the connection of paternal and kingly authority on the grounds that "Allegoryes are no good arguments" Sir Robert Filmer famously elaborated a genealogical narrative of the power of kings which rested entirely on inheritance.[20] However, even those who challenged the resemblance of kings and fathers kept in place as though real the chains of metaphor associated with the masculine rule of the household. Henry Parker launched a prolonged attack on the equation of the rule of kings and husbands, but distinguished the roles of wife and subject, for, although "the wife is inferior in nature, and was created for the assistance of man," "it is otherwise in the state betwixt man and man, for that civil difference which is for civil ends, and those ends are, that wrong and violence may be repressed by one for the good of all, not that servility and drudgery may be imposed upon all, for the pomp of one."[21] Responding to Parker, John Spelman argued that, "Domesticall government is the very Image and modell of Sovereignty in a Common-weale."[22]

Certainly, within the debate about the nature of rule, the acceptance of all the metaphors of authority within the household as "true" and natural, and the frequent saturation of sociopolitical discourse with sexual metaphor, was accompanied by a popularized consolidation of the debate on the nature of kingship as a domestic drama. Moreover, as David Underdown argues, during the civil war, metaphors of inversion were even more common as ways of visualizing social danger and anxiety about social change than in the years before the war.[23] Thus, the metaphorical aspect of the debate provided ready and emotive vocabulary for populist polemic, and the power of metaphor could be used to bypass structured argument. That the *Mistris Parliament* plays do remain, largely, within the world of the family-as-metaphor is significant with regard to their place in political discourse. Rather than engaging in abstract debate, the *Mistris Parliament* plays maximize emotive value by limiting their political vocabulary to familial metaphors. Concretizing political theory in the events of childbirth, the playlet dramatizes and enforces the centrality of the metaphor of the family found in political debate, and therefore shapes the reader's consent without inviting him (or her) to examine analytically the connection between the family and political power. The dramatic form, by casting the whole debate into the metaphorical terms of the family, enables the shaping of complex theoretical issues as readily resoluble.

In the case of some playlets, their knowing ability to play upon their status *as* news is foreground as much as any political "message." The *Mistris Parliament* plays themselves are introduced by a figure situated somewhere between a narrator and a dramatic figure. This "temporizing" figure takes a primary role in the shaping of political arguments for the reader and therefore "educating" the reader in particular political positions. The first *Mistris Parliament* pamphlet opens by inviting the audience to prepare for the carting of a whore:

> Ring the bells backward; lusty bonfires make
> Of purest straw that from pist beds you take;
> Your musick be the screeking of a Cart,
> And your shrill songs sound sweeter than a –
> For joy that Mistris *Parliament's* brought a bed;

Pray see the *Issue* of her *Maiden-head*:
'Tis but 3 half-pence in: the *Sight* will please ye,
And of your *Grief* and *mellancholly* ease you. (A1r)

The figure of the Mercury in the *Mistris Parliament* playlets exposes and uncovers the secrets of government (here transposed from the House of Parliament to a birthing room), and offers the reader the pleasure of reading a secret history even as it simultaneously invokes the specular pleasure of a theatrical side-show. Line six, "'Tis but three pence in," plays on the price of viewing as at the theatre, or fair side-show and the price of a pamphlet. The scene we are invited to be spectators at is set up by a construction, familiar from pornographic writing, that once we have purchased we, the reader, will be "in" on the details of a whore's child-bed. The narrator frames and enables the reader's porno-political pleasure in being Peeping-Tom or eavesdropper on the private rituals of delinquent women.[24]

The commodity status of the female in the *Mistris Parliament* plays is only one – but a central one – in a sequence of exchange relationships which constitute the news.[25] The use of the female figure to stand for the debate on rule, and as the focus for the reader's opprobrium, permits intrasexual relations to metaphoricize abstract political questions, and the use of a narrator serves further to position the reader as well as "selling" the ideas in the pamphlet and the pamphlet itself.

Thus, the metaphorical dramatization of politics and the use of the narrator shape the text as play and as news, but, most significantly, make a clear position for political identification for the reader. As buyers of the pamphlet, or indeed the series, the buyers are invited to understand themselves as simultaneously participants in a political debate and in the pleasures of the news market, but this is structured within Royalist terms. The figure of the Master of Ceremonies/"character of the news," in the *Mistris Parliament* plays organizes a reader's emotional response to the representation and "handles" (in the sense of indicating or placing) the generic and political implications of the text.

A second example, *Kentish Fair*, offers a vivid example of the way in which the mechanisms of news exchange and the pleasures of purchasing political polemic were themselves dramatized in a way which both made political positions clear and emphasized the reader's pleasure in exchange. The ventriloquism of "news" found in the Temporiser of Overton's 1641 pamphlet is developed in *The Kentish Fayre* (1648) into a meta-discourse on print's role in linking abstract politics and popular markets. Dramatizing events in the Royalist Kentish rebellion of 1648, the pamphlet opens with a verse apparently in the voice of the "author," on "The Kentish Fayre. Or, The Parliament Sold to Their Best Worth": "Good *Oliver*, lend me thy nose; / "Tis darke, all lights are out: / For now I meane to write in prose, / But guided, by thy snout."[26]

This voice is followed by the Cryer, who explains that Parliament is "set to sale at Rochester in Kent," and this in turn is followed by the entry of two of the protagonists – disguised as pedlars. Following the song of Mrs Webster and Mrs Maine, two women rebels, Mrs Fame enters. A news vendor, Mrs Fame asks, "What do you lack or buy Gentlemen? any Votes, Orders or Declarations? any Plots, Covenants, or Protestations?" The relationship between vendors and news is characterized as the disguised Kentish knights choose their texts:

> Sir Thomas Palmer: Hast thou ere a Parliament man a knave? I have some use of one.
> Mrs.Fame: I have a hundred Sir; why they abound Sir; I can afford you twenty at a cheap rate; buy these half dozen of me. They are transcendent knaves Sir ile assure, or ne're buy of me more.

The rest of the pamphlet is a discussion of the parliamentarians entirely in terms of their status as scandalous texts to be sold, until the play is closed by the Cryer. Although addressing the Kentish rebellion, the text has as much to say about its own status as a print commodity and that of other texts as about events in Kent; the whole playlet dramatizes not rebellion but the making of the war in the universe of scurrilous print in which it, and its reader, participate. As one figure for the making and sale of news gives way to another – author, then Cryer, then Mrs Fame, then, implicitly, her texts – the *telling* of news in print is used to give the impression that no figure or action is unsatirized, uncirculated in print, and that the war exists primarily in the imagination of the print market. The print bawdry of Mrs Fame, selling opinions, is balanced by the positive representation of female rebels, and overall the text invites the reader to take pleasure in rather than condemn the market's power to make knowledge, even as it calls attention to the distortions of truth taking place in the way the desires of print and of readers distort the truth of that knowledge.

The place of the "voice" of the Mercury, or of news personified as a vendor or personification apparently between an "actual" event and the reader, reshapes the reading experience as not a factual account but a drama of identification and analysis. It makes print, news, and political struggle into an event which is apparently *intrasubjective*, involving the reader in a play of emotions orchestrated by the voice or voices of the news and, embedded in those processes of exchange which it represents and participates in itself, a core of political opinion – the nature of the "characters" Mrs Fame has to sell – grounds the whole in political debate. What is extraordinary about *The Kentish Fayre* is the extent to which news is its self-referential subject matter, and the "event" recedes: "[e]verything that was directly lived has moved away into a representation."[27]

In the disciplinary division of texts sharing the news market, the *Mistris Parliament* plays and *The Kentish Fayre* are not abstract political theory, though the *Mistris Parliament* plays concretize theory. However, both plays engage in polemical politics and call the reader's attention to the plays as part of the print market. In each case, part of the technique of the sale of news involves a presentation of the processes of exchange. Thus they offer political debate, but also a carefully organized potential for the reader's identification. They also offer some kind of account of their own status as part of a debate and as part of a market in news. Their address to the reader, though not necessarily their angle on the political debate, is complex and imagines a reader equipped with a set of rhetorical strategies but able to be convinced. David Underdown has rightly argued that such texts do not tell us what readers thought.[28] However, in orchestrating so carefully both the political sympathy of the reader and their place as news – arguably politics in commodity form – such texts provoke, I think, two questions. How did civil war readers understand and contextualize them as part of the political debates of the moment and, equally important, how can we, reading now, do something similar, though not exactly the same, in attempting to rethink their place in political debate?

IV

Play pamphlets imagine readers, but, as Adam Fox notes, it is hard to find evidence of readers in the lower social strata and harder to find out how such readers thought about politics and the texts in the news market.[29] As Halasz indicates, too, the desire to know the nature of the pamphlet readership is frustrated by the very nature of the pamphlet market.[30] Some things are known about the reading of pamphlet plays or the performing of satire in relatively public contexts, and emphatically public forms can be imagined for such play pamphlets.[31] Some playlets, such as *A Bartholomew Fairing* (1649), imagine themselves a playing context.[32] That texts may have been played out is suggested, too, by Fox's research on the creation and reading of manuscript scandals. He finds such scandals being read to – or performed before – "an hundred severall persons."[33]

The playing out of political issues would itself be likely to provoke further debate. However, less polemical readings involved a more uncertain process of political selection, meditation, and doubt rather than "appropriation," and some commonplace books or diaries show readers engaging with scurrilous and abstract material in the 1640s.[34] The question of *why* readers noted their reading is vexed and hotly debated but, certainly, buying and reading involved the process of imagining their own relationship to the text and therefore to its form as well as to its political "message."[35] Here I turn to an example of a news reader, though not specifically of play pamphlets, who was relatively remote from the metropolis.

John Rous was a reader of scurrilous and political pamphlets in the early 1640s and his diary presents uncertain set of reading processes.[36] Rhyming in imitation of the very rhymes he loathed, he wrote: "I hate these following railing rimes, / Yet keepe them for the president of the times." This was Rous' comment on the satirical politics of 1640, recorded in his news diary, where he stored diverse items – verses, dialogues, the whole text of the arraignment of Strafford.[37] Rous' buying in the news market shows vividly the role of relatively private reading in a political arena.[38]

For Rous, public politics is complemented by, or held in tension with, private reading; his ambivalence centres on how far the consumption, reading, and retaining of items of political news implicates him in their opinions that he wants to keep at bay. For example, he attempts to interpret a verse he received in October, "Accommodation":

> The Parliament cries "Armie;" the King sayes "no!"
> The newe Leiftenants crie, "Marche on, let us goe."
> The Citizens and Roundheads crie, "so, so."
> The people, all amazed, crie "Where is the foe?" ...
> Then he that is not for accomodation
> Loves neither God, nor Church, nor King, nor Nation[39]

Rous writes that these riddling verses, "may be conceived to be a secret taxing of the Parliament, for arming of men against the King, when he protested not to intend warre against the Parliament."[40] However, in this interpretation, he says he is "leaning to others, who perhaps may have hit the veine of him that wrote the verses."[41] His struggle to develop skills in interpretation and, to an extent, theorization, which will enable him to tell the political provenance of his reading, is marked by his production of an alternative interpretation in which the rhymes support Parliament:

> But yet I, in another charitable way, (because the author is unknowne,) can construe thus, "Then he," etc *vers. ultimo,* viz. That desires not a peaceable accommodation, Loves not god, Church, King, nor Nation. Who loves not the Parliament, loves not the Nation. Who loves not the King and Parliament, *in the way on foote from the Paliament,* loves none at all. The Parliament that be for the King, prince, &c with the safety of the nation, have given their word and promise (which is the word of the kingdome, not easily violated or to be abused,) for His Majestie's safety and honour.[42]

If Rous is not being disingenuous, his politicized exegesis suggests that some pamphlets at least made little sense beyond their initial target audience. Rous' diary shows a non-metropolitan reaction to the range of extraordinary publications emerging from London presses in 1642, it indicates confusion, but also a struggle to produce political interpretations that allow the subject to make the rhymes, satires, and political reports productive for himself without succumbing to the position of the rhymes he "hates."[43] Rous' diary indicates self-consciousness about the process of reading as both confirming and undermining political positions. In the instance of the rhyme, Rous is aware of the strategies used by print to sell itself, but unable to produce a clear position.

Rous' diary registers the moment at which a troubling issue is engaged with rather than the moment at which mastery over it is achieved. It indicates that identification played a large part in politicized reading and that alongside abstract and "serious" texts such as the arraignment of Strafford, readers might puzzle equally hard over the meanings of rhymes and other pamphlets.

As William Lamont has put it, quoting C.H. George, on the 1640s, "the sweep of the literature – 'where Hobbes and Milton rub shoulders with doggerel' – make it difficult for the historian to handle."[44] As the canon of political philosophy expands to include increasingly diverse texts, it appears that the border C.H. George saw between "doggerel" and "literature" was unclear to contemporaries and is so now.[45] As the examples of John Rous and other readers from the 1640s indicate, contemporary readers also found it testing to produce a coherent reading position from the "wealth" and diversity of printed material. The "rubbing shoulders" of abstract and concrete might be found even within one text, as is indicated by the rhyme Rous struggles with, Overton's *Lambeth Fayr*, *Kentish Fair*, and *Mistris Parliament*. Although none of these texts (except Overton's because of his Leveller associations) is likely to be incorporated in the canon of political theory, clearly they form the popular context for more abstract debates. Part of what pamphlet plays did was to make relatively clear the invitation to the reader with regard to events.

V

What are the implications of the existence of a sub-genre of the pamphlet play brought to prominence by the news market of the early 1640s? If we consider together Rous' reaction to the enigmatic rhyme and the way in which pamphlet plays dramatize both politics and the print market, the role of the pamphlet play in the news market becomes a little clearer. The ephemeral commodity-cum-genre pamphlet playlet of the post-1641–42 period has at least three notable qualities. It presents both political theory and fantasized resolution of political troubles by means of the subjective yet representative desires of the "ordinary" subject or citizen and therefore provides positions with which a reader could identify. It can evoke, for a reader or a reader aloud, dramatic production and news simultaneously. And for these reasons it can give concrete and polemical life to abstract, though crucial, political debates. Significantly, it also offers pleasure because it foregrounds the reader's participation in debate by representing itself, and its reader, as participating in "news."

The playlets of the 1640s, then, do suggest the ways in which *form* is being used by the newswriters to shape the imagined reader as a political subject and to make opinion. The publishing phenomenon of the semi-dramatic news pamphlet might not give readers the opinions they wanted, but did dramatize the debate and, as in *The Kentish Fair*, dramatized the pleasures of that debate for the reader. A reader of *Lambeth Fayre*, the *Mistris Parliament* plays, and *Kentish Fair* might disagree with their political angle yet still take a (perhaps personally troubling) pleasure in participating in the circulation of news and opinion. Concentration on the pamphlet playlet and the way it makes a place for the reader invites us to consider the market in news under the sign of an interaction between commodifying populist rhetoric and political ideas. As Arjun Appadurai argues, many things pass through a "commodity phase" in their social life, and populist pamphlet playlets demonstrate political theory in its commodity phase – imagining a buyer who is also a reader, and shaping a response.[46] Although this is also true of other populist texts sold side by side with political theory in the news market of the 1640s, pamphlet plays concretize political theory, overlap with dialogues, overlap with news and with spoken debate in a way that makes it clear that they are aware of and in relationship to those other kinds of text. They know their place in a news market and also claim a place in the making of political ideas. Voice, genre, and the claims to "be" simultaneously news, play, and an encoding of the popular voice (as the title-page of the *The Wishing Commonwealthsman* (1642) puts it, the claim to be "indeed the common Town-talk") constitute the ways in which the dialogic form commodifies news and politics.

Ultimately, the circulation of political debate in the pamphlet play consists in the text's imagining of a reader, a political subject, which it seeks to create and manipulate. And, finally, the pamphlet playlet suggests that the genres of news created and attempted to stimulate and regularize demand, not only through periodization but also through simultaneously alerting a reader to the pleasures of generic hybridity and, to an extent, simplifying (by dramatizing, concretizing, and even personifying) the very political debates it presents. If, as I think it can, the pamphlet can be understood as something between a form and a commodity, perhaps a commodity-form, in the 1640s then the pamphlet play is at the scurrilous extreme of such a form. As such, the playlet is characterized by its ability to shape the reader's political sympathies through drama (not, indeed, that the political positions assumed by pamphlet plays are always, at this distance, crystal clear). Thus, as a form dramatizing the furore of political debate yet coercing agreement, such plays paradoxically foreground *and* efface the potential for political debate, producing and anaesthetizing the politicized reading subject. The techniques such texts use mean that they are important evidence in the making of political debate, and therefore political theory, in the 1640s. If this "shaping" role for which I am arguing is accepted then there are implications for the borders at least of the canon of political theory. The fact that these texts are scurrilous, polemical, shamelessly populist and often engage only with the metaphoric and emotive aspects of debate does not mean that they should – or even can – be separated, wholly, from the texts acknowledged as political theory and with which they shared a market. Their generic genealogy is different from that of the abstract political dialogue, yet at times such playlets do overlap with such texts. Halasz's comment on sixteenth- and seventeenth-century anxiety about pamphlets, that the exclusion of things designated "pamphlets" from debate, rather than dissipating the problem they constitute, makes the "problem of pamphlets' claim to discursive authority explicit even as it attempts to assign them to another amorphous place," is also true of current attempts to designate them outside political debate. In diachronic and synchronic connection with texts marketed in other forms or now accepted as part of the canon of political theory, pamphlets including playlets were part of the vibrant market in polemic which generated the highly abstract texts. I have suggested that the relationship between political theory and populist texts is in some ways close, and in my readings of the playlets suggested the links between texts are still largely understood as distinct However, in any imagined reading context of the 1640s, it seems likely that news texts dramatizing the political debates must have coexisted with relatively abstract treatises on desks, in studies, in bound volumes, in collections, and in coffee houses. The polemical pamphlet plays, so highly hybrid and conscious of the reader, invite a further rethinking of the place of political theory, news, and, especially, the genres considered to participate in political polemic.

NOTES

I am grateful to Joad Raymond for his comments on this essay.

1. For a discussion of the staus of "ranter" writings and their interpretation see see J.C. Davis, *Fear, Myth and History* (Cambridge: Cambridge University Press, 1986). William Lamont also notes that pamphlets such as *Walwyn's Wiles* are for useful "*understanding his Calvinist opponents' perceptions of what these views were*" [his ital], p.85; one aspect of the complication of satirical pamphlet culture is the way it draws on both the reader's understanding of the debate and the reader's position within that debate.

2. Willaim Lamont, "The Puritan Revolution: A Historiographical Essay," in J.G.A. Pocock *et al.* (eds.), *The Varieties of British Political Thought* (Cambridge: Cambridge University Press, 1993), 119–45.

3. For work exploring the rhetoric of Civil War, see Elizabeth Skerpan, *The Rhetoric of Politics in the English Revolution 1642–1660* (Columbia, MS: University of Missouri Press, 1992); "Writers–Languages–Communities: Radical Pamphleteers and Legal Discourse in the English Revolution," *Explorations in Renaissance Culture* (1995): 37–56; William Lamont, "The Puritan Revolution," in Pocock *et al.* (eds.), *Varieties of British Political Thought*, 119–45.

4. Alexandra Halasz, *The Marketplace of Print* (Cambridge: Cambridge University Press, 1997), 3, 16. I am grateful to Lynn Robson for this reference.

5. Arjun Appadurai, "Commodities and the Politics of Value," in Arjun Appadurai (ed.), *The Social Life of Things* (Cambridge: Cambridge University Press, 1986), 13.

6. Richard Overton, *New Lambeth Fayre*, E.138 (26), (1642), A2r–v, B4v. This is one of the pamphlets actually signed by Overton. See also *Lambeth Fayre* (1641).

7. Leslie Shepard, *The History of Street Literature* (Newton Abbot: David & Charles, 1973); Dale Randall, *Winter Fruit: English Drama 1642–1660* (Kentucky: University Press of Kentucky, 1995), 53

8. Indeed, the same Parliament that closed the theatres so that a document in the Hartlib archive could advocate that "Playhouses and Sequestered Houses" could be made profitable as "work houses" also caused George Buchanan's play *Baptistes Sive Calumnia* to be published. Hartlib, 15/2055 "Proposition For the Better Execution of the Laws Relating to the Poor," undated. See also 15/2/51A c.1645.

9. Sheila Lambert, "The Printers and the Government, 1604–1637," in R. Myers and M. Harris (eds.), *Aspects of Printing From 1600* (Oxford: Oxford University Press, 1978), 1–29.

10. See Kevin Sharpe, *The Personal Rule of Charles I* (New Haven, CT: Yale University Press, 1992), 644–54 especially 654; A.B. Worden, "Literature and Political Censorship in Early Modern England," in A.C. Duke and C. Tamse, *Too Mighty to Be Free* (Zutphen: De Walburg Pers, 1987), 45–62.

11. Anti-Catholic news is circulated in *Newes Newly Discovered* (1641, E.1102 (3)), and religious controversy is followed up in *The Lofty Bishop, the lazy Brownist and the Loyal Author* (1641, 669.f.8(32)) and in *A Dialogue Between the Crosses in Cheap and Charing Crosse* (1641, E238(9)), *A Dialogue of Crucy Cringe* (1641, E160 (7)), *The Bishops Potion, A Rent in the Lawn Sleeves*, the very well-known *Canterbury His Change of Diet* (1641, E.177 (8)), and country–city relations dramatized in *The Country-man's Care and the Citizen's Fear*. News of the Scottish war is partly dramatized in *Vox Borealis* (1641, E.177 (5)). One of the most elaborate is *Mercurius Britanicus or the English Intelligencer: A Tragi-Comedy at Paris. Acted with Great Applause*, on which Martin Butler has written. Martin Butler, "A Case Study in Caroline Political Theatre: Brathwaite's '*Mercurius Britannicus*' (1641)," *The Historical Journal*, 27 (1984): 947–53.

12. Joad Raymond, *The Invention of the Newspaper: English Newsbooks 1641–1649* (Oxford: Clarendon Press, 1996), 202.

13. Elizabeth Skerpan, *The Rhetoric of Politics in the English Revolution* (Columbia, MS: University of Missouri Press, 1992).

14. They were collected by Thomason between 29 April and 30 November 1648 and have been edited by Professor Lois Potter. *Mistress Parliament Brought to Bed*, ed. Lois Potter,

Analytical and Enumerative Bibliography, NS 1 (3), (1987), 1–129, at 111. *Mistris Parliament Her Gossiping AEB*, NS 1 (3), 144–57; *Mistris Parliament Her Invitation AEB*, NS 1 (3), 158–70; *Mistris Parliament Presented in Her Bed, AEB*, NS 1 (3), 130–43.

15. Lois Potter's introduction to the plays elucidates their complex relationship to journalism and analyses their use of female characters. Potter indicates two specific echoes in the first playlet, connecting them to other discourses, one of Parliament's Declaration of a Day of Humiliation following 25 April, the other to a Royalist sermon cheekily preached before Parliament.

16. For a longer discussion of this correspondence, see S.J. Wiseman, "'Adam, the Father of all flesh,' Porno-Political Rhetoric and Political Theory in and after the English Civil War," *Prose Studies* 14 (1991): 134–57.

17. Potter, *AEB*, 111.

18. On theories of maternal influence on the foetus, see Katherine Park and Lorraine J. Daston, "Unnatural Conceptions: The Study of Monsters in France and England," *Past & Present* 92 (1981): 20–54; Neil Hertz, "Medussa's Head: Male Hysteria under Political Pressure," *Representations*, 1, 4 (Fall 1983): 27–55; Ambroise Pare, *The Workes of the Famous Chirurgion Ambroise Parey*, trans. Th. Johnson (London, 1634), 971–82, and Ch. 7, "Of monsters which take their cause ... by imagination."

19. Mikhail Bakhtin, *Rabelais and His World*, trans. Helene Iswolsky (1965; rpt. Bloomington, IN: Indiana University Press, 1984), 5–35. Useful criticisms of this aspect of his theory are found in Mary Russo, "Female Grotesques: Carnival and Theory," in *Feminist Studies / Critical Studies*, ed. Teresa de Lauretis (Basingstoke: Macmillan, 1986), 213–29; Peter Stallybrass and Allon White, *The Politics and Poetics of Transgression* (Methuen: London, 1986), 2–26.

20. Charles Herle, *An Answer to Doctor Ferne's Reply, Entitled Conscience Satisfied* (London, 1643), 16–17. Responding to Henry Parker, Dudley Digges made non-patriarchal monarchism. See *An Answer to a Printed Book* (Oxford, 1642), 23. John Spelman, however, argued, "Domesticall government is the very Image and modell of Sovereignty in a Common-weale," see John Spelman, *A View of a Printed Book* (Oxford, 1642), 9.

21. Henry Parker, *Observations on some of his majesty's late answers and expresses* (London, 1642), in *Revolutionary Prose of the English Civil War* ed. Howard Erskine-Hill and Graham Storey (Cambridge: Cambridge University Press, 1983), 35–63, see especially 49–50.

22. Gordon J. Schochet, *Patriarchalism in Political Thought* (Oxford: Basil Blackwell, 1975), quotes John Swan, *Redde Debitum: or, a Discourse in Defence of Three Chief Fatherhoods* (London, 1640), 5–6.

23. David Underdown, *A Freeborn People* (Oxford: Clarendon Press, 1996), 94.

24. Emma Donoghue, *Passions Between Women* (London: Scarlet Press, 1993), 25–53.

25. Luce Irigaray, *This Sex Which is Not One*, trans. Catherine Porter with Carolyn Burke (New York: Cornell University Press, 1985), 170–91; Gayle Rubin, "The Traffic in Women: Notes on the 'Political Economy' of Sex," in *Towards an Anthropology of Women*, ed. Rayna B. Reiter (New York: Monthly Review Press, 1975), 157–210.

26. William Charles Woodson (ed.), *The Kentish Fayre* (1648), *Analytical and Enumerative Bibliography* 8 (1984): 3–17.

27. Guy Debord, *Society of the Spectacle* (1967) (Exeter: Aim Publications, 1987), 1.

28. Underdown, *Freeborn*, 90–92, 99.

29. Adam Fox, "Popular Verses and their Readership in the Early Seventeenth Century," in James Raven, Helen Small and Naomi Tadmor (eds.), *The Practice and Representation of Reading in England* (Cambridge: Cambridge University Press, 1995), 125–37, 125.

30. Halasz, *The Marketplace*, 12.

31. Fox, "Popular Verses," 125–37.

32. *A Bartholomew Fairing* (1649, E.565 (6)). On the metaphorical valency of playing in the 1640s, see Louis B. Wright, *Huntington Library Bulletin* 6 (1934): 73–112.

33. See Fox, "Popular Verses," 133.

34. On appropriation, see Roger Chartier, "Texts, Printing, Readings," in Lynn Hunt (ed.), *The New Cultural History* (Berkeley, CA, and London: University of California Press, 1989), 154–75. Nigel Smith, *Literature and Revolution* (New Haven, CT: Yale University Press,

1994), has examined commonplace books as "the dominant means of gathering information and recording precisely the kind of literature that could be expected to have a limited public life," 31.

35. Richard Cust has suggested that in private diaries "it is possible to see the news being both recorded and discussed" and understood in terms of conflict, whereas Kevin Sharpe has argued that Puritans are the main keepers of diaries and, more to the point, the "keeping of a private diary reflects personality types and characteristics – be it a certain paranoia, a quest for ordering, a search for the self, a sense of isolation and alienation ... more revealing of individual personality than of public affairs or perceptions." Richard Cust, "News and Politics," *Past & Present* (1995): 83; also quoted by Kevin Sharpe, *The Personal Rule of Charles I* (New Haven, CT: Yale University Press, 1992), 690–91.

36. Where Nehemiah Wallington, one of the labouring class readers and annotators in Civil War London, was apparently confident in overlayering print news and his beliefs in God's providences, the writing of John Rous, at least in the early 1640s, is contrastingly uncertain in its subordination of events and print to a political point of view. See *Historical Notices*, 2 vols (London, 1869), 2: 156; Bl Add Ms 21,935 fol 173. See also *Historical Notices*, 2: 3, 143. On Wallington's processes of reading as the "personal experience of the godly writ large," see Paul Seaver, *Wallington's World* (London: Methuen, 1985), 155.

37. 18 Nov. 1640, *The Diary of John Rous*, 109.

38. *The Diary of John Rous*, ed. Mary Anne Everett Green (Camden Soc, no 66, 1656), x–xi. Perhaps in a defensive move to distinguish "himself" and the psycho-political incursions of print culture, certainly attempting to visually segregate the two, Rous used one writing style for the quotidian, another to mark the inclusion of extracts and verses.

39. Ibid., 124.

40. Ibid.

41. Ibid., 125.

42. Ibid.

43. Ibid., 121.

44. "Pamphleteering, the Protestant Consensus and the English Revolution," in *Freedom and the English Revolution* ed R.C. Richardson and G.M. Ridden (Manchester: Manchester University Press, 1986), 72–92; C.H. George, "Puritanism as History and Historiography," *Past & Present* 41 (1968): 87; quoted Lamont, p.73.

45. The expansion in the understandings of political theory is evident, to take one example, in Nicholas Phillipson and Quentin Skinner (eds.), *Political Discourse in Early Modern Britain* (Cambridge: Cambridge University Press, 1993). See also William Lamont's eluciadation of the historiography of genre in Pocock (ed.), *Varieties of British Political Thought*, 119–45.

46. Appadurai, "Commodities and the Politics of Value," 3–63, especially 13.

Women in the Business of Revolutionary News: Elizabeth Alkin, "Parliament Joan," and the Commonwealth Newsbook

MARCUS NEVITT

The story that women only became actively involved in the material production of news after the Restoration is one that has been re-run, re-spun, and re-edited by feminist historians and literary critics for the last twenty years. It is, variously, only with the emergence of the classic Habermasian public sphere and the wider professionalization of writing under and after the Restoration regime, or the advent of Defoe, Dunton, Steele, and Addison with their "progressive" decisions to allow women to read, correspond with, and write for their numerous periodicals, that women at last began to play a part in making and shaping the news.[1] Yet it seems strange that even in the light of the recent historiography of newsbook and pamphlet culture or the controversy surrounding the classic Habermasian model, wherein a post-Restoration public sphere is either mapped backwards onto the civil war period or abandoned completely, the image of late-seventeenth-century women attending their news presses for the first time should persist.[2] It is the purpose of this essay to go some way towards offering a corrective to this image.

It is no news that women featured regularly in the civil war newsbooks whose trade in highly gendered and misogynistic language secured both editorial notoriety and a paying audience. For both sides, the dishonesty of the times was most adequately expressed alongside the index of moral bankruptcy affixed to illicit sex, which, more often than not, featured as a female vice. Therefore, the Royalist *Mercurius Aulicus* reports of the "zealous young Maids in the Citie of Norwich who covenanted together to raise Troope of Horse for the Rebels service." That five of them were to become pregnant "by whom it is not yet signified" is of no surprise whatsoever to the writer, who subsequently implores "all Virgins [to] looke to it, for people hereafter will scarce think them honest, who are so bold and shamelesse as to joyne in a Rebellion against their own Sovereign."[3] Equally, it seems unlikely – in a market where claims to truth and facticity

Marcus Nevitt, Sheffield University

were made in tandem with the right to govern the English people – that those people would have bought any of John Crouch's Royalist newsbooks for their informative news content. His vision of "the sisterhood of Tumblers" who "exercise on their backs in many obscure alleys" would probably not have prompted the Presbyterian heresiographer Thomas Edwards to undertake an alley-to-alley search of the City of London.[4] Instead, his combination of pornography, misogyny, and titillative fiction, never for Crouch without political implications, ensured the survival of his newsbooks in hostile times.[5]

Yet if women passively featured in revolutionary newsbooks, they also actively and intelligently read them. Although by its very nature evidence of specific readership is elusive, women as different as aristocratic Brilliana, Lady Harley and the republican Lucy Hutchinson have been found reading them.[6] Further down the social scale, the Leveller Katherine Chidley, immersed in the pamphlet culture of revolutionary England, as a pamphleteer in her own right and one of the most prolific female parliamentary petitioners of the 1640s, offered a novel insight into and critique of contemporary newsbook culture. Engaged in a dispute with Thomas Edwards, she sought to discredit him by alleging the utter fictionality of all his sources in his anti-independent writings, and vilified him for his recycling of "some lying popish stories (made by some Trencher poets) for Prelates, like the stories made by *Mercurius Alicus* [*sic*] at Oxford, and some of those stories (by those who are best informed) taken to be like this booke of yours."[7] Her attack on *Aulicus* is especially innovatory and demonstrates an easy familiarity with mid-seventeenth-century newsbooks. She, in effect, turns the stock criticism of London newsbooks on its head. Whilst charges of unreliability and fictionality were frequently levelled against the latter, the word of *Aulicus* was seen by many as gospel; *The Weekly Account*, though committed to refuting *Aulicus*, even went so far as to suggest that "as the intelligence of the West is somewhat uncertaine, by reason of the Cavalier's partie, ranging from place to place to stop roads and bypaths," all those who desired "truly to be informed" should "take a view of *Mercurius Aulicus*."[8] Hence, Chidley, for political ends, conflates the "lying popish stories" of a Royalist Oxford newsbook with the perceived untruths of a staunch Presbyterian, an extremely subtle line to take in this context given that Edwards himself had chosen to conflate all newsbooks and the entire independent cause, even suggesting that newsbooks were "the pensioners of the sectaries."[9] Chidley thus seeks to counter Edwards by demonstrating that she is a more discerning newsbook reader.

Yet, as this essay hopes to show, women were not simply passive objects or consumers within an early modern public sphere; rather, they were involved at various levels in its formulation. Whether petitioning Parliament collectively, prophesying to and about the head of state, or contributing innumerable paper bullets to the succession of seventeenth-century pamphlet wars, women played an important role in early modern politico-religious activism and the formation of public opinion.[10] This is not to assert that they achieved any real degree of participatory parity therein, but rather that transhistorical patriarchal politics have – for a variety of self-perpetuative and/or sexist ends – obscured crucial and historically specific moments of female agency.[11] However, the issue of agency is complicated still further when we examine the actual means of production of seventeenth-century newsbooks. Paula McDowell has shown that, in post-Restoration newsbook culture, if there were distinct roles, such as "author," "editor," "printer," or "publisher," these were frequently undercut by the existence of "editor/publishers" and "printer/publishers" so that via an elision of roles, individual agency could be seen to be subsumed within the wider structures of a collective activity.[12] This overlap between authorship, publishing, and printing had certain advantages, both economic and strategic, for contemporary workers in the news trade, so that, whilst costs could be cut, it also made the job of the censor or licenser more difficult. How was a seditious intention to be traced amid such a complex network of creative activity, when even hawkers selling the newsbooks at a street level could be found politicizing the texts they sold in radical and seditious ways?[13] Paying attention to such collective endeavour is obviously at odds with the dominant trends of literary criticism, as McDowell explains:

> twentieth-century literary critics' interest in bourgeois subjectivity and the rise of individualism has meant that dominant literary critical models emphasize individuals (especially authors). But traditional 'man-and-his-work' approaches, with their post Romantic emphasis on individual authors, are not the most useful models for the study of non-élite men's and women's involvement in the print marketplace. This is especially true of literature in politically tumultuous periods, when authors, publishers, and other printworkers often worked closely together.[14]

Thus there is a crucial feminist imperative behind the decision to attend to the collective act of making a text, so that specific moments of female agency can be reassessed outside this oppressively patriarchal, competitively individualistic scheme with its religious or mythic force. Indeed, in the recent attempt to explode this myth and counterbalance "the canon," an attention to collectivity has served feminist literary historians well. Whether it be through studies of Leveller or Quaker women's strategies of collective petitioning, or attention to early modern scribal culture where women played an integral role in the circulation, transcription, and amending of manuscript compilations, the benefit of the eschewal of limited individualistic models of authorship has been widely felt.[15] However, the pre-Restoration newsbook has yet to receive the benefits of these deconstructions of the phallocratic politics of canonicity, it remains very much a "prehistory," a lacuna that early modern gender historians have yet to fill.[16] Hence, due to a misleading overattention to "editors," a select band of six men (Samuel Sheppard, Marchamont Nedham, Samuel Pecke, John Crouch, Daniel Border, and Henry Walker) presides over the civil war newsbook, to the obvious detriment of the women of Grub Street.[17] It is therefore ironic, but unavoidable, that the methodology involved in attempting to offer a corrective to this unsatisfactory picture of an all-male, mid-seventeenth-century newspress will initially involve a reconfiguration of the very processes of individuation it ultimately seeks to displace. A vision of the collective enterprise behind newsbook culture can only come into focus once historically specific moments of individual agency have been unearthed.[18]

II

Elizabeth Alkin, or "Parliament Joan" as she was so frequently labelled by male contemporaries, is one woman who significantly problematizes the prevalent notion of an all-male civil war newspress.[19] Like so many of her non-aristocratic female contemporaries, concrete biographical information about her is sparse. However, it would appear, from a far from reliable source, that she was born at the turn of the seventeenth century and died some time late in 1654.[20] Interestingly, some of the patriarchal force behind the obscuration of so many women's records is visible in the very process of naming and the conference of an alias. Alkin never once referred to herself as "Parliament Joan" or "Jone," preferring instead in her letters, petitions, and the newsbooks she worked on to use her full name or initials. However, from her very first appearance in the State Papers in March 1645, she features as a "Joan." It is her alias who receives her first payment from the Committee for the Advancement of Money. Thus "Elizabeth, alias Joan Alkyn" received payment of two pounds in the first week of March for "severall discoveries," and in the next week it was ordered that she received "40s more, as she avers by petition that she discovered [Geo.] Mynnes wire."[21] Yet it is the naming process which remains of explicit importance here. It would appear that although the payment was made, it was done so grudgingly, and the service or activity which Alkin performed to make that payment necessary is left ambiguous and of dubious authenticity. That she "avers" her service is apparently insufficient, although the fact that the payment is actually made surely mitigates against the supposed dubiety of her testimony.

What renders her words untrustworthy is not only the well-worn trope of the unreliability of all women, but, more specifically, her name. The author of *The Character of a Rebellion*, writing after the Restoration, was keen to expose the evils of the commonwealth regime and, when addressing some of his readers, his "Illustrious Ladies," sought to express the perils inherent in non-monarchical government in particularly revealing terms:

> And here with all due respects and differences I must address my Discourse to these Noble Persons of the Delicate Sex; 'tis an ungrateful Complement to accost them with, to tell them their Honours will be lost; but credit me, Illustrious Ladies, neither your Beauties, nor other most Attractive Charms, will be able to secure you from the Insolence of Common-wealth Ravishers: England can be no longer the Paradice of Women than it continues a Monarchy: My Lord cannot suffer, but my Lady will have a share; the Widows of Barons, by the Curiality and Curtesie of England, enjoy the Titles and Priviledges of Peerage, and the Daughters of Dukes, Earls, and Barons, do by the Favour of the same Custom enjoy the Honour and Title of Ladies; these too much fall with the Monarchy; *and in a Common-wealth Joan is as good as my Lady even by day-light.*[22]

With the privilege of rank removed, England as "the Paradice of Women" suddenly descends into a kind of post-lapsarian anarchy, beset by "Ravishers" intent on violating everything in sight.[23] Courtesy of this bizarre sexual levelling, a "Lady" is no better than her polar opposite, significantly, "Joan." Albeit two and a half centuries later, but for similar ends, J.B Williams glosses the name as "given to any ill mannered or ill kept rustic woman, or scullery maid, who had to do dirty work."[24] Such sexism and classism surely inform the reason why the Committee for the Advance of Money chose to doubt Alkin's "petition" that she had effected her "discoveries." Yet, it is pertinent to remember that it was the (all-male) Committee and their male contemporaries who first bestowed the alias in this instance, and the issue of re-naming becomes even more interesting once we discover the nature of Alkin's "discoveries." Elizabeth Alkin was a spy, and as such was involved in providing "Intelligence," the lifeblood of state security and newsbooks.

Her involvement in the discovery of George Mynne again earned her two pounds in September 1647, when the Order Book for the Committee for the Advance of money records "40s to be paid to Joan —, she pretending to have made a discovery of Mynne's delinquency."[25] What was earlier rather vaguely termed the "discovery of Geo Mynne's wyre," now re-termed his "delinquency," was a crucial piece of parliamentary intelligence. Mynne, a prominent iron master of Surrey, was engaged in supplying the King with the raw materials for warfare; he supplied Royalist forces with four hundred tonnes of iron at the start of the war, and had iron and wire secreted in various parts of the country amounting to some £40,000.[26] What is as significant as the meagre sum Alkin was paid for her work in March 1647, is the fact that in a profession that was so reliant on auricular as well as written testimony, her word should still remain "pretended" or untrustworthy.[27] Indeed, there is a sense that through the conference of her denigratory alias, the very authorities who were paying her for the veracity of her intelligence were simultaneously denying its validity, equating it with the mere gossip of a rustic or scullery maid. This complex attempt to deny Alkin any agency whilst seemingly using her as an agent exemplifies the precarious position of a woman venturing forth into the early modern public sphere.

Alkin's negotiation of restrictions placed upon her, restrictions intensified by the hypocrisy which meant that her position, as far as the authorities were concerned, must remain unacknowledged, is fascinating. In the early to mid-1640s her husband was acknowledged as being involved in the Parliamentarian spy network, but on being caught by Royalist forces he was duly hanged at Oxford.[28] Alkin chooses to mobilize his legitimate image to gain financial recompense, and thereby official recognition, for her illegitimate sorties into the public sphere. The following petition is particularly revealing:

> To the right Honourable Committee for Compositions sitting at Goldsmiths Hall
> The humble petition of Elizabeth Alkin Widdowe,
> Sheweth,

> That for her many faythfull and hazardous services she hath done for the Parliament they were favourably pleased to recommend her to the Comittee of Examinations, that she might have a Sequestered house of one Stephen Fosett that was in actuall Warr against the Parliament and Chirurgeon to Sir Arthur Ashton, whoe most cruelly caused her husband to bee hanged in Oxford for doeing service for the State, in which house she yet remaynes.

> But for it is that the said Fossett by some meanes haveing compounded her doth now goe about to imprison your poore petitioner and to that purpose hath entred actions against her and endeavours nothing lesse than to ruyne her and her many Fatherless Children.

Her humble suite unto this honourable Committee is that you will take her into consideration who hath neither spared estate nor paines to doe the State service, as is evidently knowne to the Members of both houses of Parliament and to Order that she may continue still in the said house without any molestation.

And she shall pray &c.[29]

Alkin's husband appears as the guiding spirit of this petition, he, or at least the remembrance of his loyal activities, initiates all the action and proceedings. Accordingly, Alkin offers herself as the loyal member of the commonwealth, which in gender terms means playing the part of the dutiful wife and mournful "Widdowe"; she is a "poore petitioner" beset not only by the vengeful Royalist Fossett but by "many Fatherless Children." Patriarchally speaking, she registers herself as a comforting, conformable presence; as the fecund woman who desires only to remain in a domestic realm "without molestation." Yet such ostensibly quiestistic purpose is undercut by the very public form of the petition itself, and furthermore by the fact that whilst eschewing publicity she is actually offering more intelligence to the authorities by revealing the continued presence of yet another disaffected Royalist in the commonwealth. That Fossett was called in "to answer" on the day the petition was read is testament to Alkin's skill as a petitioner.[30] Whether or not she retained the house is unclear, but by October that year the Committee had granted Alkin a further fifty pounds and "a fit house to dwell in."[31]

Wherever she was living, it is clear that Alkin did not opt for a widow's retirement indoors, and in fact over the next two years continued to remember that she had "lost her husbands life in the service of the Parliament" in public petitions, and thereby succeeded in gaining more payments, improved accommodation (eventually at Whitehall itself), and protection from counter-petitioners.[32] All of this time she was still providing intelligence to the state. The (significantly underacknowledged) high point of her involvement came as late as 1653. On 22 November that year the brother of the Portuguese Ambassador, Don Pantaleon Sa, and a group of Portuguese and Maltese friends were engaged in a fierce dispute at the New Exchange with some locals. A fight ensued wherein men from either side were injured. On the following evening, the Portuguese returned to the Exchange and yet more violence erupted. On this occasion, a passer by, one Mr Greneway, was caught up in the disturbance and was fatally shot. Sa was eventually apprehended and incarcerated in Newgate by July the following year, after an attempted escape, he was moved to the Tower to be eventually tried and executed.[33] The incident was sensational, prompting an intense legal wrangle involving Lord Chief Justice Rolle himself, about whether it was possible for the family of a foreign diplomat to be tried by English law, and if so whether it was to be before a jury. The incident also prompted a welter of pamphlet and newsbook literature. In the second week of December both Pantaleon de Sa himself and the sister of the murdered Greneway published pamphlets which condemned the other party's actions whilst exonerating their own.[34] Similarly, from the last weeks of November to the first week of December the newsbooks picked up on the incident for a variety of nationalistic ends, whereby Sa was variously presented as returning to the Exchange with a coachload of ammunition and grenades, with boats waiting on the Thames to whisk him to safety, emphasizing the premeditated nature of the attack. Whilst others stressed the utter randomness of the incident, some even went so far as to claim that diplomatic relations with Portugal were now so strained that an alliance with the Spanish was imminent.[35] Amid the welter of competing narratives, the truth of the matter became elusive and it was difficult for the authorities to decide upon appropriate action. Crucially, Elizabeth Alkin played an integral role in that decision, since it was solely because of her advice, intelligence, and "Information ... concerning the murder committed by the Portugalls upon the Exchange" that the Council of State set up a committee to consider all of the information.[36] The relevant entry in the Council's order book shows that at the time she was delivering such intelligence, not only did her word go undoubted (in contrast to the Mynne case) but that the Whitehall-based Alkin had been transfigured from a "Joan" to the more respectable "Eliz: Alkin Widdow."

III

In 1649 Alkin consolidated her relationship with "Intelligence" and became a book trade informant, searching out unlicensed or seditious presses for the authorities.[37] In the July of that year, *A Perfect Diurnall* makes reference to "one Jone (a clamerous woman) whose husband was hang'd at Oxford for a spie, & she sometimes imployed in finding out the presses of scandalous pamphlets."[38] A year later, John Crouch was complaining of the intrusive activities of Parliamentarian press informants and singled two out for particular attention: "Gentlemen pray have care of a fat woman, aged about fifty, her name I know not, she is called by many Parliament Jone, and one Smith, Printer, a tall thin chapt Knave, if any such persons come pretending to search, looke to yourselves and money, and say Towzer gave you warning."[39] Whether Crouch knew Alkin's name or not, he was all too eager to assist in both the circulation of her denigratory alias and in the allegation that her activities were nothing more than a kind of legitimized robbery.[40] About a year earlier, another Royalist newswriter, Samuel Sheppard, had bewailed the fact that he had been "Routed out of my lodgings and acquaintance by *Parliament Beagles* and whole squadrons of *rebellious Mermidions* & forc't to build my nest in another angle where now I am, and (God willing) doe intend to satisfie the Kingdome weekly of the wicked *Consultations* of Parliament."[41] Yet whilst these comments reflect the general disdain with which newstrade informants were viewed, Sheppard goes on to demonstrate the ineffectiveness of their performance of the insurmountable task. It is ironic that a newsbook which opens by damning the contemporary climate of censorship should go on to lambaste George Wharton, the "Railing, Buffleheaded Calfe of Essex," for publishing a counterfeit issue of *Mercurius Pragmaticus* which merely reprinted that week's edition of Wharton's *Mercurius Elencticus*.[42]

A less sensationalized view of the material operations of news trade informers comes from the pen of Alkin herself. Ever the skilled petitioner, she appeals to Parliament to recoup some of the money she has spent in their "service":

> To the Right Honourable the Comittee of Haberdashers Hall for Advance of Money
>
> The Humble Petition of Elizabeth Alkin, a poore distressed widdow. Sheweth,
>
> That your petitioner at the beginning of the warre, and for divers yeares since was imployed as a spye by the Earle of Essex, Sr Wm Waller, and the now Lord Generall Fairfax, hath performed much service for the State in that kind, to the hazard of her life, had her husband hanged at Oxford by the late Kings party.
>
> That your petitioner hath of late done good service for the State by discovery of printing and publishing of Scandalous books, and but the last weeke your petitioner discovered fouwre presses in one Dugards Custody, in Mearchant Taylor School, weare all seized upon, and the said Dugard committed to Newgate, for which, nor any other service of the like nature, your petitioner never receaved any recompense, Albeit shee hath expended all that ever shee was worthe in the world, in the pursuance of your service.
>
> That more particularly your petitioner did discover the delinquency of Mr Minnes and divers others, to one William Mills late a collector at Cambden House, the whole benefit of which discovery the said Mills received to his owne use, to the value of 2 or 300 *l*, and never allowed your petitioner one penny for the same. That now your petitioner understanding yet there is about 40 *l* belonging to the said Mills, in the hands of the Treasurer belonging to this honourable Comittee.

> Your petitioner most humbly prays that this Honourable Comittee wilbee pleased (in consideration of her former good services, your petitioner being ready to bee cast into prison for debt, to the utter ruine of her 3 children) to order her the said 40 *l* remayning in the said Treasurers hands, for the releife of her.
>
> And shee shall pray etc.[43]

The importance of this manuscript petition for any reassessment of the role of women in the seventeenth-century newstrade, indeed for early modern women's agency more generally, ought not to be underestimated. Close attention to the rhetorical structures of the petition reveal that Alkin is exploring the limits of the concept of "good service," subtly counter-balancing the image of the "poore distressed widdow" fending off jail and the "utter ruine of her three children," that is, the comforting image – for patriarchy – of the caring, vigilant mother, alongside that of the "spye" "hazard[ing] ... her life" for the benefit of the commonwealth. Motherhood and espionage are thereby accorded a certain equivalence, so that as the boundaries between public and private are breached, spying is presented not as alien, exclusively masculine terrain, but as an activity that is particularly suited to the feminine.[44] Yet what also makes the manuscript of such interest as an historical document are the very material demands and revelations that Alkin can make courtesy of this rhetoric. Whilst it is gradually becoming evident that women were involved in the intelligence trade, the secretive nature of the work, and a hypocritical patriarchal attitude to female involvement in the public sphere has generally obscured or destroyed the records. Thus to find a woman publicly declaring that she was "for divers yeares since employed as a spye" and then going on to detail the names of her employers, activities, and requested rates of pay ("about 40 *l*") is sensational.[45] Nonetheless, this did not signal the end of Alkin's activities as a trade informant as at the end of November 1651 it is recorded that she was paid £13 8*s* by the Council of State "in Consideration of the good service done by her in the discoverie of the booke *manus testium, lingua testium*," a pro-Royalist exegetical work which appeared in the July of that year, written by the Presbyterian Edward Hall, which defends the memory of "our gracious Sovereign King Charles, King of Great Britain, Defender of the Faith, and supreme head of the Church in all causes, and over all persons."[46]

IV

It is crucial to realize therefore that "Intelligence" in its various manifestations was what sustained Alkin and her children in the economically depressed 1640s and 1650s. In spite of the prevalent historiographical account outlined earlier, wherein there were no women attending to the newspress in the middle decades of the seventeenth century, it need be no surprise, therefore, to find Alkin eventually turning to the publication of newsbooks herself. Thus, between 21 June 1650 and 30 September 1651 she is involved in the publication of ten issues of different newsbooks.[47] The first occasion she puts her name to a newsbook is with *The Impartial Scout* primarily concerned with naval and military news, and hitherto associated almost exclusively with the Daniel Border, and his printer Robert Wood.[48] Border was one of the more resilient and prolific journalists of the commonwealth and protectorate, having some fourteen different serials to his name. Whilst he was certainly no Marchamont Nedham, and whilst he will never be remembered for any pioneering work at journalistic frontiers, he was a competent newsman perhaps best remembered for his skirmishes with Henry Walker.[49] These began in March 1649 and tended to focus upon Walker's disdain for Border's imitative journalistic style, his replication both of the former's extravagant use of Hebrew and his habit of printing the London bills of mortality.[50] Border responded with a vitriolic personal attack ridiculing his rival's ginger hair, calling him "the Judas bearded iron monger," at the same time as he criticized his newswriting as "pernicious and destructive."[51] Walker's counter is especially interesting, it includes an attack by the deputy censor Theodore Jennings:

> I desire all people to take notice that I denie to give any authority to a pamphlet called *The Kingdomes Scout*, because the Commonwealth hath been so abused by it, by Robert Wood of Grub Street who contrives false invectives at an Alehouse to add to it what he fancies as news after M. Border the author hath write it, ... and the author doth now disclaim it refusing any more to write it for him; if he be so impudent still to publish it, I desire all those whom it concerns to suppress it that the people may not be cheated by it.[52]

Border is berated for his inability to subscribe to the dominant, individualistic models of authorship, for allowing the text to slip from his privileged grasp to be pawed and sullied by others in "an Alehouse." The terms of Walker's and Jennings' critique are fascinating for a number of reasons. Firstly, it provides interestingly problematic anomaly for Steve Pincus' study of the emergence of the public sphere in the *later* seventeenth century with the discussion and circulation of news in English coffeehouses.[53] Secondly, it shows the difficulties and limitations of effective censorship and licensing at a time when both practices were rather haphazard or careless.[54] Thirdly, and more importantly for the consideration of women's involvement in the civil war newstrade, the newsbook features as a collective enterprise, one in which a text can be politicized and re-authored in a variety of different, and frequently contradictory, ways, by a number of different, and frequently untraceable, authors. In the face of such a melee of intentions and narratives, the strategy of the deputy licenser was to attempt to define the roles within the newsbook more clearly, and in the process promote a divisive acrimony amongst the team that produced the *Scout*. Jennings' tactic was unsuccessful, as the newsbook continued to be approved, and Border and Wood worked together until the mid-1650s.

It is difficult to ascertain whether the Border's and Wood's working relationship is representative, but the fact that they produced seven newsbooks between them suggests, Jennings' criticism notwithstanding, that it was an effective one. For four weeks in June and July of 1650 their relationship was altered by the presence of Elizabeth Alkin on the team of *The Impartial Scout*. It is interesting to speculate as to the reasons for the incorporation of Alkin on the *Scout*, as not only did the serial represent a new journalistic enterprise for both Border and Wood following the closure of their *The Faithful and Impartial Scout* in the preceding autumn, but she was also replacing the printer/publisher George Horton, who had been involved with the *Scout* since its fifth issue.[55] The two had certainly known of her for over a year, since in the first week of June 1649 they reprinted the following "Order" from the Council of State: "*Saturday June 2*. Ordered that it be referred to the Councel of State to bestow a house upon Mrs Alkeen (a Widdow) whose Husband dyed in the Parliament's service, and consider of some competent maintenance for her and her children, which is ... needful, for they are in a very low condition until relieved."[56] What is at first striking about this item is that it is perhaps the first non-derogatory reference to "Mrs Alkeen" (not "Parliament Joan") in a newsbook. That its obvious un-newsworthiness had become newsworthy attests to one of two things; either Alkin had achieved such a celebrity status by mid-1649 that every detail of her life was deemed significant, or the item became news because Alkin was the personal acquaintance of one or both of the parties involved in the *Scout*. All information points to the latter suggestion since no other newsbook that week reprints the Order, an odd fact if Alkin's name had indeed accrued an immense cultural capital, an even odder fact once we remember that neither Border nor Wood were the sharpest news-hounds.[57]

Whatever her relationship with the two men, it seems unlikely that she was brought in purely as a financial presence, given that just three days before the appearance of the first issue of *The Impartial Scout* Alkin was once again petitioning Parliament for money and accommodation since, as she protested, as "an aged woman ... having three children to maintain" she had "no meanes of subsistence but what she is faine to take great paines for."[58] Yet perhaps this is too simplistic a reading of the situation since, as we have already seen, Alkin was the consummate parliamentary petitioner and was adept at deploying poverty and weakness topoi in a variety of ways. Nonetheless, when the first issue of the *Scout* appeared, it was printed "for" her "by Robert Wood," and as such she had presumably financed, or at least part-financed, the new venture.[59] Even if her petition is taken at face value, the costs involved in the publication of a newsbook were not necessarily prohibitive. In 1642 the printer Robert White charged Francis Coles and Thomas Bates 18*s* for printing 1,500 sheets of Roger Pike's *A True Relation of the Proceedings of the Scots and English Forces in the North of Ireland.* Joad Raymond has adapted this "improbably low" figure to demonstrate that if a newsbook print run was the "plausible minimum" of 250 copies, the print cost would probably be no more than 9*s*, which, if the newsbook were sold for a penny, would provide a profit of 11*s* 10*d* to be divided amongst the publisher/editor and the distributing hawker or mercury woman.[60] It seems likely, therefore, that for a penurious Alkin, all too aware of the erratic nature of state payment to petitioners, the publication of a newsbook represented a way in which she could make a small, but immediately realizable, profit in an industry of which, as we have seen, she had considerable knowledge.[61]

Irrespective of costs, it is highly plausible that Alkin's reputation as an "intelligencer" preceded her and that she joined with Border and Wood in order to inject some much needed life and information into a rather unspectacular publication.[62] At another level, Alkin's incorporation represents a rather broad political as well as editorial alliance. As had already been noted, she had long been involved in the exposure of dissident Royalists, a more perilous and committed manifestation of the standard anti-Royalism Border and Wood had expressed in their earlier collaborations.[63] Yet Alkin's arrival also heralded a change in the newswriting of the *Scout* enterprise. *The Faithful and Impartial Scout* had been peppered with somewhat platitudinous editorial comment and asides which served to provide the reader with a specific lens through which to view the events of the week. Therefore, whilst the use of unwieldy, martialized body politic imagery was becoming a Border/Wood trademark, we come across undigested chunks of piety alongside facile Hobbesianism:

> Necessity is not ruled by Law, the force is so great; through many dangers she finds out the way, but it sufficeth not to the strength of armes, to have flesh, blood, and bones, unless they have also sinews to stretch out, or pull in for defence of the body: so an Army consisting of many men, and furnished with war-like habiliments is but lame and unserviceable if God give not a blessing of their undertakings.[64]

However, once Alkin becomes involved in the enterprise such patches of purple prose all but disappear. Instead of an editorial comment, the first words of the newsbook Alkin is involved with are the rhetorical commonplace of "This day we received Intelligence."[65] The contrast with what Border and Wood had produced earlier is stark, so that instead of being forced into a particular perspective, the reader's attention is immediately drawn to the fact that this is a collative and collective act.[66] Indeed, there is a sense in which the distinction between author and reader is reconfigured so that instead of any privileged, self-reflexive acts of author-ity, what we are faced with is the realization that the writing, reading, and discussion of newsbooks are, in fact, part of the same process, are all essential moments in the circulation and renewal of "Intelligence." This is entirely concordant with, and received its most profound expression in, Alkin's activities as a trade informant, wherein exemplary acts of reading prompted the discussion and discovery of seditious literature and presses, which acts in turn became the material of future newsbooks. Throughout her career, therefore, Alkin can be seen impressing the preeminence of "Intelligence" above mere "Information."[67]

The material of *The Impartial Scout* itself reaffirms this notion of the circular and collative nature of news. Through the almost total absence of any ostensible "authorial comment" the newsbook itself privileges the act of collation, by reprinting its sources wholesale. The strategy is perhaps a later manifestation of John Dillingham's first professed editorial commitment to "represent an exact weekly of such things as come to knowledge, and are fit for publike view ... which shall ever be according to intelligence, and without invectives."[68] Thus, the first three issues Alkin worked on were replete with "official" parliamentary news, Acts, and innumerable newsletters from around the country, continuing to reprint the London bills of mortality, despite the fact that Henry Walker, the originator of the practice, had ceased to do so in his concurrent *Severall Proceedings in Parliament* and *Perfect Passages of Everie Daies Intelligence*. Whilst this may prove unspectacular journalism, as in an instance where over half of the second issue of *Impartial Scout* is given over to the slavish reprinting of the Act passed on 28 June "for the better preventing of prophane Swearing and Cursing," the attention to collectivity that such wholesale collation necessarily entailed opened up a discursive framework which women could exploit.[69] It is interesting to speculate as to whether this apparent denial of agency, employed in a way which surreptitiously and paradoxically reintroduces it, can perhaps be viewed as a secularized, and less rhetoricized, counterpart to the self-effacing strategies which many sectarian prophetesses were using at this time to gain a place in the public sphere.[70]

Irrespective of whether this is the case, it is nonetheless surprising to find the sudden emergence of a distinct editorial voice at the opening of the fourth issue of *The Impartial Scout*:

> It is a Princely Alchumy, out of necessary War to extract an honourable peace; and more beseeming the Majesty of a Prince, to thirst after Peace, than Conquest: *Blessedness is promised to the peace-maker*, not to the conqueror: That is a happy State, which hath a peaceful hand, and a martial heart; able both to use peace and manage War: Even so it is with the Parlament of *England*, who have not been wanting in the offer of all fair and amicable means, for composing the differences and obtaining due satisfaction.[71]

The florid rhetoric, the ungainly martial versions of body politic imagery set rather precariously alongside pacifistic biblical quotation – which is not a quotation at all, but merely an echo of Matthew 5.9's "blessed are the peacemakers" – alerts us to the fact that we are back in the realms of Border and Wood's *Kingdomes Faithful and Impartial Scout*. If this were not un-Alkinian enough, then the noncommittal, moderate nature of the political rhetoric, pandering at once to expectant Royalists and Parliamentarians alike surely drives the point home. For a woman who had had her husband and the father of her three children hanged by the Royalists at Oxford, and who had spent the majority of her life exposing dissident Royalists, references to "Princely Alchumy" and the "honourable peace" and "Majesty of a Prince" were surely anathema.[72] It is telling therefore that this is the last involvement that Alkin was ever to have with a Border/Wood newsbook, so that, whilst the next issue opened with similar militaristic metaphors of the body politic, it, significantly, did not bear her name.[73]

Whether or not Alkin left the *Scout* enterprise because of its neutralism or because she was at odds with the direction its journalism had once again taken, most of her remaining forays into newsbook publication were made in direct opposition to Border and Wood. Between September 1650 and September 1651 Alkin was involved in the production of single issues of *The Moderne Intelligencer*, *Mercurius Anglicus*, and *The Modern Intelligencer*, all newsbooks closely associated with none other than Henry Walker. Walker's brand of anti-Royalism was much more committed than Border and Wood's, and as such was more allied with that of Alkin.[74] Whilst he had been an excited onlooker at Charles' trial, Walker had also been in trouble with the authorities in 1641 when he was arrested for hurling a copy of his pamphlet *To Your Tents O Israel* into Charles I's coach.[75] Politically Independent, he was an accomplished and prolific pamphleteer in his own right and had probably been publishing newsbooks since the autumn of 1644. By September 1650 he had developed into a skilled, relatively even-handed, newsman and had acquired a reputation as a rather showy classicist who persistently and ostentatiously revealed his authorial hand through Greek, Latin, and Hebrew quotations and etymological word play.[76]

It is interesting to note, therefore, that none of the newsbooks that Alkin published with Walker contain any of these supposedly Walkerian traits. When the first of the two issues of *The Moderne Intelligencer* appeared in September 1650 it was remarkable only in its likeness to *The Impartial Scout*.[78] Once again, the focus was on naval and military news; "Information" was downgraded as editorial comments and asides were forced out by the collative and collective processes of "Intelligence."[78] There is a sense that imbalance between Intelligence and Information did not suit Walker, that with Alkin involved *The Moderne Intelligencer* was decidedly too un-Walkerian for the newsman. Hence, the following postscript is hastily appended at the end of the newsbook:

> Courteous Reader,
> I thought it convenient (as formerly) to give you a brief account of the most modern and material proceedings in several parts. And though at present, (by reason of the slackness of Intelligence this Week) I am forced to break of abruptly; yet I thought good to divulge these few lines as a caution to my future intentions; not doubting but to give you satisfaction next Tuesday for my neglect in this.[79]

Walker himself here presents the newsbook as atypical of his work. As is intimated, the postscript replaces the functional summary that Walker had introduced to his newsbooks some years earlier. He implies that in this Alkinian issue readerly "satisfaction" will be low because "Intelligence is slack." However, to some extent this is disingenuous as the newsbook contains extremely detailed information about the activities and engagements of the Parliamentarian and Royalist armies in Scotland, a similarly precise account of the movements of the naval fleet, five items of foreign news, three letters, a reprint of a letter of "pious advice" by Fairfax, and an item on the death of "Lady Elizabeth Stuart Daughter of the late King."[80] Whilst it would be difficult to make a case for this newsbook as the most news-crammed of the week, it is similarly difficult to substantiate Walker's claim that it was underinformed. Yet it *was* underinformed in a more specific respect, in the sense that it was of a low informational quality, due to the paucity of editorial matter. The terms in which Walker accounts for this are significant; he has been "forced to break of abruptly," that is coerced by some external agent to desist from regaling the newsbook with florid editorial rhetoric and classical references. It is my contestation that this external agent is less a quiet news week – this was, after all, the week after the battle of Dunbar – than the publisher, Elizabeth Alkin, pressing as ever for the collative and collective nature of "Intelligence." In contradistinction with the present issue, Walker promises his readers "satisfaction next Tuesday" and, sure enough, when the second issue appeared, published this time by Jane Coe, not only had the concluding news summary returned, but so had the intrusive editorials, larded with classical allusion.[81]

It is therefore difficult to ascertain why Alkin and Walker published another two issues of different newsbooks after their collaboration on *The Moderne Intelligencer*. The virulently anti-Royalist *Mercurius Anglicus* appeared nine days later and, strikingly, once again conformed to the Alkinian privileging of Intelligence above Information. When it first appeared for two weeks in 1644 *Anglicus* set itself the unenviable task of being London's and Parliament's *Mercurius Aulicus*.[82] More surprising, however, is the fact that the name was revived in August 1648, this time as a Royalist serial bent on persuading "the besotted City ... to rescue his Majesty from his base Imprisonment, to restore him to his just Rights, and the people to their lost Religion, Laws, and Liberties."[83] Its news content was, by its own admission, questionable to say the least, but it did devote some space to criticizing Walker, the "*Hebrew Ironmonger, Judas-bearded Harrunney*," and his anti-Scottish writings.[84] In effect, then, Walker's and Alkin's enterprise is an attempt to reappropriate the name of *Anglicus* for the Parliamentarian, and an anti-Royalist, anti-Scottish cause, in the process, reassociating it with trustworthy intelligence, all urgent causes which allied both newsworkers. Whilst the new *Anglicus* certainly outdid its predecessors on all these counts, it was an unspectacular production, relying heavily on official documents, letters, and items that could largely be found in most other newsbooks of the time. Nonetheless, the collective nature of this endeavour perhaps allowed Alkin, with her expert knowledge of contemporary book trade intelligence networks, to show her journalistic hand that week, when the Ranter Lawrence Clarkson's book *The Single Eye* had been published, seized, burnt in public, and its readers forced to report to their Justice of the Peace, *Anglicus* offered an account of the event which surpassed all of its competitors. It reprinted, like most of the other newsbooks, the report from the Commons Journal of the day when the report was presented to Parliament. Yet it went further, attempting to offer brief descriptions of both the pamphlet and Clarkson himself, and actually went so far as to offer this as the sole important news item of the day.[85]

As no other issue of *Anglicus* appeared from the stable of Alkin and Walker, one can only assume that it proved as unsuccessful as its predecessors. Nonetheless, this did not signal the end of the Alkin/Walker collaboration, which announced itself once again the following year with a single issue of a revamped, re-spelled *The Modern Intelligencer*.[86] Once again this seems to have proved a dismal failure, the strict privileging of

Intelligence over Information proving to be no great selling point for a Walkerian newsbook, used as the public were to his flamboyantly obtrusive editorial style. This may have heralded the end of Alkin and Walker's journalistic relationship but it did not signal the end of Alkin's involvement in the material production of newsbooks, since less than three weeks after *The Modern Intelligencer, Mercurius Scoticus, or the Royal Messenger* appeared bearing Alkin's imprint as publisher. As the content of this newsbook was typically Alkinian, in that it was concerned primarily with naval and military news and espoused a strongly anti-Royalist position, J.B. Williams has speculated, with a great deal of vitriol and little evidence, that the title of this newsbook was intended solely to flush out contemporary Royalist newsbook readers. Alkin was:

> Able to approach any persons noted as strangers and royalists, get them into conversation extract all she knew from them, and afterwards utilise the information thus gained. Naturally the unlucky royalist, thus stealthily approached, would at once hide in his pocket a copy of this newsbook which he had purchased ... and his conference gained by this attractive title would hold a whispering conversation with the hawker, and not until reaching home and drawing out his little newsbook would he discover that he had been swindled.[87]

Ignoring that by a process as mysterious as the divine right of kings, Williams' reading "persons" somehow become exclusively male, it is difficult simply to dismiss this account because there is a lack of substantiating evidence either way. Whilst such speculation accords well with Alkin's history as an informer for the authorities, the chances are that the number of readers who considered a 1651 newsbook which clearly printed on its title page that it was "Examined by the Originalls, published by Authority" to be Royalist were few and far between.[88] That said, what is most striking about the final newsbook Alkin published is its profoundly un-Alkinian quality. It is crammed with editorial comments and classical allusion, even going so far as to include Latin encomia by Francis Nelson on Cromwell and the recent victory at Worcester.[89] As *Mercurius Scoticus* was initially a Royalist newsbook which had appeared in 1648, what is most likely, is that, ever aware of civil war newsbook culture, Alkin is repeating the strategy she had earlier experimented with on *Anglicus*, continuing the process of reappropriating Royalist titles for Parliamentarian consumption.

V

If *Scoticus* intimates that Alkin was lessening her involvement in London newsbook culture, official records confirm this. After discovering Hall's

Manus Testium two months after publishing her final newsbook, she moved to Dover to become a naval nurse, perhaps drawing on the intricate knowledge of the Fleet she had acquired in her journalistic endeavours. Whilst tending to the sick and wounded here she once again began petitioning Parliament for maintenance and lodgings, and the various letters and petitions that survive attest that the career of the nurse was not as renumerative as that of the newswoman.[90] Her last letter, dated February 1654, is to Robert Blackbourne, a member of the Council for the Navy, and is a heartfelt plea for assistance in illness. It concludes:

> my sickness & manie infirmities being procured by my continuall watchings night and day to do service for this Commonwealth ... I have beene inforced to sell my bed and other goodes to make ... satisfaction & to prevent ... clamor, I therefore humbly request I maie [have] a little monie or else be put in some Hospitall my daies being but short & to prevent a miserable ending of them my charge being very great for Physick and necessarie attendance for my preservation.
>
> And Sir I shall think my selfe ever bound to you for all your favours hoping I shall be no more troublesome to you, but shall while I live pray for you and yours & rest
>
> your poore servant in distress,
Elizabeth Alkin.[91]

Just as she had in her spying days, Alkin reworks the notion of good "service" in an attempt to obtain relief, and, as previously, she was successful, receiving £40 that year for her "reliefe" and "services," and a further "twenty markes" in the next.[92] After these payments we hear nothing more of her for over two hundred years, when J.B. Williams offers his study of the newsbook complete with his claim that there is an undated petition in which Alkin asks to be "buried in the cloisters of Westminster Abbey without charge."[93] Whether or not this is the case, the fact that there is no record of her name in the Abbey registers depressingly reveals that just as during her lifetime there was an agency-denying countermeasure for every one of her various acts of Intelligence-gathering, so too, posthumously, Elizabeth Alkin's body and memory are forcefully denied any place in the public sphere.

NOTES

I am grateful to Rachel Falconer, Mark Greengrass, Anthony Milton, David Norbrook, Joad Raymond, Erica Sheen, and Sue Wiseman for their comments, assistance, and encouragement during the preparation of this article

1. Alison Adburgham, *Women in Print: Writing and Women's Magazines From the Restoration to the Accession of Victoria* (London: George Allen and Unwin, 1972); Kathryn Shevelow,

Women and Print Culture: The Construction of Femininity in the Early Periodical (London and New York: Routledge, 1989); Olwen Hufton, *The Prospect Before Her: A History of Women in Western Europe 1500–1800* (London: Harper Collins, 1995), 438–51; Paula McDowell, *The Women of Grub Street: Press, Politics, and Gender in the London Literary Marketplace 1678–1730* (Oxford and New York: Oxford University Press, 1998).

2. Newsbook historiography has occasionally referred to English women in the journalistic culture of the civil war, but as yet there is no extended treatment. See J.B. Williams, *A History of Journalism to the Foundation of the Gazette* (London: Longman, 1908), 131–42, 152–54; Wilbur C. Abbot. "The First Newspapermen" [*sic*], *Proceedings of the Massachusetts Historical Society* 66 (1942): 50; William M. Clyde, *The Struggle for Freedom of the Press from Caxton to Cromwell* (London: Oxford University Press, 1934), 178, 200; Joseph Frank, *The Beginnings of the English Newspaper 1620–1660* (Cambridge, MA: Harvard University Press, 1961), 146, 305, 301, 356; Joad Raymond, *Making the News: An Anthology of the Newsbooks of Revolutionary England, 1641–1660* (Moreton-in-Marsh: Windrush Press, 1993), 122–68; idem, *The Invention of the Newspaper: English Newsbooks 1641–1649* (Oxford: Oxford University Press, 1996), 151, 161, 241–2, 250–51. On women and the civil war pamphlet culture more specifically, Maureen Bell, "Mary Westwood, Quaker Publisher," *Publishing History* 23 (1988): 5–66; idem, "Hannah Allen and the Development of a Puritan Publishing Business 1646–1651," *Publishing History* 26 (1989): 5–66; idem, "Women Publishers of Puritan Literature in the Mid-Seventeenth Century: Three Case Studies" (unpublished Ph.D. thesis, Loughborough, 1987); Dagmar Freist, *Governed by Opinion* (London: Tauris Academic Studies, 1997). On the Habermasian controversy, see Joad Raymond's essay in this volume and his extensive bibliography pp.133–4, and for a proposed abandonment of the Habermasian model, see Robert B. Shoemaker, *Gender in English Society 1650–1850* (London and New York: Longman, 1998).

3. *Mercurius Aulicus* 2, 7–13 Jan. 1644, cited in Raymond, *Making the News*, 132.

4. *Mercurius Democritus* 17, 21–28 July 1652.

5. On Crouch see Williams, *History*, 145–8; Frank, *Beginnings*, 195–231; Raymond, *Invention*, 66–74, 180–83; David Underdown, *A Freeborn People* (Oxford: Clarendon Press, 1996), 90–111. For further examples of women featuring in newsbooks, see Raymond, *Making the News*, 122–68.

6. Raymond, *Invention*, 250–51.

7. *A New Yeares Gift, Or a Brief Exhortation to Mr Thomas Edwards* (1644), 7.

8. Cited in Anthony Cotton's "London Newsbooks in the Civil War: Their Political Attitudes and Sources of Information" (unpublished D.Phil. thesis, Oxford University, 1971), 92. The partisan *Mercurius Britanicus* even suggested that the monarch himself dictated to *Aulicus*; *Mercurius Britanicus* 92, 28 July–4 Aug. 1645, 1022.

9. *Gangraena*, Book I (1646), 44.

10. The literature on these topics is extensive. Perhaps the best overview is still Elaine Hobby, *Virtue of Necessity: English Women's Writing 1649–1688* (London: Virago, 1988). For more recent work with extensive bibliographies, Patricia Crawford, *Women and Religion in England 1500–1720* (London and New York: Routledge, 1993); Hilary Hinds, *God's Englishwomen: Seventeenth-Century Sectarian Women's Writing* (Manchester and New York: Manchester University Press, 1996); Megan Matchinske, *Writing, Gender, and the State in Early Modern England: Identity Formation and the Female Subject* (Cambridge: Cambridge University Press, 1998).

11. For a feminist critique of the classic Habermasian public sphere, see Joan B. Landes, *Women and the Public Sphere in the Age of the French Revolution* (Ithaca, NY: Cornell University Press, 1988); Nancy Fraser, *Unruly Practices: Power, Discourse and Gender in Contemporary Social Theory* (Cambridge: Polity, 1989); idem, "Rethinking the Public Sphere: A Contribution to the Critique of Actually Existing Democracy," in Craig Calhoun (ed.), *Habermas and the Public Sphere* (Cambridge, MA: MIT Press, 1992), 109–42. For the argument that women did actually achieve participatory parity in the public sphere at a later stage in the seventeenth century, see Steve Pincus, "'Coffee Politicians Does Create': Coffeehouses and Restoration Political Culture," *Journal of Modern History* 67 (1995): 807–34.

12. McDowell, *The Women of Grub Street*, 1–121. Contemporary seditious libel cases suggest that as it was the printer who affixed his/her name to frequently anonymous works, and was accordingly punished, it was printers who were frequently tarred with the brush of originative agency. See Joseph F. Lowenstein, "Legal Proofs and Corrected Readings: Press Agency and the New Bibliography," in D.L. Miller, S. O'Dair, and Harold Weber (eds.), *The Production of English Renaissance Culture* (Ithaca, NY: Cornell Unversity Press, 1994), 93–122.

13. McDowell, *The Women of Grub Street*, 84–5.

14. Ibid., 12

15. On the narrative strategies deployed by women petitioners, see Ann Hughes, "Gender and Politics in Leveller Literature," in S.D. Asmussen and M.A. Kishlansky (eds.), *Political Culture and Cultural Politics in Early Modern England: Essays Presented to David Underdown* (London: Manchester University Press, 1995), 162–88; Catie Gill, "Individuality and Collectivity in the Quaker Petition of Tithes (1659)," (forthcoming). On manuscript culture and women's involvement therein, see Harold Love, *Scribal Publication in Seventeenth-Century England* (Oxford: Clarendon Press, 1993); Wendy Wall, *The Imprint of Gender: Authorship and Publication in the English Renaissance* (Ithaca, NY, and London: Cornell University Press, 1993); Arthur F. Marotti, *Manuscript, Print, and the English Renaissance Lyric* (Ithaca, NY, and London: Cornell University Press, 1995), 39–61.

16. The obvious exception here is Dagmar Freist's *Governed by Opinion*, which goes some way towards offering an account of women and pre-Restoration print culture. Her section on women hawkers, who may have peddled newsbooks as well as pamphlets is especially relevant. See 110–124.

17. J.B. Williams, "Henry Walker, Journalist of the Commonwealth," *The Nineteenth Century* (March 1908): 454–464; Frank, *Beginnings*, 379–83; idem, *Cromwell's Press Agent: A Critical Biography of Marchamont Nedham 1620–1678* (Lanham, MD: University Press of America, 1980); Raymond, *Making the News*, 332–79; idem, *Invention*, 371–4; Blair Worden, "Marchamont Nedham and the Beginnings of English Republicanism, 1649–1656," in David Wooton (ed.), *Republicanism, Liberty and Commercial Society, 1649–1776* (Stanford, CA: Stanford University Press 1994), 45–81.

18. For a more theoretical perspective, the general tendency in literary criticism prematurely to reify the author, see Michel Foucault, "What is an Author?" in Josué V. Harari (ed.), *Textual Strategies: Perspectives in Post-Structuralist Criticism* (London: Methuen, 1980), 141–60; Lowenstein, "Legal Proofs and Corrected Readings," 93–122.

19. The only extensive treatments of Alkin to date are J.B. Williams, *History*, 131–54; G.E. Manwaring, "Parliament Joan: The Florence Nightingale of the Commonwealth," *The United Service Magazine*, 57 (1918): 301–10; Isabel MacDonald, *Elizabeth Alkin: A Florence Nightingale of the Commonwealth* (Keighley: Wadsworth and Co., 1935).

20. In February 1650 the far from impartial John Crouch records her age as "about fifty," whilst her last surviving letter, detailing chronic illness is dated 27 February 1654.

21. Public Record Office, State Papers (hereafter SP), 19/4/72; SP 19/4/77.

22. *The Character of a Rebellion* (1681), 11 (emphasis added).

23. For the author (perhaps John Nalson), the "Common-wealth Ravisher" *par excellence* was, predictably, the Republican Henry Marten.

24. J.B. Williams, *History*, 131. "Joan" was also the derrogatory name given to the fabled female Pope of the ninth century, famed not only for her supposed licentiousness, but also for her untrustworthy words and capacity to prevaricate and deceive. See Sarah Lawson, "From Latin Pun to English Puzzle: An Elizabethan Translation Problem," *The Sixteenth Century Journal* 9 (1978): 27; C.A. Patrides, *Premises and Motifs in Renaissance Thought and Literature* (Princeton, NJ: Princeton University Press, 1982), 152–81.

25. PRO SP 19/5/284.

26. G.E. Manwaring, "Parliament Joan," 302.

27. Compare Alkin's payment with that of Sir Edward Nicholas, the royal Secretary of State, who was paid an amazing £200 a month for his Intelligence. See, Alan Marshall, *Intelligence and Espionage in the Reign of Charles II, 1660–1685* (Cambridge: Cambridge University Press, 1994), 1–19.

28. SP 19/98/80; SP 23/62/228; SP 23/62/232; *The Kingdomes Faithfull and Impartiall Scout* 19, 1–8 June 1649, 2014; *A Perfect Diurnall of Some Passages in Parliament* 310, 2–9 July 1649, 2635.

29. SP 23/62/228.

30. Ibid. The order is scrawled in a different hand at the bottom of the manuscript of the petition.

31. SP 23/62/233.

32. SP 25/87/61; SP 25/63/16; SP 23/62/235; SP 23/62/232; SP 23/8/151; SP 25/65/238.

33. On the incident at the Exchange see *CSPD 1653–1654*, 360, 427; *CSPD 1654*, 151, 156, 169, 214; *CSPVen 1653–1654*, 153, 162, 166, 180, 236–8.

34. Don Pantaleon Sa, *A Narration of the Late Accident in the New Exchange*, (1653); Frances Clarke, *A Brief Reply to the Narration of Don Pantaleon Sa* (1653).

35. *The Moderate Publisher* 6, 19 Nov.–2 Dec. 1653; *Severall Proceedings of State Affairs* 217, 17–24 Nov. 1653; Ibid., No. 218, 24 Nov.–1 Dec. 1653; *The Perfect Diurnall* 207, 21–28 Nov. 1653; *The Faithful Scout* 139, 18–25 Nov. 1653.

36. SP 25/72/174. The decision is all the more interesting for the fact that none of the contemporary pamphlet or newsbook sources mention Alkin as a significant presence upon the Exchange.

37. Offering no evidence, J.B. Williams claims that Alkin was involved in the capture and committal of Thomas Budd, editor of *Mercurius Catholicus*, in 1648; *History*, 152. For a discussion of the role of "female trade informants" after the Restoration, see Paula McDowell, *The Women of Grub Street*, 90–118.

38. *A Perfect Diurnall* 310, 2–9 July 1649, p.2623.

39. *The Man in the Moon* 43, 13–20 Feb. 1650, p.342.

40. Whilst Alkin is easily recognizable from Crouch's comments, the identity of the "Smith" he refers to is far from certain. Plomer has demonstrated that there were at least eight different Smiths registered as printers and booksellers in London in the 1640s and 1650s, however, there are no extant records which prove that any of them were employed as press informants. H.R. Plomer, *A Dictionary of the Booksellers and Printers who Were at Work in England, Scotland and Ireland from 1641–1667* (London: London Bibliographical Society, 1907), 166–8.

41. *Mercurius Pragmaticus* 43, 20–27 Feb. 1649.

42. Ibid.; the counterfeit issue has exactly the same date but bears the issue number 46. It is a reprint of *Mercurius Elencticus* 69, 21–28 Feb.1649.

43. SP 19/98/80

44. This is at odds with contemporary and traditional twentieth-century views of the world of espionage. It is surely no accident that as patriarchy was attempting to erase or devalue the role of women in the early modern public sphere, both sides in the civil war sought to consolidate and demonstrate their power by inscribing their authority on the bodies of captured *male* spies in spectacular public executions. For instance, Richard Symonds recalled an occasion when the Royalist army was deliberately marched under a gallows so that they could see the body of a Parliamentarian spy above. Similarly, David Kniverton, a Royalist spy, was publicly hanged outside the Royal Exchange, and copies of parliamentary ordinances forbidding unlicensed travel were stuck to various parts of his body. See C. Carlton, *Going to the Wars: The Experiences of the British Civil Wars 1638–1651* (London and New York: Routledge, 1992) 263–4; Alan Marshall, *Intelligence and Espionage*, 1–18.

45. However, attention to such details raises the problem of the dating of the manuscript. Whilst it is currently, albeit tentatively, dated at September 1647 and is archived with a bundle of other manuscripts from that period, the specific historical details of the petition suggests a later date of early February 1650. Specifically, the petition refers to "last weeke your petitioner discovered fouwre presses in one Dugards Custody, in Mearchant Taylor School" and that "the said Dugard [was] committed too Newgate." This is the same William Dugard who began editing and printing the French newsbook *Nouvelles Ordinaires de Londres* in July 1650, yet to most early modernists he is remembered as the first printer of Milton's *Eikonoklastes*. Less well known is the fact that in January 1649, before his appointment as "Printer to the State," he also published Salmasius's *Defensio Regia*, the French scholar's famous attack on the regicides, and in the March of that year also published an expanded

edition of *Eikon Basilike*, for which offences the authorities had him committed to Newgate on 20 February 1650. As this was Dugard's only period of incarceration whilst he was headmaster of the Merchant Taylor's School, and Alkin was handsomely rewarded in the March of that year with Whitehall lodgings, it seems most likely that Alkin's petition actually dates from the third week of February 1650, the same week in which Crouch was vilifying her in *The Man in the Moon*. On Dugard, see *Dictionary of National Biography*, XV, 133–4; W.R. Parker, *Milton: A Biography* (Oxford: Clarendon Press, 1996), 263–4; Leona Rostenberg, *Literary, Scientific, Religious and Legal Publishing, Printing and Bookselling in England, 1551–1700: Twelve Studies* (New York: Burt Franklin, 1965), 130–60.

46. SP 25/24/68; SP 25/24/71; *Manus Testium Movens: Or a Presbyteriall Glosse Upon many of those obscure prophetick texts* (1651), p.2. This was a response to Nathaniel Holmes's *A sermon [on Psal. cxlix. 9] preached before the ... Lord Maior ... and severall companies of the city of London upon the generall day of thanksgiving, Oct. 8. 1650.* which claimed that the actions of the regicides, and Cromwell's defeat of the Scots was actually the fulfilment of scripture.

47. Carolyn Nelson and Matthew Seccombe (eds.), *British Newspapers and Periodicals, 1641–1700: A Short Title Catalogue of Serials Printed in England, Scotland, Ireland, and British America* (New York: MLA, 1987), 705.

48. For Border, see Frank, *Beginnings*, 211–28.

49. Ibid., 176–8.

50. The arguments continued until around the end of the year. Ibid., 178.

51. *The Kingdomes Faithful and Impartial Scout* 20, 8–15 June 1649, 154, 160.

52. *Perfect Occurences of Parliament* 129, 15–22 June 1649, 1128.

53. Pincus, "'Coffee Politicians Does Create,'" 811.

54. Frank, *Beginnings*, 178.

55. Border had also been involved in the publication if a second weekly serial at this time, producing *The Perfect Weekly Account* every Wednesday with the highly skilled printer, Bernard Alsop.

56. *The Kingdomes Faithfull and Impartiall Scout* 19, 1–8 June 1649, 147.

57. Border's promise in the first issue of *The Kingdomes Weekly Post* that it would print news that the other newsbooks missed was, like the majority of his predictions, unfulfilled.

58. SP 23/62/232.

59. *The Impartial Scout* 53, 21–28 June 1650. On the traditional role of a newsbook publisher, see Frank, *Beginnings*, 8, 23, 28, 234, 269. For a more dynamic view which intimates at a more creative involvement, see Paula McDowell, *The Women of Grub Street*, 30–45, 60–71.

60. In his *Glossographia* (1656), Thomas Blount clarifies the distinction between hawkers and mercury women: "Those people which go up and down the streets crying News-books, and selling them by retail, are also called Hawkers and those Women that sell them wholesale from the Press, are called Mercury Women," cited in D.F. McKenzie, "The London Book Trade in the Later Seventeenth Century" (unpublished Sandars Lectures, 1976), 25.

61. See Cotton, "London Newsbooks in the Civil War," 8; *Commons Journals*, ii: 612, 613, 615; Raymond, *Invention*, 233–4. Although Raymond's figures are for the early 1640s, the fact that *The Impartial Scout* did not procure any advertising revenues during Alkin's involvement surely makes his calculations applicable.

62. On the unoriginal, "facile," and "noncommittal" nature of the Border/Wood newsbook see Frank, *Beginnings*, 128.

63. Ibid., 91–2.

64. *The Kingdomes Faithful and Impartial Scout* 36, 28 Sept.–5 Oct. 1649, 257.

65. *The Impartial Scout* 53, 21–28 June 1650, 217.

66. Border had also regularly dropped editorial comments and asides from his collaboration with Bernard Alsop. See Freist, *Governed by Opinion*, 104–7.

67. On the "Intelligence"/"Information" distinction see Raymond, *Invention*, 162, wherein Intelligence constitutes the news, the raw material of the newsbook and Information features as editorial matter.

68. *The Moderate Intelligencer* 1, 6–13 March 1645, 1.

69. *The Impartial Scout* 2 (54), 28 June–5 July 1650, 225–8. Tantalisingly, another woman, Jane

Coe, who does not appear to have had as sustained a relationship with "Intelligence" as Alkin, but was more expertly involved in the material printing of pamphlets and newsbooks, was systematically denied these benefits of collectivity. Her involvement between June 1644 and November 1647 in the production of *The Kingdomes Scout, Mr Peters Report, The Moderate Messenger,* and *Perfect Occurrences* is obscured not only by the obtrusive editorial voices of a younger Daniel Border and Hugh Peters but by the fact that she was frequently working in tandem with, and was introduced to the printing industry by, her husband, Andrew Coe. On the Coes, see Henry R. Plomer, *Dictionary,* 471; D.F Mackenzie, *Stationer's Company Apprentices, 1605–1640* (Charlottesville, VA: Bibliographical Society of the University of Virginia, 1961), 22.

70. On the potentially liberating effects of such self-effacement, see Christine Berg and Philippa Berry, "Spiritual Whoredome: An Essay on Female Prophets in the Seventeenth Century," in Frances Barker *et al.* (eds.), *1642: Literature and Power in the Seventeenth Century* (Colchester: University of Essex Press, 1981), 37–55; Marcus Nevitt, "'Blessed, Self-Denying, Lamb-Like'? The Fifth Monarchist Women," *Critical Survey* (forthcoming).

71. *The Impartial Scout* 4 (56), 12–19 July 1650, 241.

72. In fact, Border's attitude to Royalism had always been complexly neutral. For instance, *The Weekly Account* refused either to praise or condemn "the number of people that resorted to his Majesty for cure of the Evill." *The Weekly Account* 8, 17–24 Feb. 1647; see also *Weekly Account* 46, 28 Oct.–4 Nov. 1646 and *Weekly* Account 13, 24–30 March 1647, cited in Frank, *Beginnings,* 128.

73. *The Impartial Scout* 5 (57), 19–25 July 1650, 249.

74. In fact, there is a sense that he liked to maintain a certain radicalism in his working relationships on newsbooks, so that between January 1644 and October 1649 he could be found working on the *Perfect Occurences* with the antinomian John Saltmarsh. Nelson and Seccombe, *STC,* 308–314, 702; Raymond, *Invention,* 199.

75. Henry Walker, *Collections of Notes taken at the Kings Tryall, at Westminster Hall*s (1649); Ernest Sirluck, "'To Your Tents, O Israel: A Lost Pamphlet," *Huntingdon Library Quarterly,* 19 (1955–56): 301–5. Furthermore, the Walkerian *Perfect Occurences* of early 1646 continually stressed the need for local vigilance and legislative action against Royalist plots. See Frank, *Beginnings,* 108–12. The picture of his radical edge may be sharpened with the realization that he gave more space than any other contemporary editor to the Levellers. In 1645, *The Great Assises Holden In Parnassus* accused him of a kind of social levelling, that he "with censures bold, / The actions of his betters had controld," 19, ll. 11–12; Raymond, *Invention,* 199, 217.

76. *Perfect Occurences* 63, 10–17 March 1648, 516. For a discussion of Walker's classicism, see Frank, *Beginnings,* 81, 109, 150.

77. Whilst Nelson and Seccombe do not venture an attribution of *The Moderne Intelligencer,* both Frank and J.B. Williams positively identify Walker as its editor.

78. This was not the first time that Walker had effaced himself as an editor. Between March 1648 and January 1649, Walker was probably involved in the production of *Packets of Letters from ... to members of the House of Commons* and *A Declaration, Collected Out of the Journals of Both Houses of Parliament.* These, too, had no editorial content. See Raymond, *Invention,* 69.

79. *The Moderne Intelligencer* 1, 11–18 Sept. 1650, 8.

80. The only other newsbook to pick up on this last item at this time was Walker's other journalistic enterprise. See *Perfect Passages* 10, 9–13 Sept. 1650, 78.

81. *The Moderne Intelligencer* 2, 18–25 Sept. 1650. As has already been mentioned, Jane Coe appears to be an interesting contrast to Alkin, in that she continually allows her involvement in the newsbooks she worked on to be obscured. Amazingly, she worked on the *Perfect Occurences* with Walker and Saltmarsh for the entire period between June 1644 and November 1647. See n.69.

82. *Mercurius Anglicus* 1, 31 Jan.– 7 Feb. 1644. On other London-based newsbooks which set themselves up in opposition to *Aulicus,* see Raymond, *Invention,* 26–36.

83. *Mercurius Anglicus*1, 27 July–3 Aug. 1648, 1.

84. Ibid. "Luke Harruney" was the, not entirely successful, anagram Walker used to mask

himself when working on *Perfect Occurences.*

85. Lawrence Clarkson, *A Single Eye: All Light, no Darkness; or Light and Darkness One* (1650); *Mercurius Anglicus* 1, 24 Sept.–1 Oct. 1650; *Perfect Diurnall* 42, 23–30 Sept. 1650, 553–4; *Mercurius Politicus* 17, 26 Sept.–3 Oct. 1650, 286; *Severall Proceedings of Parliament* 53, 23 Sept.–3 Oct. 1650, 790.
86. *The Modern Intelligencer* V, 26 Aug.–3 Sept. 1651.
87. Williams, *History*, 142.
88. *Mercurius Scoticus*, 23–30 Sept. 1651, title-page.
89. This has led Nelson and Seccombe to attribute *Scoticus* to Francis Nelson; *STC*, 388. This *Scoticus* survived for only one issue and is not to be confused with Scotland's first newspaper of the same name which also appeared that year.
90. There is no record of Alkin petitioning for relief at any stage during the period she was publishing newsbooks.
91. SP 18/66/74.
92. SP 25/75/258; 25/75/545; 25/76/73.
93. Williams, *History*, 154. However, I have not been able to locate this petition.

The Newspaper, Public Opinion, and the Public Sphere in the Seventeenth Century

JOAD RAYMOND

In a proclamation of January 1676, withdrawing his recent and ineffectual interdiction on coffee-houses, Charles II required all coffee merchants to act as state spies, discouraging the spread of libellous papers and reporting on those who introduced "False and Scandalous Reports of the Government, or any Ministers thereof" into their establishments.[1] In 1667, during the second Anglo-Dutch war, the Archbishop of Glasgow wrote to Joseph Williamson, Under-Secretary of State and supervisor of *The London Gazette*, requesting a copy of the "weekly intelligence" so as to contradict the demoralizing news spread by "ordinary newsmongers."[2] These examples typify a shift in attitudes since James' proclamations against "lavish speech."[3] The Carolean regime had learnt how to respond pragmatically to the pressure of public opinion. The British had secured the right, albeit assumed and unprotected by legislation, to read the news of their troubled country. After the Restoration, whatever interventions Parliament and King subsequently made to restrict the dissemination and public debate of news, politics, and opinion, a substantial proportion of the public pursued in print and coffee-houses events and issues that interested them. Political debate and communication were less likely to be confined to diaries, private correspondence, and intimate chat, and more likely to appear in the open.[4] Later Stuart governments did not try to control public opinion by suppressing or preventing the forums for news entirely, but by manipulating them to their advantage. As the loyalist Roger L'Estrange commented in 1681: "'Tis the *Press* that has made 'um *Mad*, and the *Press* must set 'um *Right* again. The Distemper is *Epidemical*; and there's no way in the world, but by *Printing*, to convey the *Remedy* to the *Disease*."[5]

The early modern British public had a nearly pathological interest in reading and hearing news: literary critics and historians confirm the charged comments of contemporaries on the itch of news, its potency and prevalence. They also suggest that interest in and discussion of news – the formation of public opinion – played an increasingly important part in society and political culture. The "public sphere" of Jürgen Habermas has

Joad Raymond, University of Aberdeen

become in recent decades the most influential model of popular debate and public opinion as a social force in early-modern Europe. Originally published in 1962, though not translated into English until 1989, *The Structural Transformation of the Public Sphere* presents a nuanced and energetic picture of a growing space for public debate coterminous with the development of bourgeois society; a space which, with the onset of a later form of capitalism in the nineteenth and twentieth centuries, is transformed into an instrument of state manipulation of the public.

Habermas' account speaks to all of Europe, but Britain is, conveniently, his model case. Britain precedes Europe in the development of a public sphere, and Habermas places its incipience there in the years 1694–95.[6] Research on public opinion in the seventeenth century, and particularly on pamphlet culture, has led recent commentators to question both the chronological specificity and the usefulness of Habermas' model. Most significantly, several writers have suggested that a public sphere appeared in Britain prior to the 1690s, and have drawn Habermas' account back into earlier periods.[7] I shall return to the issue of public opinion and its relation to the public sphere later in this essay, after dealing with the model Habermas outlines and its historical relevance.

In his 1961 preface Habermas commented on the specificity of the model which is both sociological and historical:

> We conceive [of the?] bourgeois public sphere as a category that is typical of an epoch. It cannot be abstracted from the unique developmental history of that "civil society" originating in the European High Middle Ages; nor can it be transferred, idealtypically generalized, to any number of historical situations that represent formally similar constellations.[8]

This qualification is significant. An ideal type is an abstract model or system which, in the manner of the work of Max Weber, can be used to explain a social dynamic in any number of situations. And if Habermas' public sphere cannot be turned into a sociological ideal type, and thereby chronologically shifted, then accounts which empirically falsify it make the model redundant. The theory is as vulnerable to historical as to theoretical disproof.[9] Raising this possibility himself, Habermas has subsequently expressed doubts "about how far we can push back the very notion of the public sphere into the sixteenth and seventeenth centuries without somehow changing the very concept of the public sphere to such a degree that it becomes something else."[10] It might be argued that we do not have to agree with Habermas' proscription against appropriating his model as an ideal type, and that he is himself inconsistent in his approach; yet the most important question – for the literary critic, historian or sociologist – must surely be whether the shoe fits.[11] My purpose here is not to explore the relation between social theory and history; or to question whether an historical account which relies on a much-contested Marxist view of a seventeenth-century bourgeoisie bears much currency today. Rather I shall use historical and literary evidence and perspectives to examine the value of Habermas' model for explaining the role of the newspaper in generating and constituting public opinion in the seventeenth century.

II

The "structural transformation" of Habermas' title is not, as some commentators imply, the appearance of the public sphere: by this phrase Habermas refers to the later developments that narrow the operation of the public sphere.[12] The title is too quotable for its own good, and the last three-fifths of the book sometimes suffers under its shadow. To do the book justice it is necessary to reflect upon its entirety, and to consider its message as it bears upon the twentieth century and the critical practice of the intellectual; in a sense the earlier, historical passages of the book establish the foundations of a bigger argument. Nevertheless, it is the appropriation of those passages that concern us here, so the model Habermas develops in the earlier stages of his narrative is summarized in some detail.

According to Habermas, the public sphere has three defining characteristics. First, it is an arena to which everyone has in theory a right of access. The theory is different from the practice: in fact access is only ever achieved by those in particular economic circumstances, which is not the same as saying that it is denied to those not in those circumstances.[13] According to Habermas, the gender, professional, and educational homogeneity of the participants were perceived as incidental to a common humanity; and they continue to be treated as such in his idealization. Secondly the public sphere is non-instrumental. Habermas uses the term "instrumental" specifically to describe a mechanism, medium, or agency which can be used to influence or work upon an individual or group. The public sphere is non-instrumental because it cannot be deployed or manipulated in order to achieve a particular effect; it does not serve a particular interest group. It consists of "private persons come together as a public," and hence relies on a social separation between public and private, in which private persons are not pursuing merely political ends. Though he recognizes that the status of being a private individual was subject to certain legal codifications, namely property ownership, Habermas underplays the legal origins and definition of private and public, as far as their seventeenth-century manifestations are concerned, and they remain a neglected and consequential dimension of the interface between social, intellectual, and literary history.[14] It is, according to Habermas, only later that public opinion becomes a force institutionally compelling public authorities.[15] Thus the public sphere should not be equated with organized political opposition, though such an opposition might occasionally appeal to and generally benefit by it. Thirdly, it is governed by reason. The exchanges which in part constitute the public sphere appeal to reason (rather than, for instance, rank) as their arbiter and authority. Hence, within the public sphere all persons can be considered equal.

The public sphere emerges between the domains of the private and public. It is located between arenas of public authority where the public is represented, such as the state or court, and the private realm of civil society, such as the family or private business.[16] It exists in and is inseparable from real social spaces: in debate conducted in journals and periodicals, in salons, *Sprachgesellshaften*, and in coffee-houses.[17] Notwithstanding this concrete sense of place, according to Habermas the public sphere is freed from the brute, material realities of labour and commercial exchange: in fact, he sees the commercial apparatus which in part constructs the public sphere as also endangering it.[18] For this reason, Habermas represents those journalists who participate in the public sphere as disinterested idealists, deaf to the noise of exchange relations and the desire to make money. The journalists engage with issues over which everyone has the right to a private opinion, and they do so because it is their right. This disinterest is connected to the "literary" concerns of the "world of letters" which is a precursor to the public sphere proper.[19] Habermas uses "literary" as a convenient middle term for those issues that lie between private and public; though the participants in the public sphere certainly discuss politics and parties as well as books, science, and art.[20] In this Utopian account Habermas transforms the commercial world of the coffee-house and journal into a patronage-free successor to the European republic of letters.

III

The significance of 1694–95 in Habermas' account of the emergence of the public sphere in Britain is that these years saw the founding of the Bank of England, the final expiration of the Licensing Act of 1662 (which had lapsed between 1679 and 1685) and the first cabinet government. The foundation of the Bank of England "signalled a new stage in the development of capitalism." The expiration of the Licensing Act introduced "unique liberties" for the press. Government by cabinet gave a new status to parliamentary authority in the state, and was the first stage in the process by which the public would become an institution. In this institutionalization of the public was embedded a contradiction which ultimately led, in the nineteenth and twentieth centuries, to a mutual infiltration between public and private and the collapse of the public sphere.[21]

With the ascendancy of the bourgeoisie in the early eighteenth century, critical debate achieved the political independence necessary to constitute a potent public sphere.[22] The press was central to this. Initially it offered reporting that was news-oriented and "discreet." Then it crept into the hands of the opposition, and "political journalism in the grand style" was created by the Tories in 1722 when they purchased the *London Journal*. In 1726 Bolingbroke brought out *The Craftsman*, and with this, and the *Gentleman's Magazine*, "the press was for the first time established as a genuinely critical organ of a public engaged in critical political debate: as the fourth estate."[23] Bolingbroke's association with Swift, Pope, and Gay underscores the "literary" dimension of the public sphere. In the hands of an economically and socially dominant bourgeois stratum the press constituted a kind of "pre-parliamentary forum" at a time when Parliament was also gaining a political ascendancy. Habermas claims that with the emergence of the public sphere, public critical debate superseded the resort to violence as the means of making national political intervention;[24] though in doing so he understates the reality of the Jacobite threat in 1691, 1715, and 1745. Then, during the eighteenth century, the term and concept of "public opinion" emerges, in recognition of these earlier developments.

More recent descriptions of public opinion in the later seventeenth century have offered various dates for its arrival as a significant force in politics. Gary Stuart De Krey's exposition is more or less consonant with Habermas'. He argues that 1695 witnessed a "communications revolution," through which printed media became a critical element in London politics. The circulation of early-eighteenth-century journals was greater than their predecessors, and they created popular participation and political allegiance by linking local and national issues. In 1710–15, he argues, readers were politically educated through the newspaper press and ideologically polarized along party lines; satirical images of Whig and Tory made "rational political discourse" near-impossible. His "communications revolution" arrives through a change in quantity, which distinguished early-eighteenth-century conditions from earlier "journalistic boomlets."[25]

Mark Goldie, in an analysis of the allegiance controversy of 1689–90 has suggested that the participants were probably the last group of pamphleteers not from Grub Street, indicating a move to professional (and party-politically financed) journalism in the 1700s. The circulation figures for this period show "that although the Revolution has the appearance of an aristocratic coup, it involved, through the press, a substantial part of the political nation." However thorny gauging the impact of pamphlets is, Goldie concludes, "it is hard to avoid the conclusion that the political consciousnesses of Englishmen in the late seventeenth century were susceptible to a high degree of purposeful guidance from the centre."[26] This situation probably intensified when the party mechanisms for propaganda became more structured in the 1700s; hence the turn of the century was no turning-point. Even the development of the provincial newspaper was founded on appetites and mechanisms of supply which had long been in place. Tim Harris identifies even earlier evidence of meaningful popular intervention. Both Whigs and Tories exploited the arena of politics without doors; propaganda, petitioning, and popular demonstrations during the Popish Plot and Exclusion Crisis suggest an active expression of popular interest in politics that was not merely an effect of elite manipulation.[27] Mark Knights likewise assumes that an arena for expressing and manipulating public opinion existed during the crisis of 1678–81.[28]

Michael Treadwell, analysing the emergence of the trade publisher, suggests that 1680 was a critical year in the development of the book trade, starting a concentration of distribution in a very few hands, and which ultimately led to the development of the newspaper publisher as a distinct profession: by the 1720s and the birth of Grub Street, newspapers had become a much more profitable venture.[29] This chronology suggests that monopoly forces and market concentration enhanced the role of widely circulated newspapers in public debate; I shall return to this important issue below.

These accounts both complicate the picture of a gradually emerging role for popular public opinion in political life, and suggest that changes were more precocious than Habermas proposes. There is much to indicate that popular political opinion and debate developed even earlier than the 1670s or 1680s, perhaps before the civil wars.[30] Certainly in the 1640s the press created an arena of propagandistic conflict which engaged with and stimulated public debate.[31] Seventeenth-century representations of contemporary popular discourse also anticipate Habermas' sketch of debate; though they commonly give it a dystopian or satiric colouring. In these sketches, other social spaces, especially St Paul's Walk and the Royal Exchange, appear as predecessors of the coffee-house. According to Francis Osborn, in the early seventeenth century, "it was the fashion of these times ... for the principal gentry, lords, courtiers and men of all professions ... to meet in Paul's Church by eleven and walk in the middle aisle till twelve, and after dinner from three to six, during which times some discoursed of business, others of news."[32] Likewise, in 1628 Bishop John Earle described St Paul's Walk as:

> the Lands Epitome, or you may call it the lesser Ile of Great Brittaine, It is more then this, the whole worlds Map, which you may here discerne in it's perfect'st motion iustling and turning. It is a heape of

stones and men, with a vast confusion of Languages, and were the
Steeple not sanctified nothing liker Babel. The noyse in it is like that
of Bees, a strange humming or buzze-mixt of walking, tongues and
feet: It is a kind of still roare or loud whisper. It is the great Exchange
of all discourse, & no busines whosoeuer but is here stirring and afoot.
It is the Synod of all pates politicke, ioynted and laid together in most
serious posture, and they are not halfe so busie at the Parliament. It is
the Anticke of tailes to tailes, and backes to backes, and for vizards
you need goe no further then faces. It is the Market of young
Lecturers, whom you may cheapen here at all rates and sizes. It is the
generall Mint of all famous lies ... All inuentions are emptied here,
and not few pockets. ... It is the eares Brothell and satisfies their lust,
and ytch. The Visitants are all men without exceptions, but the
principall Inhabitants and possessors, are stale Knights, and Captaines
out of Seruice, men of long Rapiers, and Breeches, which after all
turne Merchants here and trafficke for Newes.[33]

The invention of the newspaper and the appearance of coffee-houses did not
depopulate the walk. In a burlesque poem on Paul's church in 1716 Edward
Ward complained, in mortifying rhyme, of the "Mungrel-Politicians" who
met there:

To crack their shallow Brains with News;
Meer Scavengers, who load their Senses
With all the Filth the Press dispenses,
That they may shoot their Rubbish-Lyes,
And bury Truth with Falsities,
Plaguing all Places, where they're known,
With wise State-Comments of their own ...
Turning God's House, by this ill Course,
Into a Coffee-House, or worse ...[34]

Early coffee-houses were said to have a similar vitality. Describing
Miles' coffee-house in New Palace Yard, Westminster, where James
Harrington's Rota club met until February 1660, Anthony Wood wrote:
"The room was every evening full as it could be crammed ... the arguments
in the Parliament House were flat, to the discourses here."[35] In 1673 Thomas
Player wrote to Joseph Williamson that "the common people talke anything,
for every carman and porter is now a statesman; and indeed the coffee-
houses are good for nothing else." He added nostalgically: "It was not thus
when wee dranke nothing but sack and clarett, or English beere and ale.
These sober clubbs produce nothing but scandalous and censorious
discourses."[36] A similar sentiment was expressed by Thomas Brown in a

1684 poem entitled "The Claret Drinker's Song"; though an anonymous 1685 broadside suggested that drinking alcohol induced rebellious behaviour, and drinking coffee or tea was the key to obedience.[37] A 1665 pamphlet poem, *The Character of a Coffee-House* commented, in phrases resonant with Habermas, that there was "no respect of persons there," that "all degrees of persons" mingled together, though "News-mongers do drink't most hearty." One of the drinkers comments:

> Sirs unto me
> It reason seems that liberty
> Of speech and words should be allow'd
> Where men of differing judgements croud,
> And that's a *Coffee-house*, for where
> Should men discourse so free as there[38]

Our impression that the coffee-houses of seventeenth-century England were teeming with political debate among an unconstrained mix of social classes is partly derived from literary texts the attitudes of which are at best ambivalent. This represents a partial truth: though a coffee-house may have provided a literate member of the lower or middling sort the opportunity to read the newspapers for the modest cost of a cup of coffee (a penny), it seems unlikely that many artisans would have found many spare hours to while away in discussion. To walk around St Paul's was to participate in a fashionable display of leisure; perhaps coffee-house debate had a similar dimension.

The continuity in representations of St Paul's Walk across the century, and the similarities between representations of the Walk and later coffee-houses, should not suggest that little changed in the frameworks for public opinion in the seventeenth century. First, there is a striking continuity in elite expressions of anxiety about popular access to news. These expressions rely heavily on stereotypes, and in doing so they homogenize images of the news media and of the practices of passing on news. Real changes are concealed by the stable conventions of representation.[39] Secondly, the appearance of the newspaper affected the way news and views were passed on in public spaces. News was central to coffee-house culture, and many representations in plays and poems of the social encounters in coffee-houses suggest that printed media were a catalyst for debate. An act set in a coffee-house in Thomas St Serfe's comedy *Tarugo's Wiles* (1668) includes a discussion of the recently founded *London Gazette*; St Serfe was himself a newsletter-writer.[40] Roger L'Estrange complained in 1681 that "every Coffee-house [is] furnished with News-Papers and Pamphlets (both written and Printed) of personal Scandal, Schism and Treason."[41] The prologue to Nicholas Rowe's *The Fair Penitent* (1703) refers to the "distant

Battles of the Pole and Swede, / Which frugal Citizens o'er Coffee read";
and numerous other poems and plays of the period make the connection.[42]
Mercurius Civicus, later *The City Mercury*, an advertising journal of
1680–81, used coffee-houses as well as booksellers as a means of
commercial distribution.[43] *The Athenian Mercury* solicited correspondence
from its readers at coffee-houses: Mr Smith's coffee-house in Stocks-market
and the Rotterdam in Finch Lane. Allan Ramsay wrote of "Politicians, who
in learn'd Debates, / With Penetration carve out Kingdoms Fates, / Look
sour, drink Coffee, shrug, and read Gazettes."[44] Representations of
alehouses in the period also suggest that they were places for political
discussion founded on news.[45] One tavern proprietor in Kent received, in
return for information supplied to the government, a newsletter and a
weekly gazette or two to attract custom to his establishment.[46] In 1660s
Cambridge, according to Roger North writing in the early eighteenth
century, there was a single coffee-house kept by one "Kirk":

> The trade in news also was scarce set up; for they only had the public
> gazette, till Kirk got a written newsletter circulated by one [Henry]
> Muddiman. But now the case is much altered; for it is become a custom
> after chapel to repair to one or other of the coffee-houses, for they are
> diverse, where hours are spent in talking, and less profitable reading of
> newspapers, of which swarms are continually supplied from London.[47]

Accounts of the news and political culture in the seventeenth century
suggest that 1694–95 were not the critical years for the emergence of public
opinion and popular debate. The appearance of new news media, especially
in the 1640s, changed the way news was circulated in the seventeenth
century, and ensured that the political culture of the second half of the
seventeenth century was not a xerox copy of that of the first.[48] In his
chronology, Habermas seems to have gravely postdated the arrival of the
public sphere.

IV

But can we, amidst this talk of news and caffeine, find the three factors –
reason, inclusiveness, and non-instrumentality – that Habermas claims
constitute a pre-parliamentary space and that make it an important forum for
discussion and effective critique? Or is there simply a general similarity
between popular discussion in the seventeenth century and Habermas'
public sphere? This section discusses the realities of reason and inclusion;
in the next section I turn to the question of instrumentality.

   The elements of reason and inclusion are linked in practice and need to
be tackled together. It is reason that guarantees the effectiveness of debate,

providing an external principle to which all agree to submit; none are *a priori* excluded provided they agree to its rule. There are three problems with these ideals, three constraints upon speech which severely impair the relevance of the Habermas model: the printing trade, with its legal and economic constraints; the realities of interaction in a stratified society; and the discursive status of reason itself.

The circumstances of seventeenth-century publishing interfered with the free exercise of reason. Prior to 1695, licensing laws conditioned public debate in one way or another.[49] Yet pressure did not end once and for all in 1695. The lapse of the Licensing Act was not intended to be a permanent cessation of press control, and even though Parliament failed to devise a replacement act, there were numerous subsequent attempts at statutory regulation, including Stamp Tax. The harassment, financial and legal, of the Jacobite press was effective.[50] Economic circumstances perpetuated government and party interest in publishing. Moreover licensing laws were only one aspect of the control of, or pressure on, speech. When they lapsed, such as in 1679, the unwary author or publisher simply faced the threat of prosecution for seditious libel or treason; though this was a peril many were prepared to face. Parliamentary privilege was also a constraint upon journalists. Anonymity figures reveal complex patterns. Authorial anonymity of all publications ran at about eight per cent in 1614; in 1644 it was sixty per cent; in 1688 it was fifty-seven per cent.[51] Printer and publisher anonymity were also very high through the second half of the century, even when licensing regulations lapsed, which suggests that licensing laws were not a significant determinant at least of publisher and printer anonymity; though libel laws may have been. Of a sample of 600 pamphlets published in 1679–81 under three per cent reveal their author's name; just over five per cent present initials.[52] By this time anonymity had become a convention among pamphleteers, part of a tradition that had emerged through creative and pragmatic responses to changing circumstances during the century.[53] There were sundry pressures, legal and otherwise, on public speech.

The London Gazette, which exercised a monopoly of English printed periodical news from September 1666 to December 1678, provides a useful case study here.[54] The means by which the government used the *Gazette*, and Williamson's supplementary manuscript newsletter, to squeeze out competition were not solely market-based, as the Archbishop of Glasgow's comments, quoted above, might suggest, but legal and supra-legal.

The behaviour of the news writer Henry Muddiman suggests the malpractices which were common in his trade. His newsbooks, *Mercurius Publicus* and *Parliamentary Intelligencer*, disappeared in late 1663 when Roger L'Estrange was granted a monopoly of news. Thereafter, he set about establishing a manuscript newsletter which he sent out with copies of L'Estrange's newsbooks. Williamson, covetous of Muddiman's profits, planned to circumvent L'Estrange's monopoly and to publish a printed newspaper; he succeeded with *The Oxford Gazette* in November 1665. Though relations between the two were strained, Williamson sagely appointed Muddiman as the first editor; but they soon fell out, and not long after the paper became *The London Gazette*, in February 1666, Muddiman resigned and returned to his newsletters.[55] He obtained the right to free postage, which stirred Williamson's envy. Thereafter Muddiman's service was systematically hindered by James Hickes, a clerk in the Letter Office. The interference with Muddiman's business was partly commercially motivated, and partly impelled by the government's desire to control the presentation of domestic news. Hickes wrote to Williamson in December 1667 that:

> There is a general complaint of the Gazettes wanting domestic intelligence; some in the office, who sent 14 or 16 dozen weekly, now only send half the number; 20 dozen less than formerly are sent form the office, they having nothing in them of the proceedings of Parliament, which Mr. Muddiman writes at large. Muddiman gives far larger accounts to his correspondents than you do, which makes them much desired.[56]

Hickes intercepted Muddiman's letters, sometimes passing them on to the editors of the *Gazette*.[57] The practice of intercepting letters, which had caused concern in the civil war years, continued after the Restoration, as Charles II developed a sophisticated and sometimes minatory intelligence service. This intelligence service even resorted to the organized violence of mercenary gangs. The intense personal pressure that could be applied is illustrated by the prevention of the posthumous publication of Milton's *De Doctrina Christiana*.[58]

Muddiman was not alone in being victimized by Williamson. One correspondent wrote to Williamson in 1667 thanking him for suppressing the "newsmonger at Nottingham, as they go about their business better for it" and added "if he suppressed all Muddiman's papers to the postmasters, it would be a good service, the itch of news being grown a disease."[59] The business practices which determined the supply of news, in print, alehouse, and coffee-house, suggest the limitations on free and reasoned conversation.

The desire to restrict the extent of access to news suggests another halter upon the public exercise and observance of reason amongst those participating in debate, namely social hierarchies. Habermas suggests that in the ideal of the public sphere submission to the governing principle of reason entails a blindness to social status within debate.[60] Though actual prejudices may be present, they are incidental to the functioning of that sphere and can be sociologically bracketed off from analysis. Feminist criticism has suggested that in fact gender hierarchies were central to, rather than incidental to, the working of the public sphere, and thus cannot be discounted.[61] The incomplete separation of gender roles into separate spheres in the later seventeenth century perhaps played itself out in the expectations which limited female participation in public debate, in both the press and coffee-house.[62] There is much evidence that women participated in coffee-house debate,[63] in contrast to Earle's earlier account of St Paul's.[64] But though women participated, it is likely they were less than fully recognized or had subordinate status.[65] And those women who did enter a coffee-house risked accusations of having flirtatious or professional motivation, of being identified as "a Tawdry Woman, a wanton daughter, or a Buxome Maide."[66]

The same dilemma exists with respect to social rank, the concerns of which were inscribed within those spaces in which Habermas' public sphere was conducted. Many coffee-houses were places of fashion as well as of discourse and political intrigue. Edmund Arwaker's poetic fable, "The Coffee-House: Or, A Man's Credit, is his Cash," depicts a familiar fashion-driven world: "At Will's, where Troops of flutt'ring, gaudy Beaus / Parade, to pick up scraps of Wit and News."[67] An old soldier enters, "His Hat ill cock'd, his Cravat as ill ty'd," and, in response to the inevitable question "what strange news?," he reports on a military victory at Flanders, in which he has participated:

> With Patience they the Story let him tell,
> But not a Man believ'd a Syllable:
> One, with an Oath, says, I'll not heed a Word
> He speaks; he can't tell how to wear his Sword.
> Another (of his Friend's Persuasion) cries,
> 'Tis such a shabby Curr, I'm sure he Lyes.

Soon after there enters "a little Prig, / Powder'd to th'Eyes, and almost drown'd in Wig," who reports the same news and is believed: "all for Gospel from his Mouth receive: / Wealth more persuades, than Probability; / And One so Rigg'd they fancy'd could not Lye." The moral of the poem underlines the deference paid "To Fools well Dress'd."

This is, of course, a literary representation, albeit a suggestive one. But in non-literary writings the veracity of an eyewitness account was commonly underscored by the social status of the witness. In scientific writings there was a perceived connection between social status, honour, and veracity.[68] In any newspaper there was a direct relationship between credit and credibility, which may have encouraged the principle of anonymity.[69] Partly because of their widespread availability, printed news media were for many years proverbially unreliable. News in the hands of the vulgar was likely to be corrupt, mere opinion; the educated were more likely to be sceptical.[70] Though the itch was widespread, it was scratched in different ways. The preface to a multi-volume collection of historical works published in 1706 admitted the universal appeal of news, but drew a distinction between popular and elite responses to news: "That busie Humour which makes People curious to know what others have done, or are doing, which furnishes common Conversation, and puts every Body upon Enquiries after News, invites Men of Leisure and Tast to search the Records of their own and former Ages."[71] Attendance at a coffee-house could impair the reputation for probity of even a man of status: Henry Ball wrote in 1673: "this I dare nott affirme for gospell, being told it only by Sir Thomas St George, who frequents much coffee-houses."[72] The role of social status in the presentation of truth, even in a journal such as *Philosophical Transactions*, would not only have impinged on reason, but would have circumscribed its authority.

The third form of pressure on speech which undermines Habermas' model is the discursive status of reason, the principle which governs debate in the public sphere. Locating, defining, and quantifying reason is not a practicable task; yet even if we accept modern criteria, Habermas' approach is evidently tendentious. While judging twentieth-century opinion by the standards of the television and mass-media, Habermas evaluates seventeenth-century opinion through the standards of Hobbes and Locke. Locke did engage with pamphlets and newsbooks; Hobbes self-consciously rejected them; but a more comprehensive overview of seventeenth-century popular print suggests a less elevated view than Habermas offers, one in which L'Estrange, Marchamont Nedham, William Sherlock, and Henry Sacheverell are more representative.[73] Particularly when licensing laws were not in operation, newspaper and pamphlet debates were frequently described as having been invaded by madness.[74] The trope reflects disunity not just about issues, but about the terms of debate. The figure of madness indicates a lack of common ground. If pamphlet exchange created a new Babel, as was widely suggested, then debate inflamed divisions rather than resolved them.[75] A poem of 1642, possibly written by the King's printer Leonard Lichfield, nicely captures both reality and metaphor in an account of a press being overturned at the battle of Edgehill:

> Yet those that found it on that Boysterous day
> Tooke't for some Dread Commission of Array; ...
> So Anagrammatized each Comma in't
> That Babel-London has not put in Print
> More confused Nonsense ...[76]

Henry Ball wrote to Williamson in 1673: "There is a general dissatisfaction among the merchants and the coffee-houses, dayly venting malicious censures of the actions of this present warr, their fears of breaking with Spaine driveing them beyond reason."[77] The satirical pamphlet *The Women's Petition Against Coffee* (1674) denied the presence of reason in coffee-house debate: "yet in all their prattle every one abounds in his own sense, as stiffly as a Quaker at the late *Barbican* Dispute, and submits to the Reasons of no other mortal: so that there being neither *Moderator* nor *Rules* observ'd, you may as soon fill a Quart pot with *Syllogismes*, as profit by their Discourses."[78] The satire is highly conventional, and perhaps all the more expressive for being so. Accounts of the incipient conflicts of 1641–42 emphasized the role of "fears and jealousies" in breaking down negotiations; and during the Popish Plot the same emotions were said to govern behaviour.[79] By presenting stereotypes and engaging in fierce satire and controversy, newspapers as often undermined as championed reason. Politics and religion were not usually weighed and measured with the careful scrutiny of experimental science.[80]

These comments do not suggest that reason was not used in debate; rather they suggest that reason was not generally recognized as an arbiter of debate. This is not to say that appeals to reason as a shared value were unknown in political and religious discourse. Though the universal right of freedom of speech may not have been a rallying cry, the right to discuss politics was defended with appeals to reason; in fact they inform the rhetoric used to support liberty of speech and of the press after 1660. The point was made strongly by the author of the 1665 pamphlet-poem *The Character of a Coffee-House* when s/he claimed that "It reason seems that liberty / Of speech and words should be allow'd."[81] The conventions and limitations of this rhetoric of liberty is suggested by its deployment in relation to parliamentary proceedings. That "every one's ears" were "itching to hear the proceedings in Parliament," as Samuel Key wrote, was repeatedly testified to in the Restoration period. In March 1681 the House of Commons ordered the printing of its votes, an abridged version of its journals which were then only available in manuscript. Sir Francis Winnington opined: "I think it neither natural, nor rational ... that the People who sent us hither, should not be informed of our actions."[82] The intention was to generate popular support. The 1689 Convention Parliament temporarily reversed the decision. A parallel debate had taken place in Parliament in November 1641 over the Grand Remonstrance, a document that expressed Parliament's grievances against Charles I in the form of an historical account of his misdoings, together with a petition addressed to the "people." The same month saw the appearance of the first printed newsbook, probably as part of a concerted parliamentary publicity exercise.[83] In both cases the liberty to read the proceedings of Parliament was proposed with specific ends in mind; these were appeals to the public. Subsequently L'Estrange claimed that the printing of votes led to misunderstandings, animosity, and misery; and he exploited the parallel between the uses of print in 1681 and 1641.[84] The universal validity of reason was no more present in seventeenth-century political culture than the abstract principle of unqualified freedom of speech as a human right. To look for it is to mistake the patterns and conditions through which debate was conducted. Reason played its role in political transactions, and was used forcefully to argue for the inclusion of the public in debate "without doors." But this does not mean that its role was systemically central, and thus worthy of a place in an ideal type. Nor can we bracket as mere contingencies the circumstances of the book trade, the realities of social status, and the explicitly limited currency of reason in actual debate.

Research on literacy suggests that the readership of pamphlets and newsbooks, and the numbers of those who had access to the contents through hearing them read aloud, was higher than Habermas had cause to think. Though there is evidence that there was a lively and widespread culture of reading in the seventeenth century that expanded with time, such breadth of participation does not encompass or guarantee an equality of participation.[85] This dichotomy between quantity and quality is of fundamental importance, and I shall return to it. The public debate of the seventeenth century was wide, but it was also uneven, and its conduct reflected the hierarchical principles of society at large. *The Character of a Coffee-House* describes a "great concourse / Of all degrees of persons, even / From high to low," but it does not celebrate this intermixing.[86] Instead it offers a social satire on the inelegant participants, and deplores the insult to gentle breeding. The same evidence that suggests that there was a wide degree of participation indicates that the nature of that participation was far from egalitarian.

Anthony Wood wrote that "The decay of study, and consequently of learning, are coffee-houses, to which most scholars retire and spend much of the day in hearing and speaking of news, in speaking vilely of their superiors."[87] Contempt for vulgar opinion ironically permeated the newsbooks and pamphlets that helped to foster it. The debate continued notwithstanding the stratification within its boundaries, perhaps sometimes spurred by those inequalities. The Putney and Whitehall debates, a record of the dynamics of mid-seventeenth-century out-of-doors political debate, which is inclusive of soldier and officer, are at moments driven by the social gulf between participants.[88]

In an account of public debate, both quality and breadth of participation should be considered. The fact of inequality represented in texts or within the dynamics of debate, and the absence of an abstract principle of reason, however, does not mean that debate was merely staged, or an act of containment, or that those who were subordinated were effectively marginalized. Research on the history of reading has shown how manipulative and active readers could be: readers read against the grain; they poached and appropriated texts; they culled fragments from magnitudes and construed general propositions from particulars; they reworked and rewrote texts through their reading.[89] This suggests that the prejudices implicit in newspaper publishing, for example, did not determine who read which papers, nor did it restrict the uses to which those newspapers could be put. Habermas's ideal of inclusion was not realised in seventeenth-century Britain because of the quality of participation; yet this may not have mattered in practice. The resourcefulness of the public is an important element in the construction of public opinion, to which I shall return in the conclusion.

V

The third crux in the case against Habermas' public sphere involves instrumentalism. The public sphere existed as a pre-parliamentary forum of popular political debate capable of sustaining critical and rational exchange, according to Habermas, because it was free from censorship and from commercial and party-political interests. He distinguishes between criticism and pamphleteering, yet acknowledges that in Britain "a press devoted to the debate of political issues developed out of the pamphlet."[90] This admission is an accurate one, though if critical debate emerges out of pamphleteering, we might ask, is it reasonable to draw a line between the two and categorize one as a form of manipulation and the other as reasoned exchange free from interest? For, in Britain, it was surely instrumentality that created as well as curtailed debate. Religious and political differences prompted the interested exploitation of the commercial mechanism of the press which then occasioned lively and heterogeneous political discussion.

Coffee-houses were used for political plotting; newsbooks and papers were instruments of politics.[91] Samuel Butler satirized those who, working for the Long Parliament, "draw up all News, / And fit it to our present Use."[92] Whereas the corantos of the 1620s seem to have been purely commercial enterprises, though not always lucrative ones, the first printed newsbooks were transparently in the parliamentary interest and were initially unofficially sponsored by the Pym circle.[93] The early *Heads of Severall Proceedings* and *Diurnal Occurrences* established a context for reading Parliament's Grand Remonstrance, one of the milestones on the road to civil war. Some 1640s newsbooks appear to have been targeted at specific audiences, such as London citizens and Presbyterians; perhaps thereby creating smaller arenas of public debate.[94] Others, however, were transparently instruments of propaganda, spinning news of the war as part of the military effort.[95] Nonetheless, popular discussion during the 1640s seems to have been considerable, and to have influenced the outcome of parliamentary debates.[96] It may seem that this was an exceptional period, when the war of words was preserved by the eclipse of the Stationers' Company and the consequent absence of monopoly forces. The connection between monopoly and controversy was not straightforward, however. Dispute did not narrow in 1679–80, when the newspaper trade, liberated by the lapse of the Licensing Act, became concentrated into the hands of a very few trade publishers.[97] The single greatest factor determining the evolution of the book trade in England was the monopoly held by the Stationers' Company; yet that evolution nonetheless facilitated the creation of public debate.

Two case studies of the circumstances of news monopoly in the seventeenth century suggest that there was no automatic antagonism between effective propaganda, control of the printed news market, and open discussion of news events. The first concerns *Mercurius Politicus*, the predominant newsbook in the 1650s. Its editor, Marchamont Nedham, was a pioneer in the development of journalism, whose editorials in the period 1650–52 are also essential texts in the history of Republicanism, striking not least because of the role they played in disseminating political theory. In 1652 Nedham dropped these editorials, and his newsbook, it is usually imputed, became a tamer beast. In 1655 Nedham's dominance in the market-place was legislated into a near-monopoly, when new licensing restrictions silenced the competition.[98] Three simultaneous developments suggest the coercive, instrumental power of *Politicus* in this period. First, the establishment of its sister periodical, *The Publick Intelligencer*, the Monday alternative to Thursday's *Politicus*, which duplicated about half of the contents; this sibling journal was presumably intended to squeeze out what was left of the market. Secondly, Nedham's increasing exploitation of the advertising sections of his journals. Thirdly, *Politicus* not only excluded editorials, but became increasingly focused on overseas news. The slighting of domestic news suggests a deliberate attempt to manipulate public opinion by defrauding readers with harmless and less interesting reports.

In fact, the popularity of *Politicus* does not seem significantly to have declined in this period. The coverage of overseas news was excellent. Nedham's contributors consisted of the extensive intelligence network of John Thurloe, Secretary to the Council of State, plus correspondents Nedham had himself cultivated. Their reports frequently expressed opinions at odds with Nedham's own politics. This heterogeneity of perspective, while it may lack the Machiavellian intensity of the earlier editorials, was nonetheless the basis for a practical political education. Nedham may have left out the theory, but *Politicus* in this period can be seen as a practical enactment of his belief that different opinions needed to be overcome rather than silenced, in a kind of *concordia discors* which represented Britain's (or England's) new place in the European order. Though commercial and ideological interests may have ranked very highly in the design of the newsbook, it still provided thought-provoking materials; heterogeneity and diversity were compatible with instrumental political intentions.[99]

The second example involves the official bi-weekly newspaper of the Restoration government, the *Gazette*. From 1666, for about a decade, the *Gazette* enjoyed a near-monopoly and considerable financial success.[100] It also focused on foreign news, and, more transparently than *Politicus*, was an instrument of state propaganda, intended to control rumour and occlude alternative news services. The editors of the *Gazette* were restricted by their superiors and prevented from publishing materials that had fallen into their hands. In 1673 Robert Yard, then editor, wrote to Williamson complaining that he was denied access to reports he felt he should have, "so that att such times wee must be either silent, or hazard running into errors." He gave a specific example concerning a naval encounter with the Dutch:

> The narrative being sent yesterday to the presse, by Mr. Newcombes means, I gott a sight of it (which I could not doe before) and made a short extract out of it for the newsbook, yet, being unwilling to doe any thing of that kind my self, I acquainted Mr. Bridgeman with it, who very angerly asked me how I came by that extract, and that he wondered Mr. Newcomb durst lett any body have a copy of the narrative, with whom he was likewise very sharp on the same account; and on all other occasions they are so farr from communicating anything to us, which is necessary should be made publick, that when we ask them they make difficulty to tell us.[101]

His protestations had little impact; we find him airing similar ones two months later.[102] Muddiman's newsletter service was also required to meet government expectations; on a number of occasions in the 1660s he found himself reprimanded for presenting unacceptable or confidential materials.[103]

As a positive form of manipulation, the *Gazette* included petitions and addresses to curry popular support for the regime.[104] Narcissus Luttrell, Sir Samuel Luke, and Henry Care all acknowledged that this constituted a form of propaganda.[105] Notices in newspapers, including the *Gazette*, were recognized as a means of catching criminals.[106] There were frequent requests for publicity in the *Gazette*, some by government officials; and several requests for anonymity or silence on an issue.[107] The *Gazette* was a model of publicity, essential to the coffee-house culture of the day, and it is through its success, and the accomplishments of other news periodicals, that we can understand the proverbial epithet "as publick as a News-book."[108]

Some readers suggested that in devoting so much space to foreign news, the editors of the *Gazette* intended to manipulate the public and ignored their real interests. Hickes's letter to Williamson in 1667, quoted above, counselled that the decline in sales was because of their lack of domestic news, especially of Parliament.[109] A Dublin reader objected to the lack of London news.[110] Complaints were common. Other readers, however, praised the proclivity as a form of specialization and suggested that this distinguished the *Gazette*. Williamson received letters of compliment as well as of criticism. Dr Thomas Smith wrote in 1665 that the *Gazette* "gives much more satisfaction to all readers than L'Estrange's two whole sheets do"; Sir George Downing advised that he "would try to cry up the Gazette, but nothing can be added to its reputation"; Pepys admired it.[111] John Tutchin criticized the Paris *Gazette* in *The Observator* in 1702, adding that "our English Gazette has hitherto given us the most faithful account of foreign news; nay it has kept so much within the bounds to truth, that in any advantage the Confederates have had over the enemy; it has rather not told all than said too much." Newsletter writers and amateur correspondents explicitly left foreign news to the *Gazette*.[112] Its sales did not drop after 1695, the supposed watershed which saw the end of censorship and the onset of free-market journalism; it was not until the 1710s that distribution significantly declined.[113]

The presenting of foreign affairs was not a cynical substitute for domestic; the reading public was interested in overseas news. Reports of popular discourse during the early 1670s show genuine concern with international issues.[114] Charles II's government considered suppressing the coffee-houses during the second and third Anglo-Dutch wars (1664–65 and 1672–74).[115] In polemical and literary representations of popular interest in news and coffee-house talk the emphasis is often on foreign matters.[116] The prologue to Nicholas Rowe's *The Fair Penitent* suggests that readers were interested in what could not possibly concern them: "Like distant Battles of the Pole and Swede, / Which frugal Citizens o'er Coffee read."[117] According to Mercury's epilogue in John Dryden's *Indian Emperor*, the "proper bus'ness" of the "Coffee-wits ... is to Damn the *Dutch*."[118] A 1680 drinking song by John Oldham, entitled "The Careless Good Fellow," comments on popular anti-French sentiment:

> The Bully of *France*, that aspires to Renown
> By dull cutting of Throats, and vent'ring his own;

Let him fight and be damn'd, and make Matches, and Treat,
To afford the News-mongers, and Coffee-house Chat:[119]

Other sources report the expression of Francophobia in coffee-houses.[120] Though the *Gazette* was intended as an extension of the government, it participated in stimulating precisely the discussion which the government wished to curb from time to time. The scrutiny of international affairs is not a politics-free zone. Hence the obsolescence of licensing regulations in 1695 did not fundamentally change the role of the *Gazette*.

Even from the perspective of advertising, where commercial interests are most tangibly tied with the business of periodical publication, it is difficult to conclude that materialistic intentions prevented newspapers from stimulating a free and open encounter. Newspaper advertising began in the late 1640s when publishers and printers filled empty space with notices of other books emerging from their houses. Soon the dedicated advertising periodical emerged, in the form of *The Publick Adviser*, along with its London offices that fulfilled the Utopian vision of advertising outlined by Montaigne and Hartlib.[121] In the 1650s Nedham further explored the possibilities of advertising. But it is difficult to conclude that the books or services Nedham advertised were exclusively (let alone exhaustively) ones he endorsed. The advertisements in the *Gazette*, however, were partly controlled by the office of the Secretary of State, and reflected the attitudes of the government.[122] Writing in 1710, Joseph Addison had no doubt of the role of advertisements in "the Management of Controversy": "above half the Advertisements one meets with now-a-Days are purely Polemical. The Inventors of *Strops for Razors* have written against one another this Way for several Years, and that with great Bitterness; as the whole Argument *pro* and *con* in the case of *Morning-Gowns* is still carried on after the same Manner."[123] These examples suggest that the manipulative power of the periodical increased during this period, as editors became more sensitive to the uses of publicity and ways of exploiting it. This is hard to square with the principle of disinterested reason and a model of a public sphere which is intrinsically non-instrumental.

VI

This essay has suggested that 1695 was not a watershed in the emergence of a public sphere of popular political opinion; it was the 1640s that saw the most rapid development of informed popular debate, building on an expansion of political communication dating from the early 1620s. Licensing legislation played a comparatively minor role in the development of public opinion after the 1640s, perhaps because of the widespread assumption of the right to read, hear, and discuss news. It has also been suggested that the historico-sociological model that Habermas outlines is more attractive, perhaps because of its relevance to the twentieth century media, than it is accurate. Though there may have been broad participation in debate, this did not guarantee equality within it, nor did it ensure that discussion was governed by reason. Debate was driven by heterodoxy of religious belief, and by conflicting discourses of social and political thought; a conflict that was less likely to be seen as the encounter of reason with reason than as the deranged non-communication of Babel. The quality rather than the quantity of participation brings Habermas' account into question. Finally, the principle of non-instrumentality ill fits the realities of seventeenth-century debate, which was sponsored, rather than impeded, by commercial and ideological interests; which grew not from the desire to create an environment of free and open communication, but from the desire to manipulate and rhetorically persuade.

It is time for a more nuanced model of popular political opinion founded on the realities of seventeenth-century discussion, on the nature and languages of debate and on the practical economic circumstances that channelled communication. This final section briefly outlines the role that the printed news media might play in such a model. This will foreground the significance of the nature as well as the extent of participation, and thus acknowledge the valuable contribution Habermas made to the subject without dragging his version back half a century or more.

Accounts of public opinion, such as those offered by De Krey, Goldie, and Harris, markedly emphasize the breadth of the circulation of printed materials. But circulation is not necessarily directly proportional to influence, nor is it easy to evaluate. Defoe's *Review* appeared in runs of 425–50; yet it was granted considerable significance.[124] Looking at newspaper circulation between 1700 and 1730, James Sutherland concludes that, while the journal reading public probably expanded in the 1720s, it was only the guarantee of sales to coffee-houses that made many periodicals commercially viable, and that smallish print-runs were enhanced by numerous readers.[125] Henry Snyder, building on Sutherland's work, argues that newspapers played a role in public opinion only after 1695; but his evidence for print-runs suggests that circulation substantially declined in 1712 with the introduction of Stamp Tax (though losses were subsequently restored).[126] J.A. Downie further complicates the picture by suggesting that periodicals may no longer have been profitable in the 1710s, and were kept afloat not by coffee-house subscriptions but by party subsidies. This requires that we not only rethink the issue of influence but also recognize, as Dr Johnson did, that even literary journals such as the *Spectator* had a party-political dimension.[127] These figures for the later seventeenth and early eighteenth century show not a transformation in the newspaper's role in sponsoring critical debate but an uneven and unsteady building on foundations laid earlier. The development of the market-place for newspapers and pamphlets, together with new technologies of reporting and persuading, created new and enhanced modes of manipulation that opened up rather than closed down communication.[128]

The reasons for this lie in the history of reading, and we should outline the development of popular opinion with one eye on this context. If we are to add the dimension of quality to our understanding of popular participation in political culture, and if we are to understand how widespread political debate could have emerged through commercial interests and party-political propaganda, the neglected factor is the reader. Newspapers (and earlier newsbooks) played an important part in constructing readers' sense of neighbourly and national identity by spanning linguistic constituencies and geographical entities. Even with a focus on overseas news, the periodical press assisted in defining an "imagined community."[129] Thus the newspaper constructed the basis of a series of interlocking and overlapping spheres of political debate and action in different communities of readers.

To digress briefly, it is worth noting that nowhere is the plurality of arenas of debate, some interlocking, some overlapping, some concentric, more evident than in the complex relations between information, geography, and nationhood. Habermas' model is resolutely metropolitan, and is based on social spaces which occur in large urban centres, and on periodicals that are putatively national but implicitly centred on the capital. There is evidence of coffee-houses outside London, in Bristol and York, for instance,[130] but London clearly had a critical mass of them; newspapers were distributed nationally, but they originated in, and tended to reflect the concerns of London. The New British History has opened up new questions – or at least begun to answer more comprehensively old questions – about the centralizing processes of state formation, as well as the development of national and regional identities.[131] This invites us to consider seriously the socio-political basis of the evolution of newspapers in Scotland, Ireland, and Wales. The newspapers of these nations tended to begin as reprints of English journals, which were the natural successors to the commercially successful distribution of London-printed texts.[132] Then reprints were displaced by indigenous newspapers, which facilitated the construction of a sense of national community and thus national identity. The process was less linear than Benedict Anderson's account of imagined communities suggests.[133] It is a curious fact that while the histories of Scottish and Irish newspapers begin in the middle of the seventeenth century, soon after the English, that of the Welsh is delayed for another hundred years. What can this tell us about the existence of a "public sphere" in Britain? Perhaps only that for the model to fit current notions of state formation, it would have to be transmuted to allow for several separate spheres in Scotland, Ireland, and Wales, all strongly influenced by London, which function concurrently with a "British" sphere. Perhaps the loss of this metropolitan focus renders problematic the metaphor of the "sphere" itself. It is far without the scope of this intervention to address such questions as these, but this geographical and national dimension must colour future accounts of public opinion and the parameters of debate.

Readers were not simply the passive products of the ideologies of print-capitalism. For example, changes in the forms of journalism were always deflected by continuities in reception; just as continuities in the anti-news rhetoric across the seventeenth century conceal radical transformation in the news media. Readers were always capable of using texts for their own ends, of improvising arguments on the basis of printed texts.[134] It was perhaps by encouraging this that the newspaper made the strongest contribution to the informed and reasoned debate in seventeenth-century Britain.

The newsbook, newspaper, and periodical had three essential attributes that cultivated critical debate among their readers. First, and most obviously, publicity itself. Justifying his planned monthly review, *The Works of the Learned*, Jean de La Crosse wrote in 1691:

> If some Authors and Booksellers pretend to damn this design, and ask by what right I take upon me to give out an impartial judgment over their Books, and erect my self into an Universal Critick. I'll answer, by the same right as they have publish'd 'em. Is not a Book common as soon as it comes into the world, and may not every Reader say, it is good or bad?[135]

Publication in print made a book fair game for any reader's judgement; de la Crosse claimed no greater authority than this. The duties of authorship outweighed the rights; a sentiment also voiced in *Remarks upon the London Gazette* (1693), a pamphlet which attacked the *Gazette* for an inaccurate report, carefully measuring the evidence against other sources. The author condemns the *Gazette* for exceeding "the Liberties of a Romance. ... To imagine such wretched Stories as these will pass Muster, is to treat the Nation with the utmost Scorn and Contempt, and, in effect, to proclaim them Fools in Print." Because of the fact of publicity, interest was bound inextricably with reason: "the naked Representation of Fact is a sufficient Advantage. Indeed, great Kings scorn to embase their publick Intelligence with such incredible Alloy. For in soft Language, to deceive and misrepresent, to maim and murther Truth, are mean and inglorious Practices."[136]

Secondly, periodicity. Like clubs, the regularity with which newspapers appeared guaranteed a continuity of information and therefore of debate.

Even when there was no news, space had to be filled. Readers supplied with a weekly, bi-weekly, or daily dose of news and views were required to relate items back to previous issues, to follow stories as they unfolded (such as ongoing election polls[137]). This is more likely to develop patterns of remembering and active involvement than the culture of passivity and forgetfulness for which the impact of the periodicity of the early newspaper is sometimes blamed.[138]

The third nurturer of critical debate, and one which followed from the exigencies of periodicity, was the heterogeneity of the newspaper and periodical. Precisely because they juxtaposed unrelated items, newspapers offered a textual space which required the reader to make sense of, to recognize and synthesize diversity. Joseph Addison archly described the audience for news as "gathering together Materials for thinking."[139] This diversity became the focus of commercial enterprise in *The Athenian Mercury* (initially *Gazette*) in 1691. Its brief was to answer its readers' queries and to avoid any possibility of embarrassment by enlisting the anonymity of print.[140] It offered to answer questions upon any subject sent in by either sex (it was the first periodical that specifically addressed women readers) in all languages. The editorial committee partly admitted that they were only telling the world what it already knew, qualifying this: "there are very many *Questions* here, some of moment, which were never before *publickly decided*, especially in *Morality*, which is by far the most *usefull part of Knowledge*."[141] It justified the variety of its concerns: "*The Complaint we have met with from some Persons that we touch upon Subjects too high for the* Publick View, *and that 'tis not fit for such Questions as some we answer, to lye for common* Chatt and Entertainment on a Coffee-house-Board ... *further, Why may'nt Discourses of this Nature be as proper for* Coffee-houses *as others?*"[142] Perhaps the most remarkable aspect of the *Athenian Mercury* was the space for heterogeneity which it created for questions on a world of topics, following the lead of its readers, notwithstanding its commercial orientation. In doing so it was utilizing a framework long-established by the newsbook.

It was in this way that early newspapers were not instrumental, were intrinsically unlikely to impose upon and coerce their readers into acceptance of a single, simple perspective on the news. War stories, parliamentary proceedings, travel accounts, political editorials, book adverts, lost property, bills of mortality, cargoes of ships, biographies, bibliographies, Hebrew anagrams, lottery numbers, assize reports, literary criticism, and social comment all stood side by side, and in doing so invited rather than compelled the reader to construe a view of the world from the page before them. It was through the reception of their publicity, periodicity, and heterogeneity that newspapers contributed most to the development of political opinion. Notwithstanding the gestures made to coffee-houses and newspapers, their material culture is signally absent from Habermas' idealist account of a public sphere. The participation of the newspaper and other printed forms in public opinion in the later seventeenth century cannot be quantified until we have more studies based on exact empirical analysis of reception; but its quality was both informative and polemical, idealistic and instrumental, accessible and discriminating, reasoned and Babelish, and it was through these dichotomies, intrinsic to the book trade, that the appetite of the popular reader for political opinion and debate was fed.

NOTES

Thanks to Lauren Kassell and Fritz Levy for their comments on this paper; and to the participants at "The News" conference for creating public critical debate.

1. *By the King. An Additional Proclamation Concerning Coffee-Houses*, 8 Jan. 1675/76. Though there were sporadic attempts to place a halter on debate; James Sutherland, *The Restoration Newspaper and its Development* (Cambridge: Cambridge University Press, 1986), 52.
2. *Calendar of State Papers, Domestic Series* [hereafter *CSPD*] *1667* (London: Longman, 1866), 243.
3. See Fritz Levy's essay in this volume.
4. Richard Cust, "News and Politics in Early Seventeenth-Century England," *Past and Present* 112 (1986): 60–90; Kevin Sharpe, *The Personal Rule of Charles I* (New Haven, CT, and London: Yale University Press, 1992), ch. 11; Steve Pincus, "'Coffee Politicians Does Create': Coffeehouses and Restoration Political Culture," *Journal of Modern History* 67 (1995): 807–34; Andrew Mousley, "Self, State, and Seventeenth Century News," *The Seventeenth Century* 6 (1991): 149–68.
5. *Observator* 1, 13 April 1681.
6. Jürgen Habermas, *The Structural Transformation of the Public Sphere: An Inquiry into a Category of Bourgeois Society*, trans. Thomas Burger with the assistance of Frederick Lawrence (Cambridge, MA: MIT Press, 1989), 58
7. Sharon Achinstein, "The Politics of Babel in the English Revolution," in James Holstun (ed.), *Pamphlet Wars: Prose in the English Revolution* (London: Frank Cass, 1992), 14–44, and *Milton and the Revolutionary Reader* (Princeton, NJ: Princeton University Press, 1994), 3–26; Kevin Dunn, *Pretexts of Authority: The Rhetoric of Authorship in the Renaissance Preface* (Stanford, CA: Stanford University Press, 1994), 7–9; Joseph F. Loewenstein, "Legal Proofs and Corrected Readings: Press-Agency and the New Bibliography," in David Lee Miller, Sharon O'Dair and Harold Weber (eds.), *The Production of English Renaissance Culture* (Ithaca, NY: Cornell University Press, 1994), 93–122; David Norbrook, "*Areopagitica*, Censorship, and the Early Modern Public Sphere," in Richard Burt (ed.), *The Administration of Aesthetics: Censorship, Political Criticism, and the Public Sphere*, Cultural Politics, vol. 7 (Minneapolis, MN, and London: University of Minnesota Press, 1994), 3–33; Pincus, "Restoration Political Culture"; Alexandra Halasz, *The Marketplace of Print: Pamphlets and the Public Sphere in Early Modern England* (Cambridge: Cambridge University Press, 1997); Sue Wiseman, "'Adam, the Father of all Flesh,' Porno-Political Rhetoric and Political Theory in and After the English Civil War," in Holstun (ed.), *Pamphlet Wars*, 134–57; and *Drama and Politics in the English Civil War* (Cambridge: Cambridge University Press, 1998), 35–8; David Zaret, "Religion, Science, and Printing in the Public Spheres of Seventeenth-Century England," in Craig Calhoun (ed.), *Habermas and the Public Sphere* (Cambridge, MA: MIT Press, 1992), 212–35. For a case made for France, see Jeffrey

K. Sawyer, *Printed Poison: Pamphlet Propaganda, Faction Politics, and the Public Sphere in Early Seventeenth-Century France* (Berkeley, CA: University of California Press, 1990).

8. Habermas, *Structural Transformation*, xvii.

9. Lloyd Kramer, "Habermas, History, and Critical Theory," in Calhoun (ed.), *Habermas and the Public Sphere*, 236–58, argues that an historian using Habermas' model necessarily adopts his methodology and is therefore required to adopt a critical perspective on the present, transformed public sphere; for him historical falsification seems petty.

10. Habermas, "Concluding Remarks," in Calhoun (ed.), *Habermas and the Public Sphere*, 465.

11. Through much of *Structural Transformation* Habermas does indeed treat the public sphere as an ideal type, notwithstanding this caveat. Zaret, "Religion, Science, and Printing," 212–13, explicitly adopts an ideal-type approach while persuasively challenging Habermas' neglect of earlier public spheres.

12. Habermas, *Structural Transformation*, 192, 202, 250. The sections on the seventeenth century describe the "genesis" of this bourgeois public sphere.

13. For feminist criticisms of this approach, see Joan B. Landes, *Women and the Public Sphere in the Age of the French Revolution* (Ithaca, NY: Cornell University Press, 1988), 3–7, 39–45; Nancy Fraser, "Rethinking the Public Sphere: A Contribution to the Critique of Actually Existing Democracy," in Calhoun (ed.), *Habermas and the Public Sphere*, 109–42, esp. 118–28; Nancy Fraser, *Unruly Practices: Power, Discourse and Gender in Contemporary Social Theory* (Cambridge: Polity, 1989). See also Habermas' comments in "Further Reflections on the Public Sphere," trans. Thomas Burger, in Calhoun (ed.), *Habermas and the Public Sphere*, 427–9.

14. Habermas, *Structural Transformation*, 31–43, 73–9.

15. Ibid., 27, 25–6, 196–211.

16. Ibid., 27–31.

17. In their revisions of Habermas' model, Achinstein (*Milton and the Revolutionary Reader*) suggests that a public sphere was created in 1640s reading encounters; Halasz (*Marketplace of Print*) that it existed even earlier in an abstract arena of discourse.

18. Habermas, *Structural Transformation*, 159–95.

19. Ibid., 29; "Concluding Remarks," 465; see also Paul Trolander and Zeynep Tenger, "Criticism against Itself: Subverting Critical Authority in Late-Seventeenth-Century England," *Philological Quarterly* 75 (1996): 311–38.

20. For science, see Stephen Shapin and Simon Schaffer, *Leviathan and the Air-Pump: Hobbes, Boyle, and the Experimental Life* (Princeton, NJ: Princeton University Press, 1985); Adrian Johns, *The Nature of the Book: Knowledge and Print in Early Modern England* (Chicago, IL: Chicago University Press, 1998).

21. Habermas, *Structural Transformation*, 57–88, 141–51.

22. Ibid., 58–9. For a contemporary association between moderate freedom of the press and parliamentary government, see John Toland's "Proposal for better regulating of Newspapers," BL: MS Add 4295, ff. 49–50; printed in Laurence Hanson, *Government and the Press, 1695–1763* (1936; Oxford: Clarendon Press, 1967), 135–8.

23. Habermas, *Structural Transformation*, 59–60.

24. Which is how Habermas sees the civil wars in Britain; ibid., 62–4.

25. De Krey, *A Fractured Society*, 213–22, quotes 213, 221, 219, 214.

26. Mark Goldie, "The Revolution of 1689 and the Structure of Political Argument: An Essay and an Annotated Bibliography of Pamphlets on the Allegiance Controversy," *Bulletin of Research in the Humanities* 83 (1980): 473–564, quotes 518, 520.

27. Harris, *Politics Under the Later Stuarts*, also *London Crowds in the Reign of Charles II: Propaganda and Politics from the Restoration to the Exclusion Crisis* (Cambridge: Cambridge University Press, 1987), *passim*, and "The Parties and the People: The Press, the Crowd and Politics 'Out-of-doors' in Restoration England," in Lionel K.J. Glassey (ed.), *The Reigns of Charles II and James VII & II* (London: Macmillan, 1997), 125–51.

28. Mark Knights, *Politics and Opinion in Crisis, 1678–81* (Cambridge: Cambridge University Press, 1994).

29. Treadwell, "London Trade Publishers," 128, 131–2.

30. Alastair Bellany, "'Rayling Rymes and Vaunting Verse': Libellous Politics in Early Stuart

England, 1603–1628," in Kevin Sharpe and Peter Lake (eds.), *Culture and Politics in Early Stuart England* (London: Macmillan, 1994), 285–310, and "Mistress Turner's Deadly Sins: Sartorial Transgression, Court Scandal, and Politics in Early Stuart England," *Huntington Library Quarterly* 58 (1996): 179–210; Thomas Cogswell, "The Politics of Propaganda: Charles I and the People in the 1620s," *Journal of British Studies* 29 (1990): 187–215, and "Underground Verse and the Transformation of Early Stuart Political Culture," in Susan Amussen and Mark Kishlansky (eds.), *Political Culture and Cultural Politics in Early Modern Europe* (Manchester: Manchester University Press, 1995), 277–300; Pauline Croft, "The Reputation of Robert Cecil: Libels, Political Opinion and Popular Awareness in the Early Seventeenth Century," *Transactions of the Royal Historical Society*, 6th ser., 1 (1991): 43–69; Cust, "News and Politics"; James Holstun, "'God Bless thee, Little David!': John Felton and His Allies," *ELR* 59 (1992): 513–52; also n.7, above.

31. Nigel Smith, *Literature and Revolution in England, 1640–1660* (New Haven, CT, and London: Yale University Press, 1994); Joad Raymond, *The Invention of the Newspaper: English Newsbooks, 1641–1649* (Oxford: Clarendon Press, 1996); Achinstein, *Milton and the Revolutionary Reader.*

32. Quoted in Cust, "News and Politics," 70.

33. John Earle, *Micro-Cosmographie. Or, A Peece of the World Discovered; In Essayes and Characters* (London, 1628), sigs. I11-K.

34. [Edward Ward], *St Paul's Church; Or, The Protestant Ambulators* (London, 1716), 23–4.

35. Quoted in Bryant Lillywhite, *London Coffee Houses: A Reference Book of Coffee Houses of the Seventeenth, Eighteenth and Nineteenth Centuries* (London: George Allen and Unwin, 1963), 366.

36. W.D. Christie (ed.), *Letters Addressed from London to Sir Joseph Williamson while Plenipotentiary at the Congress of Cologne in the Years 1673 and 1674*, 2 vols., Camden Society, n.s. 8–9 (1874), II: 67–8.

37. *The Remains of Mr. Thomas Brown* (London, 1720), 11–13; *Rebellions Antidote: Or a Dialogue Between Coffee and Tea* (London, 1685).

38. *The Character of a Coffee-House* (London, 1665), 2, 4, 6; for more on coffee-houses, including their non-observance of social hierarchies, see Pincus, "Restoration Political Culture."

39. For pre-newsbook attacks on printed news, see *The Staple of Newes*, and *Newes From the New World Discover'd in the Moone*, in *Ben Jonson*, ed. C.H. Herford and Percy and Evelyn Simpson, 10 vols. (Oxford: Clarendon Press, 1925-50), vols. 6 and 7; Richard Brathwait, *Whimzies: Or, A New Cast of Characters* (London, 1631), 22; Donald Lupton, *London and the Covntrey Carbanadoed* (London, 1632), 142; Joad Raymond (ed.), *Making the News: An Anthology of the Newsbooks of Revolutionary England* (Moreton-in-Marsh: Windrush Press, 1993), 11–15.

40. Thomas St. Serfe [or Sydserf], *Tarugo's Wiles: Or, The Coffee-House. A Comedy* (1668), 26.

41. Quoted by Lois G. Schwoerer, "Liberty of the Press and Public Opinion: 1660–1695," in J.R. Jones (ed.), *Liberty Secured? Britain Before and After 1688* (Stanford: Stanford University Press, 1992), 211.

42. Nicholas Rowe, *The Fair Penitent. A Tragedy* (1703), prologue; John Gay, "Fable XIII," l. 23, in *Poetical Works* (London: Oxford University Press, 1926), 300; William Oldisworth, *State Tracts* (1715), 1: 184; Edward Ward, *The Character of a Covetous Citizen* (1702), 5 and *passim*; *A Dialogue Between Tom and Dick* (1680), 4.

43. *The City Mercury: from the Office at the Royal Exchange* 274, 14 April 1681, recto.

44. "Content. A Poem," ll. 100–102, in *The Works of Allan Ramsay*, ed. Burns Martin *et al.* (London: Scottish Text Society, 1944), 1: 93.

45. G[eorge]. M[eriton]., *The Praise of York-shire Ale* (1685). The authorship is doubtful: a note by Francis Douce in the Bodleian copy (Douce M559) attributes it to Giles Marrington of North Allerton. Alan Marshall, *Intelligence and Espionage in the Reign of Charles II, 1660–1685* (Cambridge: Cambridge University Press, 1994), 105 and *passim.*

46. *CSPD 1666–67* (London: Longman, 1864), 511.

47. *The life of the Honourable Sir Dudley North* (London, 1744), quoted by Peter Fraser, *The Intelligence of Secretaries of State and their Monopoly of Licensed News, 1600–1688* (Cambridge: Cambridge University Press, 1956), 117–18.

48. As argued by Jonathan Scott, *Algernon Sidney and the Restoration Crisis, 1677–1683* (Cambridge: Cambridge University Press, 1991), 6; and contradicted by Pincus, "Restoration Political Culture," 833.

49. For press control in the period, see Cyprian Blagden, *The Stationers' Company: A History 1403–1959* (Stanford, CA: Stanford University Press, 1960); Cyndia Susan Clegg, *Press Censorship in Elizabethan England* (Cambridge: Cambridge University Press, 1997); Hanson, *Government and the Press*; J.A. Downie, *Robert Harley and the Press: Propaganda and Public Opinion in the Age of Swift and Defoe* (Cambridge: Cambridge University Press, 1979), 1–15; Sheila Lambert, "State Control of the Press in Theory and Practice: The Role of the Stationers' Company Before 1640," in Robin Myers and Michael Harris (eds.), *Censorship and the Control of Print: in England and France, 1600–1910* (Winchester: St. Paul's Bibliographies, 1992), 1–32; Schwoerer, "Liberty of the Press"; F.S. Siebert, *Freedom of the Press in England 1476–1776: The Rise and Decline of Government Controls* (Urbana, IL: University of Illinois Press, 1952); William Speck, "Politics and the Press," in Michael Harris and Alan Lee (eds.), *The Press in English Society from the Seventeenth to the Nineteenth Centuries* (Cranbury, NJ: Associated University Presses, 1986), 47–63. For accounts of the effect of licensing on literary discourse, see Lucasta Miller, "The Shattered Violl: Print and Textuality in the 1640s," in *Essays and Studies*, 2nd ser., 46, *Literature and Censorship*, ed. Nigel Smith (Cambridge: D.S. Brewer, 1993), 25–38; Annabel Patterson, *Reading Between the Lines* (London: Routledge, 1993), and *Censorship and Interpretation* (Madison, WI: Wisconsin University Press, 1984); A.B. Worden, "Literature and Political Censorship in Early Modern England," in A.C. Duke and C.A. Tamse (eds.), *Too Mighty to be Free: Censorship and the Press in Britain and the Netherlands* (Zutphen: De Walburg Pers, 1987), 45–62.

50. C.G. Gibbs, "Press and Public Opinion: Prospective," in Jones (ed.), *Liberty Secured?*, 231–64; J.C.D. Clark, *Samuel Johnson: Literature, Religion and English Cultural Politics from the Restoration to Romanticism* (Cambridge: Cambridge University Press, 1994), 149.

51. For 1614, see my forthcoming article, "'The Language of the Public': Print, Politics, and the Book Trade in 1614"; for 1644 and 1688, see D.F. McKenzie, "The London Book Trade in 1644," in John Horden (ed.), *Bibliographia: Lectures 1975–1988 by recipients of The Marc Fitch Prize for Bibliography* (Oxford: Leopard's Head Press, 1992), 131–52, at 136.

52. Knights, *Politics and Opinion*, 157–9; Donald F. McKenzie, "The London Book Trade in 1668," *Words*, 4 (1974): 81 and *passim*; Schwoerer, "Liberty of the Press," 207–8.

53. For a brief history of anonymity, see my forthcoming study of the pamphlet between 1588 and 1688.

54. Actually a *near*-monopoly: *Poor Robin's Intelligence, City Mercury,* and *Mechanick Exercises* invaded the pitch, along with a number of serials which offered foreign news, price indices and so on.

55. J.G. Muddiman, *The King's Journalist, 1659–1689: Studies in the Reign of Charles II* (London: John Lane and the Bodley Head, 1923), 161–7; J.B. Williams, *A History of English Journalism to the Foundation of the Gazette* (London: Longman, 1908), 177–98; P.M. Handover, *A History of the London Gazette, 1665–1965* (London: HMSO, 1965), 5–17.

56. *CSPD 1667–8*, 102.

57. *CSPD 1665–1666* (London: Longman, 1864), 484, for Hickes' own account; see also 17, 251, 280, 306, 322, 398; also Mary Anne Everett Green's comments on ix.

58. Marshall, *Intelligence and Espionage*; Fraser, *The Intelligence of Secretaries of State*; Gordon Campbell, Thomas N. Corns, John K. Hale, David Holmes, Fiona Tweedie, "Milton and *De Doctrina Christiana*," available at <http://voyager.cns.ohiou.edu/~som alley/ddc.html>; Mark Goldie, "The Hilton Gang and the Purge of London in the 1680s," in Howard Nenner (ed.), *Politics and the Political Imagination in Later Stuart Britain: Essays Presented to Lois Green Schwoerer* (Rochester: University of Rochester Press, 1997), 43–73.

59. *CSPD 1667*, 415.

60. Habermas, *Structural Transformation*, 27–30.

61. Fraser, "Rethinking the Public Sphere," 118–21.

62. Robert B. Shoemaker, *Gender in English Society 1650–1800: The Emergence of Separate Spheres?* (London and New York: Longman, 1998); Helen Berry, "'Nice and Curious

Questions': Coffee Houses and the Representation of Women in John Dunton's *Athenian Mercury*," *The Seventeenth Century* 12 (1997): 257–76.

63. Pincus, "Restoration Political Culture," 815, 834.

64. See above. See also Ian Atherton's essay in this volume.

65. Representations of coffee-houses, such as St Serfe's *Tarugo's Wiles*, tend to exclude women, or to delimit their participation by giving it sexual overtones; the coffee-house is a centre for rakes on the Restoration stage. Also Richard Ames, *The Bacchanalian Sessions* (1693), 15–16; Thomas Southerne' *The Wives Excuse* (1692); Charles Johnson, *The Generous Husband: Or, The Coffee House Politician* (London, 1711), where women participate in disguise (though there are additional reasons for this); Berry, "John Dunton's *Athenian Mercury*," 261–2.

66. *The Men's Answer to the Women's Petition* (1674), 2.

67. Arwaker, *Truth in Fiction: Or, Morality in Masquerade* (London, 1708), 234–6.

68. Shapin and Schaffer, *Leviathan and the Air-Pump*; Stephen Shapin, *A Social History of Truth: Civility and Science in Seventeenth-Century England* (Chicago, IL, and London: Chicago University Press, 1994).

69. Michael Treadwell, "London Trade Publishers 1675–1750," *The Library*, 6th ser., 4 (1982): 113–14; see also Jonathan Barry, "Popular Culture in Seventeenth-Century Bristol," in Barry Reay (ed.), *Popular Culture in Seventeenth-Century England* (1985; London: Routledge, 1988), 68–9.

70. For the unreliability of 1640s newsbooks see Raymond, *Invention*, 276–9.

71. *A Complete History of England*, 3 vols. (London, 1706), I: preface.

72. Christie (ed.), *Letters*, 1:7 3, also 176 and 2: 67–8; cp. *The Women's Petition Against Coffee* (London, 1674), 4–5; Nicholas Amhurst, *Protestant Popery* (1718), 66; Zeynep Tenger and Paul Trolander, "'Impartial Critick' or 'Muse's Handmaid': The Politics of Critical Practice in the Early-Eighteenth Century," *Essays in Literature* 21 (1994): 30.

73. For Locke, see Richard Ashcraft, *Revolutionary Politics & Locke's Two Treatises of Government* (Princeton, NJ: Princeton University Press, 1986), *passim*, but esp. 6–11; for Hobbes see Raymond, *Invention*, 290–95

74. Smith, *Literature and Revolution*, 61–2.

75. See Earl, quoted above; Lucasta Miller, "The Shattered *Violl*"; Zaret, "Religion, Science, and Printing in the Public Spheres"; Achinstein, "The Politics of Babel in the English Revolution."

76. *A Proclamation of His Majesties Grace* (1642), quoted, Loewenstein, "Legal Proofs," 101.

77. Christie (ed.), *Letters*, 1: 88.

78. *The Women's Petition Against Coffee*, 4.

79. For example: Edward Cooke, *Memorabilia: Or, the most Remarkable Passages and Counsels* (London, 1681), 1; John Nalson, *An Impartial Collection* (London, 1682), I: lii; John Rushworth, *Historical Collections … The Third Part* (London, 1691), I: 248.

80. Gary Stuart De Krey, *A Fractured Society: The Politics of London in the First Age of Party, 1688–1715* (Oxford: Clarendon Press, 1985), 219; Zaret, "Religion, Science, and Printing," 227–30.

81. *The Character of a Coffee-House*, 6.

82. Knights, *Politics and Opinion*, 179–80, also 153–92 on public opinion and the press.

83. I have argued this at length in Raymond, *Invention*, 80–126.

84. Fraser, *The Intelligence of Secretaries of State*, 126–7.

85. On reading see Habermas, "Further Reflections," 425–7; Raymond, *Invention*, 241–4 and references there for literacy; Tessa Watt, *Cheap Print and Popular Piety, 1550–1640* (Cambridge: Cambridge University Press, 1991); Dagmar Freist, *Governed by Opinion: Politics, Religion and the Dynamics of Communication in Stuart London, 1637–1645* (London and New York: Tauries Academic Studies, 1997); Tim Harris, *Politics Under the Later Stuarts: Party Conflict in a Divided Society, 1660–1715* (London: Longman, 1993), 178–88.

86. *The Character of a Coffee-House*, 3–4; see also Edward Ward, *The School of Politick* (1690); *The Rules and Orders of the Coffee House* (1674).

87. Anthony Wood, *The Life and Times of Anthony Wood*, ed. Andrew Clark, 5 vols. (Oxford: Clarendon Press, 1891–1900), 2: 300.

88. They are reproduced in A.S.P. Woodhouse (ed.), *Puritanism and Liberty* (1938; London: Dent, 1986); Woodhouse's introduction presents the debates as a dynamic, agonistic encounter of ideologies.

89. There is a wealth of literature on this subject, but in addition to n.85, above, see: Robert Darnton, "History of Reading" in Peter Burke (ed.), *New Perspectives on Historical Writing* (Cambridge: Polity Press, 1991), 140–67; Carlo Ginzburg, *The Cheese and the Worms: The Cosmos of a Sixteenth-Century Miller*, trans. John and Anne Tedeschi (New York, 1982); H.J. Jackson, "Writing in Books and Other Marginal Activities," *University of Toronto Quarterly* 62 (1992/93): 217–31; Lisa Jardine and Anthony Grafton, "'Studied for Action': How Gabriel Harvey Read his Livy," *Past and Present* 129 (1990): 30–78; Ann Moss, *Printed Commonplace Books and the Structuring of Renaissance Thought* (Oxford: Clarendon Press, 1996); James Raven, Helen Small and Naomi Tadmor (eds.), *The Practice and Representation of Reading in England* (Cambridge: Cambridge University Press, 1996); William Sherman, *John Dee: The Politics of Reading and Writing in the English Renaissance* (Amherst, MA: University of Massachusetts Press, 1995).

90. Habermas, *Structural Transformation*, 93.

91. For plotting, see Harris, *Politics Under the Later Stuarts*, 84; Knights, *Politics and Opinion*, 172–3; Lillywhite, *London Coffee-Houses*, 18–19; Keith Feiling and F.R.D. Needham, "The Journals of Edmund Warcup, 1676–84," *English Historical Review* 40 (1925): 240–41, 249–59 *passim*.

92. Butler, *Hudibras* (Cambridge: Cambridge University Press, 1905), 263.

93. On corantos, see George Barwick, "Corantos," *The Library*, 3rd ser., 4 (1913): 113–21; Laurence Hanson, "English Newsbooks, 1620–1642." *The Library*, 4th ser., 18 (1938): 355–84; Folke Dahl, *A Bibliography of English Corantos and Periodical Newsbooks 1620–1642* (London: Bibliographical Society, 1952); Michael Frearson, "The Distribution and Readership of London Corantos in the 1620s," in Robin Myers and Michael Harris (eds.), *Serials and their Readers, 1620–1914* (Winchester: St Paul's Bibliographies, 1993), 1–25. For 1641 newsbooks and Pym see Raymond, *Invention*, 108–26.

94. The suggestion that rather than one inclusive public sphere there were/are several smaller public spheres is made by Fraser, "Rethinking the Public Sphere," 121–8.

95. Raymond, *Making the News*, ch. 2; Joseph Frank, *The Beginnings of the English Newspaper, 1620–1660* (Cambridge, MA: Harvard University Press, 1961), 32–115; Joyce Lee Malcolm, *Caesar's Due: Loyalty and King Charles 1642–1646* (London: Royal Historical Society, 1983), 124–48.

96. Anthony Fletcher, *The Outbreak of the English Civil War* (London: Edward Arnold, 1981); cp. John Miller, "Public Opinion in Charles II's England," *History* 80 (1995): 376–81.

97. Treadwell, "London Trade Publishers," 128–31.

98. Siebert, *Freedom of the Press*, 230–32; *CSPD 1655* (London: Longman, 1881), 319; Frank, *Beginnings*, 253–8.

99. *The Observator* 1, 24–31 Oct. 1654, 2–3. Nedham accepted, or resigned himself to, the monopoly, though that is hardly surprising; he submitted an unidentified document concerning printing to the Council of State in April 1655. In August, Cromwell ordered commissioners to put into action the Ordinances against unlicensed printing of June 1643 and September 1647, and the act against street vending of October 1643. It is tempting to assume that Nedham had some hand in this, though there is no substantive evidence. Thurloe, Nedham's overseer, presented rules to regulate printing at the end of August, so it is possible that the impulse to silence the press was his, and Nedham played a passive rule in these plans. *CSPD 1655*, 139, 300–301, 309. This argument is developed at greater length in Raymond, "'A Mercury with a Winged Conscience': Marchamont Nedham, Monopoly and Censorship," *Media History* 4 (1998): 7–18.

100. See letter from Hickes to Williamson, 8 Aug. 1666, reporting that "the single gazette far exceeds in profits L'Estrange's double sheets"; *CSPD 1666–67*, 21; Christie (ed.), *Letters*, 1:139.

101. Christie (ed.), *Letters*, 1: 174. Newcombe, printer of the *Gazette*, was also a government printer in the 1650s, responsible for *Politicus*: he is one of the unsung political survivors of the seventeenth century.

102. Christie (ed.), *Letters*, 2: 32.
103. Miller, "Public Opinion," 365.
104. For example, *London Gazette* 2016, 16 March 1684[5]; 2018, 23 March 1684[5].
105. Thomas O'Malley, "Religion and the Newspaper Press," in Harris and Lee (eds.), *The Press in English Society*, 44–5.
106. Andrew Browning (ed.), *Memoirs of Sir John Reresby* (Glasgow: Jackson, 1936), 235.
107. *CSPD 1665–6*, 391; *CSPD 1666–67*, 6, 384, 562; *CSPD 1667*, 393, 413, 427, 546–7; *CSPD 1667–68*, 1, 138, 198, 224, 303, 416, 417–95 *passim*, 504, 515, 527, 565, 603, 604; for requests for exclusion see *CSPD 1665–66*, 518, 535, 589; *CSPD 1666–67*, 74, 570.
108. Knights, *Politics and Opinion*, 171 and n.127.
109. *CSPD 1667–68*, 102; quoted above.
110. *CSPD 1666–67*, 282; cp. 376.
111. *CSPD 1665–66*, 90, 213; for L'Estrange's newsbook cp. *CSPD 1666–7*, 21; *The Diary of Samuel Pepys*, ed. Robert Latham and William Matthews, 9 vols. (London: Bell, 1970–76), 6: 305; 7: 116, 405, 406; 8: 216; 9: 38.
112. *The Observator* 31, 5–8 Aug. 1702, quoted in Hanson, *Government and the Press*, 84.
113. Hanson, *Government and the Press*, 85, 141–3; James R. Sutherland, "The Circulation of Newspapers and Literary Periodicals, 1700–30," *The Library*, 4th ser., 15 (1935): 113–4; see also Henry Snyder, "The Circulation of Newspapers in the Reign of Queen Anne," *The Library*, 5th ser., 23 (1968): 206–35.
114. Christie (ed.), *Letters*, 1: 88, 133–4; 2: 67–8; see also Gibbs, "Press and Public Opinion," 259–60.
115. Pincus, "Restoration Political Culture," 822.
116. *The Women's Petition*, 5; Arwaker, "The Coffee-House"; Richard Ames, *Islington-Wells; or the Threepenny Academy* (1691), 12.
117. Rowe, *The Fair Penitent* (1703), prologue, ll. 12–13.
118. Dryden, *The Indian Emperor* (1667), epilogue, ll. 19–20.
119. *The Poems of John Oldham*, ed. Harold F. Brooks with the collaboration of Raman Selden (Oxford: Clarendon Press, 1987), 237–8, ll. 31–4; also published as "The Claret Drinker's Song" in *The Remains of Mr. Thomas Brown* (London, 1720), 11–13.
120. Christie (ed.), *Letters*, 2: 1; cp. Pincus, "Restoration Political Culture," 828.
121. *The Publick Adviser* 1, 19–26 May 1657; Raymond, *Invention*, 11.
122. O'Malley, "Religion and the Newspaper Press," 40–41; Harris' essay in this volume.
123. *The Tatler* 224, 14 Sept. 1710; *The Tatler*, ed. Donald F. Bond, vol. 3 (Oxford: Clarendon Press, 1987), 166; cp. *The Tatler* 240, 21 Oct. 1710; *Tatler*, ed. Bond, 3:232–6.
124. Snyder, "Circulation of Newspapers in the Reign of Queen Anne," 209.
125. Sutherland, "Circulation of Newspapers and Literary Periodicals," 123–4.
126. Snyder, "Circulation of Newspapers in the Reign of Queen Anne," 206–35, esp. 215.
127. J.A. Downie, "Periodicals and Politics in the Reign of Queen Anne," in Myers and Harris (eds.), *Serials and Their Readers*, 45–61; Clark, *Samuel Johnson*, 235.
128. For an account of these developments see my forthcoming study of the pamphlet.
129. Benedict Anderson, *Imagined Communities: Reflections on the Origin and Spread of Nationalism* (1983; London: Verso, 1991), esp. 33–46.
130. Pincus, "Restoration Political Culture," 813–14; Barry, "Popular Culture."
131. See for instance John Morrill's essays in Brendan Bradshaw and John Morrill (eds.), *The British Problem, c.1534–1707: State Formation in the Atlantic Archipelago* (Basingstoke: Macmillan, 1996), and Steven G. Ellis and Sarah Barber (eds.), *Conquest and Union: Fashioning a British State, 1485–1725* (London: Longman, 1995).
132. Printing follows distribution networks; it does not create markets *ex nihilo*: see John Feather, "The Country Trade in Books," in Robin Myers and Michael Harris (eds.), *Spreading the Word: The Distribution Networks of Print, 1550–1850* (Winchester: St Paul's Bibliographies, 1990), 165–72.
133. See n.129, above; Raymond, *Invention*, 76, 238–41; Robert Munter, *The History of the Irish Newspaper, 1685–1760* (Cambridge: Cambridge University Press, 1967); Carolyn Nelson and Matthew Seccombe, *British Newspapers and Periodicals, 1641–1700: A Short Title Catalogue* (New York: Modern Language Association, 1987).

134. See nn.85 and 89, above.
135. Stephen Parks, "John Dunton and *The Works of the Learned*," *The Library*, 5th ser., 23 (1968): 13–24, quote 16.
136. *A Collection of Scarce and Valuable Tracts [Somers Tracts]*, 16 vols. (London, 1748–52), 11: 227–8, 224.
137. De Krey, *A Fractured Society*, 216–17.
138. For example, C. John Sommerville, *The News Revolution in England: Cultural Dynamics of Daily Information* (New York: Oxford University Press, 1996[7]).
139. *The Spectator* 10, 12 March 1711; ed. Donald F. Bond, vol. 1 (Oxford: Clarendon Press, 1965), 46.
140. *Athenian Gazette* vol. 1, 17 March 1690[1]. See also Gilbert D. McEwen, *The Oracle of the Coffee House: John Dunton's Athenian Mercury* (San Marino, CA: Huntington Library, 1972); Berry, "John Dunton's *Athenian Mercury*."
141. *Athenian Mercury,* second volume, preface (1691); *Athenian Mercury* 2: 17, 21 July 1691.
142. *Athenian Mercury,* third volume, preface (1691).

Timely Notices: The Uses of Advertising and its Relationship to News during the Late Seventeenth Century

MICHAEL HARRIS

Advertising material has been the subject of what might be described as contemptuous disregard over a long period. Its presence has been seen at best as a necessary evil and at worst as a corrupting manifestation of commercial values. Yet the universal presence of advertising in all periods identifies its value to the producer and the consumer of various forms of media; and the modern superstructure of agencies, account executives, and endless marketing strategies indicates a social and cultural force which requires analysis. This paper is about advertising in the primary medium of public communication of the late seventeenth century, the printed news serial. It attempts to suggest how advertising worked at street level. This is a tough assignment and requires a detailed reading of difficult material across a broad range of publications. Its meaning, like that of news, is hard to assess. Even so, in terms of its relationship to the printed serial alone, advertising must be given the same sort of attention as other elements of their content.[1]

The first and inescapable characteristic of the advertising in the printed serials, including what were later described as newspapers, was its bulk. From the first appearance of an in-house notice of publication in the mid-1620s the volume of advertising in serial print continued to escalate. This was not an isolated phenomenon. Other ways of bringing material into public view remained in use in an apparently massive way. In the late seventeenth century most people's sense of the marketing process would have come from the handbills which flooded the streets of London but remain unidentified through natural wastage, by cries which caused such annoyance to some and amazement to others or simply by word of mouth or reputation. The confusing character of London as a monster city was offset by the clustering of activities and the known locations of the main centres of business and trade. Everybody knew about the Royal Exchange and how to find it, and advertising in this case would have been surplus to requirements.[2]

Michael Harris, Birkbeck College

It is reasonable to categorize the advertisement as ephemeral, most were either thrown away or never had any substantive existence in the first place. Consequently, because most of the advertising that has survived has done so through the printed serial, kept as part of the semi-official record of events, it is tempting to overestimate the force of the relationship. Advertising in the serial was only the tip of the iceberg. At the same time, though the bulk of serial advertising is substantial and it appears in the bound volumes to link up with all the main areas of commercial, social, political, and cultural activity, this is to some extent an illusion. Like all forms of serial content, the published advertisements are both selective and repetitive so that part of the quantity is made up of apparently endless duplication. On the other hand, although the quantity is huge, the relationship of the advertising in the serials to any of the things or activities advertised is to some extent marginal. Vast areas of the London trading community were never represented in the serials at all, while most of the advertisements were occasional, short-term, one-off notices which provided information to be followed through elsewhere. This reflects the nature of the news serial more generally, in which the whole story can seldom be found. Bits of information, often not located anywhere else, are present in this form of publication, but for a clear perspective other parts of the record, if available, have to be brought into play.

This sort of underlying characteristic makes the advertising hard to evaluate. Various attempts have been made at quantification and classification without getting to the heart of the matter.[3] Such studies can indicate the generalized increase in advertising which is painfully evident on the page. It can also identify those lines of advertising which ebb and flow through the pages of the London serials over time as well as indicating absences, though the unfortunate use of a miscellaneous category can be confusing. Quantification can provide useful information. However, what it fails to do is indicate how the different kinds of advertising were used. By applying a framework classification, the quantifier inevitably narrows the range of analysis. Not all advertisements for books are doing the same thing, nor are all advertisements relating to crime, and this reservation applies across the whole range of material.

Through the serials the advertisers participated in the core activities of capitalist enterprise, buying and selling. This was a selective process, and some commodities and services were never offered in this way. But while buying and selling focused on the marketing of such commodities as books and medicines, the advertisements appearing in the printed serials fulfilled more complex functions. This paper contains a brief examination of some of these and suggests how the advertisements fitted into a general mix of news and information which was channelled into the market towards the end of the seventeenth century.

One of the defining elements of the serial output as developed in London from the 1620s was its close engagement with its readers. In this respect, the printed sheets shared some of the open-access characteristics of the internet. Content was not a product of a top-heavy internal structure of full-time employees. Usually the printer or publisher assumed responsibility for compiling the publication. As the material flowed in from different directions, there is not much evidence of editorial intervention beyond the correction of mistakes and the rejection of personal controversy.

Readers acted as both consumers and contributors, creating circuits of communication around which flowed all forms of material. Serial publication had always been a commercial process in which the reader had a continuous commercial interest. Survival of any title required the continuous renewal of engagement through small commercial transactions, usually the giving or receiving of one penny, endlessly renewed. Whether this was mediated by a coffee-house proprietor or some other public institution, the printed serials were subjected to continuous market testing and engaged with the producer in a particularly direct way.[4]

However, it was as contributors that readers stood in the most dynamic relation to the producer. Without the resource of a structure of information gathering, readers inevitably became a primary source for all sorts of news and information as well as advertising. Some of the overlap in supply blurs the way in which the content of serials can be understood. Advertising by anyone not involved in the publication was always paid for, though the terms were variable and negotiated through the printing office. Sometimes basic rates were given, but frequency, location on the page, and the use of emphasis and illustration were probably among the variables in determining the cost. A difficulty arises here in relation to news items paid for in the same way. The extent and character of this form of material is hard to gauge, but it seems clear that a proportion of the news cover, probably a small part, equated with advertising both in its intention and method of payment. In the 1740s readers were also paying for news to be left out and this was probably a long-standing service.[5]

The blurred frontier between news and advertising reflects a similar deliberate fudging of the division in the commercial newspapers of the 1680s themselves. Advertising was sometimes separated out by the inclusion of a heading or by a printed rule or both. Reading the papers, it is immediately evident that advertising is included outside the frame. There does not seem to be any intent to deceive, but clearly an agreement was reached with the producer over placement and whether this related to the content of the advertisement or the inclination of the advertiser or some other unknown local factor is never certain.

Advertising was an integral part of the content of most, if not all, of the printed serials of the late seventeenth century. Its presence was one, perhaps the only, clear content division between the manuscript newsletter and the printed serial. It seems a fairly safe bet to say that none of the newsletters which were labour-intensive to produce and limited in circulation, as well as directed to a diffuse national readership, carried such items. London-based print was the natural medium for the promotion of goods and services, though its public character also gave it value in a wider context. The presence of advertising can be seen as a vital support to the finances of publications running in the 1680s on small profit margins. It also provides a guide to the success of individual titles which filled up with notices as readers increased. Even so, the volume of advertising was restricted by the limitation of the single-sheet form of most serials and both too little and too much of this form of content could disrupt the circuit.

However, advertising had a more complex position in relation to the conduct of serials than to provide its producers with a recurrent profit. It was also a form of material through which the relationship between producer and consumer could be mediated. Through advertising readers spoke to each other by way of the producer or received messages from commercial or political interests who were, in their turn, able to plug into the established circuits of printed communication. This function indicates a submerged role for the paid advertising carried by the serials. It offered a means of public access to the serial text. Whatever the editorial limitations on information and correspondence supplied by readers, there was always the capacity for consumers, both individuals and groups, to get material into the public sphere by this route.

The way in which this worked in practice related to the way in which advertising was shaped by the intervention of the state during the later seventeenth century. Under the licensing system, reintroduced through the Printing Act of 1662, the control of serial news was linked to that of public advertising. Licensing was to some extent focused on the supply of news and information in serial form and represented a means of establishing and securing an official narrative of events. The exclusion of a controlled and restricted print trade from this form of output was linked to the publication of a sequence of official news serials of which the *London Gazette*, first published in 1665, was the most durable. Publication was based on monopoly grants in which news and advertising were yoked together.[6] In practice the two components soon began to be filtered into separate strands.

Unlike the equivalent continental gazettes, the *London Gazette* was a hybrid. On the one hand it was a commercial enterprise, run on behalf of individuals in and out of the Secretary of State's offices and sold by subscription or through the pamphlet shops in the same way as other forms of print. At the same time, it remained a state-sponsored medium for the circulation of public information of all kinds. This was a characteristic form of compromise but it created tensions within the content of the paper itself, not least in relation to advertising. All the printed serials assumed a position in which public service was identified as a primary justification for publication. In the *Gazette* this characteristic, which flickered unevenly through the commercial serials, had a more intense and serious expression.

In serial publication, advertising was already established by the mid-1660s as an integral part of the content. Profit and public interest were served by it. In the pages of the *Gazette* a serious attempt was made to exclude specific categories of advertising as inappropriate. An early issue stated: "Being daily prest to the Publication of Books, Medicines and other things, not properly the business of a Paper of Intelligence. This is to notifie once for all, that we will not charge the Gazette with Advertisements, unless they be matter of State."[7] This attempt to hold the line against "ordinary" advertisements was doomed to failure. By 1670 books and even medicines were being advertised, a sure sign of compromised principle. Medical advertising remained a high-profile component of this form of material, profitable but likely to cause some reader resistance through repetition and over-use.[8]

None the less, the compilers of the *Gazette* extended its primary public service function of providing an authoritative if selective news narrative into the advertising content. Through its bi-weekly publication schedule, the *Gazette* was able to facilitate and support what might be described as information chronologies. This process was visible in all forms of serial publication, but in the *Gazette* it had both a higher profile and a greater emphasis. All serials established a rhythm of production and distribution synchronized with the inward and outward movement of postal services. The mechanism was consistent and reliable and through this line of communication it was possible to construct the timetables of public administration which in the *Gazette* provided a counterpoint to the official narrative.

In this way the *Gazette* was plugged into several different levels of public activity radiating outwards from the court of Charles II. In its news section, the *Gazette* followed the movement of the King as he travelled around the country, in particular his visits to Newmarket, supplementing this with notices about his availability to touch for the King's Evil. This healing function, experienced unsuccessfully by the young Samuel Johnson, was advertised in the *Gazette*, though more often it was the King's unavailability through the state of the weather or the end of the touching season that received attention.[9] More consistently, and usefully, the paper was geared up to relay through its notices the schedules which related to the conduct of government. The paper carried invitations to potential farmers or undertakers to apply for regional grants conveying an interest in the collection of the hearth tax or the issuing of wine licences. Each season, these notices were renewed through the *Gazette* with follow-up items urging and demanding the submission of accounts and identifying problems with the accounting procedures.[10] Similar requests for tenders were made for military and naval equipment sometimes, as in the case of importers of such foreign supplies for the navy as hemp, tar, and masts, laying out a timetable which could extend a year ahead of the notice.[11] In time of war the *Gazette* had a particular value to government. During the Dutch wars it was possible through notices in the paper to respond to the rapidly changing circumstances of the time. Deserters were advertised, arrangements for dealing with Dutch seamen coming ashore after sea battles were outlined, and the general organization of prisoners of war brought into public view.[12] If the timetables of war were shorter and more disjointed than the more leisurely schedules of national government, the rhythms established by serial publication were still of pragmatic use.

At the same time, the access offered through the *Gazette* by way of paid-for notices provided a means for other institutions and organizations to engage with the main line of serial news. The Corporation of the City of London used the paper to promote public tenders for a string of different purposes, including the letting of City Lands and street management.[13] These notices carried a detailed series of instructions as well as a timetable for applications, and through the *Gazette* a clear sense of the management of the City was brought before the public. The activities of less formally constituted non-governmental organizations were also integrated into the schedules of the *Gazette*. University colleges, the major public schools, livery and trading companies all announced occasional or regular activities, while the annual feasts of incomers to London from York and Hereford, and even the events organized by groups of people sharing the same surname were slotted into the advertising section. The value of the *Gazette* to coordinate any timetable of activities appeared clearly in relation to what were to become the leisure industries. Notices concerned with tennis, bowling, football, and, more insistently, foot and horse racing were part of a seasonal input. Towards the end of the century the "what's on" function of the newspaper began to bring the schedules of theatrical performance into the frame of the serial publication notices.

Under the licensing system this material was focused in the *London Gazette*. During lapses in the legislation it seeped into all sectors of serial publication as the need for a generalized coverage across a range of titles became evident. The material described so far has been related to public information of general concern. Other elements of the material published in the advertising section of the *Gazette* and later of the commercial news sheets, related more directly to personal experience and was integrated with elements of the flow of events as recorded in the news narrative.

In its earliest period of publication, the *Gazette* had the flavour of a newsletter of the Court. Its advertisements were peppered with notices of dogs lost by the aristocratic inhabitants of the chambers at the Palace of Whitehall, while on one occasion the keeper of St James's Park appealed to the public for information about a lost pelican.[14] However, as the scope of the publication and the circles of readership broadened out, the elements of personal and public information coalesced around the critical areas of crime and the operation of the law. It was through the publication of criminal and related advertising that a series of secondary narratives began to be constructed giving the advertising sections of the London newspapers a specific news value of their own. They began to carry what Richard Steele described in the *Tatler* in 1710 as "News from the little World."[15]

Specificity was always the central characteristic of newspaper advertising. Places, people, times, and objects all received close and detailed description in the notices which had intention built into them. This was particularly apparent in the material initially focused in the *Gazette* and later scattered through the commercial sheets which provided accounts of crimes and criminals. This category of material has been given careful and imaginative attention by the historian John Styles, although his study centres on the material carried in English local papers in the later eighteenth century.[16] Looking at the way newspaper advertisements worked in the detection and pursuit of criminals, Styles suggests how print functioned in the storage, dispersal, and retrieval of information and provided an effective support to the operation of the law.

Styles is perhaps unduly dismissive of the importance of such material published in the news serials of the seventeenth century.[17] In terms of quantity, the difference between 1680 and 1780 is unmistakable, while the absence of any local news sheets before 1695 clearly limited the range of public involvement. However, this does not imply that the material, printed in London but relating to crimes taking place across the nation, did not have a part to play in the legal processes of detection and arrest. In fact, the increasing presence of such notices suggests at least a sense of the value of publicity. The combination of specificity, narrative, and intention can be suggested in a single notice published in the *Gazette* in 1676.

> Two Gentlemen pretending to be Persons of Quality, Rid away with two horses the 21 instant. The one was a brown Bay Nag about 13 hands and an half high Trots hard, Paces little, having a shorn Main about nine years old. The other a handsom strait dapple grey Nag, a little Flea bitten about the Head, Trots all, the height of the other. They rode away from the *King's Arms* in *Darking* in *Surrey*; The one had a brown Perriwig, his Under-lip having a deep cleft in the middle, with

Boots on, about 30 years of age, pretty tall, but slender. The other had dark brown curled hair pretty long, fresh coloured, about 22 years of age, a handsome Man, in Boots hose Stockings and Shooes. If anyone can give tydings of the Horses or Persons, to Mr. *Walsingham Heathfield* at the *Three Sugar Loaves* in *Clare-market, London*, or to the said *King's Arms* in *Darking*, shall be well rewarded. These Gentlemen go by the names of Capt. *Hopton Williams*, and Mr *Talbot*, but they are supposed not to be so.[18]

In this confined space, the notice in the *Gazette* brings the elements of public and private information into view in a way which both supplements and diversifies the content of the serial.

By providing access to readers or to members of the public who understood how serials worked, the advertisements could become closely interlocked with components of the news narrative. This was almost a routine circumstance and is difficult to illustrate in isolation. One example of the interplay of news and notices which emerged in the *Gazette* concerned a banquet to celebrate the coronation of James II. The event was reported in the *Gazette*, which, a day or two later, carried notices referring to lost spoons and other pieces of plate which were to be returned without questions.[19] Six years on, a serious but not terminal fire at the Palace of Whitehall created massive confusion and loss of property. It was reported in the *London Gazette* on Monday 13 April 1691: "*Whitehall, April* 11. On Thursday last about 9 [?] at night a Fire happened here at the lower end of the Stone-Gallery, which continued for several hours with great violence, and burnt down some private Lodgings, but was happily stopt before it came near the King's or Queen's Apartments." Immediately below, under the heading "Advertisements," came the first of a series of notices inserted by individuals who had been burned out and had lost property in the process. The first stated: "Whereas during the late Fire at Whitehall, a Walnut Chest of Drawers with several Papers in it, Prints, and drawings, some Colours and Pencils for Painters, with some few pieces of Plate, was lost out of my Lord Rutland's Lodgings; These are to give notice, That whoever shall bring the same to Mr. Cornelis Gronvelt at his Lordships said Lodgings, shall have 5 Guinea's." The second item concerned "a little strong box bound about with guilt Iron" lost from Prince George of Denmark's Treasury Office. The sequence of requests and rewards continued in the *Gazette* for several issues.[20] Any event at which the confusion of crowds led to loss or theft was likely to be accompanied by a litany of notices in the news serials. The popularity of foot races around London as well as in other parts of the country, announced and reported in the news, also gave rise to this sort of response and emphasized the interaction between readers and publishers.[21]

This relationship, developed in the *Gazette*, moved through the commercial news sheets published with the lapse in licensing in 1679. As new serials came on stream, so the printers and publishers became more directly and visibly involved as intermediaries in the flow of information round the circuits of print. From the 1680s, the producers took on an agent's role, becoming, in some sense, information brokers whose transactions were orchestrated through the advertising carried by their serials. Individual booksellers clustered round the Royal Exchange, including Robert Horne and Benjamin Harris in the 1680s, whose commercial interest included serial publication, were neatly placed to channel specific requests from readers and customers into the information nexus centred on the Exchange. Elsewhere in the central districts of London, publishers of news sheets offered the same service. Abel Roper at the Black Boy in Fleet Street figured in a large number of notices published in his serial the *Post Boy*, which related to a variety of topics. They included in the first months of 1698 requests for information about a lost notebook, the offer of particulars for a successful brew-house where Nottingham and Derby ale was prepared, and details of the services of a dancing master.[22]

Publishers were concerned as intermediaries in all sorts of transaction, and their shops, usually small in size, became the focal points for most forms of agency activity. Individual booksellers must have maintained a variety of ledgers and books of account in which the details of runaway apprentices, services to be delivered, and the whole gamut of objects lost and found were recorded and kept up to date, and in the process they moved into the area characterized by a second primary line of printed advertising. This was closely identified with personal services, though it also included miscellaneous buying and selling, which made up the business of the Register Offices or Offices of Intelligence. Combining the functions of the job centre, estate agent, and commodity broker among others, the offices became from the mid-seventeenth century onwards part of the information infrastructure that supported London's complex economic and social development.[23] The long-term importance of the Register Office, operating in general at a low level of visibility, is suggested by the surprising involvement of Henry and John Fielding in an enterprise of this kind projected in association with the *Covent Garden Journal* in the mid-eighteenth century.[24]

Under the licensing laws, the holders of official grants to publish news and advertising, notably Roger L'Estrange, subcontracted the right to publish advertising material in serial form. The forms of personal and commercial information which were not seen as appropriate for the *Gazette* became the staple of low key, often free, advertising sheets which were issued in conjunction with Register Office businesses. The combination of an office-based service with publication of a printed serial consisting mainly or entirely of advertisements created an alternative form of circuit, drawing in readers as buyers and sellers to respond or contribute to the content.[25]

The offices were scattered through the main centres of commercial activity in London and are still visible through advertisements published in the *London Gazette* as well as in the limited number of surviving copies of the advertising sheets themselves. One of the earliest surviving publications was simply headed "Mercury-Office at Charing-Cross," with the statement below: "*Next door the* Red-Lyon-Inn *at the Entrance into the* Spring-Garden, *For Buying and Selling of Estates and Places, for procuring of Money, upon Real and Personal Security, and accomodating Persons of Quality and others with Servants.*" Under a series of headings, indicative notices promoted a range of services which could be followed up at the office itself. The single sheet, printed on both sides in double columns, was probably issued in 1677. It was modelled, like all the news serials of the later seventeenth century, on the *Gazette*, and carried between rules the black letter assertion: "With Allowance."[26]

The main point to be made here about this form of advertising is that it formed a distinct strand of material, running in tandem with the more generalized, public service notices focused in the *Gazette*. To some extent, publication of the advertising sheets was supported by the operation of the licensing system. Within the deregulated market of the early 1680s and after 1695 competition and the public demand for conventional and now widely available news narratives accelerated a process of convergence between the news serial carrying advertising and the advertising sheets which began to assume some of the characteristics of the newspaper. This was initially reflected in the circumstances of the *City Mercury*, later *Mercury; or, Advertisements Concerning Trade*.[27] This routine free sheet linked to a Register Office at the Royal Exchange was merged with sequential news serials: first, *Mercurius Civicus* (1680), and, secondly, the *Impartial Protestant Mercury* (1681). The value of combining all forms of advertising with a narrative of events seems to have been clear enough.

The most original attempt to sustain a business-centred advertising serial in conjunction with miscellaneous lines of news and information was made by John Houghton, a broker living initially in Bartholomew Lane close to the Royal Exchange.[28] He constructed a commercial enterprise which was partly conducted through the medium of serial print in which advertisements became a crucial mechanism of negotiation. His *Collection for the Improvement of Husbandry and Trade* had a complex eleven-year publishing history from its appearance in 1692. The starting point of the *Collection* was neither news nor advertising but information. In this respect it resembled the commercial lists, Bills of Entry and Commodity Price Currents, published in

London since the early seventeenth century.[29] Houghton, as a Fellow of the Royal Society, had broader interests, and his publication, while it included standard information on prices and goods imported and exported, also took in such public information as the weekly Bills of Mortality.[30] The direct publication of a news narrative without the licenser's sanction would have been disastrous. However, Houghton saw his paper as a "handmaid" to the *London Gazette*, through which the news could be filtered. As he remarked:

> I find the Generality are desirous of News; I hear about 7 or 8000 Gazettes at a time are printed, which is but small for 10000 Parishes or 8 Million of People; 'twoud be for the Improvement of Trade to have them spread, and its probable, Not-Seers having a tast of the principal things contained therein (which I shall strive to shew in my following Papers) may long for more particulars.[31]

The enterprise seems to have been over-ambitious and foundered in June 1692, but with an injection of cash from subscribers it bounced back after a seven-month hiatus the following January.[32] One problem seems to have been the expense of a network of correspondents supplying information about local prices and other matters. This was in line with the organization of the *Gazette*, whose compilers also offered free copies of the paper and access to the post in return for news. At the time of the restart, Houghton determined to use his "great Correspondency" to establish an agency service.[33] Initially he offered to help *"Masters* to *Apprentices,* and *Apprentices* to *Masters."* This presumably helped to lock readers in to the project as well as to generate income. Houghton's development of his serial as a medium of advertising was partly to promote his own commodity sales as an "Apothecary." But the main thrust was into the information brokerage system, in which he acted as intermediary, balancing the elements of supply and demand. To accommodate the advertisements, Houghton extended his paper in July 1693 to four pages, using the last leaf for this material. He announced under the heading "Advertisements":

> *My Collection I shall carry on as usual. This part is to give away, and those who like it not may omit the reading. I believe it will help in particular encourage the Advertizers to increase the want of my Papers. I shall receive all sorts of Advertisements, but shall answer for the reasonableness of none, unless I give thereof a particular Character, on which (as I shall give it) may be dependence but no argument that others deserve not as well.*[34]

Houghton was unusual in providing an index to the advertisements in his regularly issued volumes.[35]

In the *Collection* he floated ideas for new services, testing market opinion before committing himself to the speculation. In April 1694 he pondered: "Whither Advertisements of *Schools,* or *Houses* and *Lodgings* about *London,* may be useful, I submit to those concerned." A month later he wrote: "I now find Advertisements of *Schools, Houses,* and *Lodgings* in and about *London,* are thought useful."[36] In 1694 he laid out his full range of services at that time:

> I sel CHOCOLATE ... which I know to be a great helper of bad Stomachs and Restorative to weak People. I'll answer for their Goodness.
>
> I also sell true *German* SPAW-WATER, and SAGO.
>
> If applied to, I'll strive to help *Masters* to *Clerks, Apprentices,* and other valuable *Servants,* and such to *Masters.*
>
> Also *Masters* of Ships to *Chyrurgeons* and they to *Masters.*
>
> I find Advertisements of *Schools,* or *Houses* and *Lodgings* to be let, are useful;
>
> I know of valuable Estates to be sold.
>
> I want several *Apprentices* for valuable *Tradesmen.*
>
> I can help to ready Money for any *Library* great or small.[37]

In August 1695 he moved into marriage broking, though he was forced to point out: "These Proposals for Matches are real; and I do promise to manage them and such like with so much Secresie and Prudence, that none shall discourse with their best Friends with more Confidence of Fidelity than with me, let them be of what Rank soever."[38] This enterprise seems to have caused more difficulty than most.

The combination of information and advertising kept the *Collection* afloat well after the lapse of licensing restrictions. Houghton also continued to provide "an Abstract of the Material things in the *Gazette*" which he considered would "be useful for History."[39] However, even this dynamic and appealing serial was too static to endure the growing competition. The personal and local character of its advertising content may in the end have been a deterrent to readers increasingly obsessed with politics and international relations and whose concerns were better reflected in more generalized notices. The only comparable enterprise was undertaken by the inveterate speculator Charles Povey. His *General Remark on Trade* was run in conjunction with his business, based at "the Traders Exchange-House in *Hatton-Garden.*"[40] The paper contained a manic combination of news, information, and the sort of Register Office advertising that had characterized Houghton's *Collection.*

After 1695 a new environment was established for the publication of news, information, and advertising. The construction of the stable, generalist newspaper, increasingly under the control of groups of London booksellers and following rapid production schedules, changed the balance of power in serial print from the state to the business community. The success of the new tri-weekly and daily papers made them the favoured medium of public discourse and consequently the focus for the notices through which middling society was organized. This shift was reflected in the rapid and progressive decline in the circulation of the *Gazette*. Increasingly stuffed with formal government-centred material and legal notices, individual subscribers lost interest. The *Gazette* still carried authority, but part of what might be called its "human interest appeal" had been relocated.

At the same time, the pattern of ownership which developed did something to distance the reader from the producer, a process reflected in the emphasis given to advertisements for books and medicine. These had figured prominently through the seventeenth century and could have some news value. Advertisements for print were, to some extent, keyed into the components of the news narrative and served to guide readers into the circles of publication which provided explanation, illustration, and general background to events. The first advertisement in a news serial in the 1620s had been for a map illustrating the progress of the war, and the advertising content of the *Gazette* was shot through with offers of maps geared to the ebb and flow of the hostilities moving across western Europe.[41] Medical advertising was less explicitly current, though it could occasionally chime with events. In 1673 an advertisement for "The Royal Stiptick Liquor," which curtailed bleeding, claimed that it "hath been since used in the last Fight at Sea with the Dutch."[42] This was an exception, and though medical notices often contained case histories and material which related to accidents or other current happenings the link with news was tenuous. In both cases, the items were more the product of a marketing strategy than of a dialogue between readers or between readers and publishers.

The separate publication of information and advertising sheets continued, though increasingly elements of their content were absorbed into the generalist London newspapers. However, it was not until the publication of the *Daily Advertiser* in 1731 that a convergence between the forms of advertising can be clearly identified.

Advertisements continued to fulfil a news-related function, running in tandem with the narrative of events but also providing readers with a view of a parallel universe. Even for those not wanting to farm taxes, catch a thief, hire a footman, or cure a disease, the advertisements were of interest. This non-specific appeal of advertising was well expressed by Richard Steele in the *Tatler* in 1710. He wrote:

> It is my Custom, in a Dearth of News, to entertain my self with those Collections of Advertisements that appear at the End of all our publick Prints. These I consider as Accounts of News from the little World, in the same Manner that the foregoing Parts of the Paper are

from the great. If in one we hear that a Sovereign Prince is fled from his Capital City, in the other we hear of a Tradesman who hath shut up his Shop, and run away. If in one we find the Victory of a General, in the other we see the Desertion of a private Soldier. I must confess, I have a certain Weakness in my Temper, that is often very much affected by these little Domestick Occurences, and have frequently been caught with Tears in my Eyes over a melancholy Advertisement.[43]

In the printed serial different parts of the content moved at different speeds. News, information, and advertising were like the cogs in a rather cumbersome machine, meshing together in the manufacture of "middling" English culture. In this way, the timely notices of a thousand intersecting transactions played their part in a complex process.

NOTES

1. The only full length study of the general use of advertising from the late seventeenth century appears in a gripping but confused study centred on the marketing of the Anodyne Necklace. Francis Doherty, *A Study in Eighteenth-Century Advertising Methods* (Leviston, Queenston, and Lampeter: Edwin Mellen Press, 1992). See also Roy Porter, *Health for Sale: Quackery in England 1660–1850* (Manchester: Manchester University Press, 1989).

2. For an account of the Royal Exchange as a centre of commercial and other intelligence, see Michael Harris, "Exchanging Information: Print and Business at the Royal Exchange in the Late Seventeenth Century," in Ann Saunders (ed.), *The Royal Exchange* (London: London Topographical Society, 1997).

3. For an example of applied quantification, see R.B. Walker, "Advertising in London Newspapers, 1650–1750," *Business History* XV, 1 (Jan. 1973): 112–30.

4. For a general analysis of the process of interaction, see Michael Harris, "Locating the Serial: Some Ideas about the Position of the Serial in Relation to the Eighteenth-Century Print Culture," *Studies in Newspaper and Periodical History* 2 (Westport, CT, and London: Greenwood Press, 1997), 3–16.

5. Information from marked up, office copies of the *London Daily Post and General Advertiser*, Michael Harris, *London Newspapers in the Age of Walpole* (London and Toronto: Associated University Presses, 1987), 59.

6. J.B. Williams, *A History of English Journalism to the Foundation of the Gazette* (London: 1908), 187–8.

7. *London Gazette* [hereafter *LG*] 62, Monday 18 June 1666.

8. For resistance from mid-eighteenth century readers to such material, see Harris, *Newspapers*, 177–8.

9. *LG* 145, Monday 8 April 1667; 154, Thursday 9 May 1667; 10828, Monday 28 May 1683. *Domestick Intelligence* 104, Friday 11 March 1681. In all the notes citing advertisements from printed serials, the aim is to give an indication of process rather than a fully representative sample of such material.

10. *LG* 42, Monday 9 April 1666; 226, Thursday 16 Jan. 1668; 229, Monday 27 Jan. 1668; 275, Monday 6 July 1668; 1414, Monday 9 June 1679.

11. Notice from the Principal Officers and Commissioners of Her Majesty's Navy in *LG* 4294, Monday 6 Jan. 1707. For an earlier example of this approach in relation to timber supply, see *LG* 2309, Thursday 5 Jan. 1688.

12. *LG* 682, Monday 3 June 1672; 685, Thursday 13 June 1672; 2574, Monday 14 July 1690.

13. For examples of lettings offered by the City Lands Committee, *LG* 1766, Monday 23 Oct. 1682; 1849, Thursday 9 Aug. 1683; 2372, Monday 13 Aug. 1688. Tenders for clearing part of the Fleet Ditch ("Turnmill-Brook") in *LG* 1831, Thursday 7 June 1683.
14. *LG* 1079, Thursday 24 March 1675. The notices about lost dogs are scattered promiscuously through the early issues.
15. *Tatler* 224, Thursday 14 Sept. 1710.
16. John Styles, "Print and Policing: Crime Advertising in Eighteenth-Century Provincial England," in Douglas Hay and Francis Snyder (eds.), *Policing and Prosecution in Britain 1750–1850* (Oxford: Clarendon Press, 1989), 50–111.
17. Styles, "Print," 57–8.
18. *LG* 1089, Thursday 27 April 1676. The twice-weekly *Gazette* carried up to three or four such notices in a single issue, while from 1679 this number was extended through the active involvement of the unlicensed news serials. Presumably in many cases separately printed handbills supplemented the serial cover.
19. Reports of the coronations in *LG* 2028, Monday 27 April 1685; 2444, Monday 15 April 1689. Notices of losses in *LG* 2029, Thursday 30 April 1685; 2444, Monday 15 April 1689. Other, less prestigious, banquets were sometimes followed by similar appeals.
20. *LG* 2652, Monday 13 April 1691; 2654, Monday 20 April 1691; 2655, Thursday 23 April 1691.
21. In 1680 a foot race between well-known runners from Barnet, a satellite market town north of London, to Smithfield was reported in the *Domestick Intelligence* 79, Tuesday 6 April 1680. The same issue carried a notice of property lost "when the Foot race was run."
22. *Post Boy* 425, Tuesday 25 Jan. 1698; 434, Tuesday 15 Feb. 1698; 447, Thursday 17 March 1698.
23. A good account of the mid-century offices is provided in Williams, *Journalism*, 167–71.
24. The Fieldings drew up a prospectus for the business which was published as *A Plan of the Universal Register Office* (1751). An introduction and complete text appears in Bertrand A. Goldgar (ed.), *The Covent-Garden Journal and A Plan of the Universal Register Office* (Oxford: Clarendon Press, 1988).
25. Williams, *Journalism*.
26. For an account of the offices and advertising sheets centred on the Royal Exchange, see Harris, "Information," 17 *et seq.*
27. Ibid., 19.
28. An account of Houghton's publication and some of its rivals appears in Larry Neal, "The Business Press," in Robert P. Maccubin and Martha Hamilton-Phillips (eds.), *The Age of William 111 & Mary 11: Power, Politics and Patronage, 1688–1702* (Williamsburg, VA: College of William and Mary, 1989), 145–9.
29. A full and detailed bibliographical account of these publications appears in J.J. McCusker and C. Gravesteijn, *The Beginnings of Commercial and Financial Journalism* (Amsterdam: NEHA, 1991).
30. The design of the paper was laid out in *Collection for Improvement of Husbandry and Trade* (*Collection*) 1, Wednesday 30 March 1692. It was published initially on Wednesday and Saturday, the Saturday issue containing material extracted from "the Custom-House Bills," which were apparently also issued by Houghton, *Collection* 6, Wednesday 27 April 1692.
31. *Collection* 16, Wednesday 1 June 1692. *Gazette* material was often left out or curtailed on the basis of its lack of interest, *Collection* 60, Friday 22 Sept. 1693.
32. Houghton had been involved in the publication of a serial under the same title in 1682. The break in publication on this occasion was between the appearance of *Collection* 24, Wednesday 24 June 1692 and the issue of 25, Friday 20 Jan. 1693. The price was dropped at this time from two pence to a penny.
33. *Collection* 27, Friday 3 Feb. 1693.
34. *Collection* 52, Friday 28 July 1693.
35. The title pages and other apparatus for the collected volumes and the volumes themselves were issued twice yearly.
36. *Collection* 90, Friday 20 April 1694; 95, Friday 5 May 1694. A similar item appeared in *Collection* 52, Friday 28 July 1693 enquiring about the level of interest in ship news, the availability of coaches and carriers and forthcoming fairs with their commodities. Houghton

specialized in the provision of lists of people providing specific services and it was at this point that information and advertising overlapped.

37. *Collection* 101, Friday 6 July 1694.

38. *Collection* 159, Friday 16 Aug. 1694. The material had begun to appear in relation to "A Gentleman about 30 Years of Age, that says he has a Very Good Estate," *Collection* 155, Friday 19 July 1695.

39. *Collection* 140, Friday 5 April 1695.

40. *General Remark on Trade* 213, Monday 7 July 1707. Part of Povey's business was in insurance and he claimed to use the profits from his paper for charitable purposes.

41. The text of many of the advertisements for maps which appeared in the *Gazette* and an account of the publishers appear in Sarah Tyacke, *London Map-sellers, 1660–1720* (Tring: Map Collector Publications Ltd., 1978).

42. *LG* 814, Monday 8 Sept. 1673. For a comparable advertisement in which "The New Sucking-Worm Engine" had been successfully used to fight a fire near Cheapside in London, *Collection* 75, Friday 5 Jan. 1694.

43. *Tatler* 224, Thursday 14 Sept. 1710.

Constructing the Frameworks of Desire: How Newspapers Sold Books in the Seventeenth and Eighteenth Centuries

CHRISTINE FERDINAND

When Roman booksellers wanted to capture their readers' attention, they used what materials they had to hand. Literally. Horace complains about the treatment his own works received at the grubby hands of the common reader:

> I want no stall [taberna] or pillar to have my little works [libellos], so that the hands of the crowd – & Hermogenes Tigellius – may sweat over them.[1]

Martial, writing later, was more enthusiastic:

> There is a shop opposite Caesar's forum with
> its doorposts from top to bottom bearing
> advertisements [*scriptis*], so that you can in a moment read
> through the list of poets.[2]

Though by no means outdated, the simplicity of the early booksellers' strategies had its limits. The books evidently served to promote themselves, arranged on bookstalls or in lists attached to the posts adjacent. Martial's vignette of the shop's posts festooned with advertisements fits with the public context Armando Petrucci has described of every available space in Rome covered with writing of one sort or another.[3] In particular, Martial suggests a market of knowledgeable readers who already knew what they wanted and where to look for it, and who would have been ready to respond to the names of the authors posted. Horace probably describes a similar group of readers, but with the gloss of satire. Hermogenes Tigellius can stand for the reader today who is forever "just looking," who would surreptitiously read a book in the shop, but not buy it.

The information required by these particular consumers might have been straightforward – little more than lists of authors and titles, the forerunners of real title pages, or a glimpse of the books available for purchase in one

Christine Ferdinand, Magdalen College, Oxford

form or another – but it could none the less be effective encouragement, whether for immediate sale of a book or for copying on demand. This relationship between bookseller and customer, though commercial, was very direct.

The trade in books obviously goes back much further, to the Greeks and beyond, but evidence of its advertising is indirect. It is known that books (in rolls, and later in codex form, developed from writing tablets by the Romans[4]) were exported from Athens to markets over the Black Sea, and it is reported that Socrates was readily able to locate and purchase Anaxagoras' writings after he had heard a reading from them.[5] Both these examples suggest the possibility of some form of advertising, as well as the networks of tradespeople, authors, and consumers that underpin book-trade economics.

Advertisements for books have therefore probably existed for nearly as long as books themselves. Strategies for promoting them have always depended on a number of factors that were generally the same for the Romans as they were for booksellers in the seventeenth and eighteenth centuries: the actual market and the potential market for reading material – both of which were naturally connected with levels of literacy – the drive and the means to expand that market, and the technologies available.

The tradition of putting up advertisements for books outside booksellers' shops was an enduring one that, more than a millennium later, happily survived the arrival of print. Indeed, the new technology encouraged marketing and distribution on a scale unknown before, almost unlimited, since any number of advertisements, followed by the books themselves, could be produced and sent wherever the book-trade networks reached. Nevertheless, it is important to remember that a context of interdependent management practices, economics, and communications within which the new print trade operated, had long been in place.

As proper title pages for books developed, and certainly by the end of the sixteenth century, it became common to print extra copies that could double as advertisements, a logical refinement on the handwritten notice posted on the bookseller's doorpost. A modern title page could provide much of the information necessary to form a decision to purchase: the title of the book, the author's name, where it might be bought or ordered, even the price. And it could be sent out before publication. R.B. McKerrow has collected early literary allusions to the practice, from Thomas Nashe's *Terrors of the Night* in 1594 (where he complains of readers who "*piteouslie torment Title Pages on euerie poast*"[6]) to Ben Jonson's *Epigram III* "To my Booke-seller" (1616):[7]

> Thou, that mak'st gaine thy end, and wisely well,
> > Call'st a booke good, or bad, as it doth sell,
> Vse mine so, too: I giue thee leaue. But craue

> For lucks sake, it thus much fauour haue,
> To lye vpon thy stall, till it be sought;
>   Not offer'd, as it made sute to be bought;
> Nor haue my title-leafe on posts, or walls,
>   Or in cleft-sticks, aduanced to make calls
> For termers, or some clarke-like seruing-man,
>   Who scarse can spell th'hard names: whoe knight less can.
> If, without these vile arts, it will not sell,
>   Send it to *Bucklers-bury*, there 'twill, well.[8]

The strategy was more prosaically described in one of the periodicals in 1682: "*It being usual and long-accustomed for* Book-binders *Servants on Saturday-nights, to Post up the Titles of such Books as their Masters have to Bind, and which are to be Publisht in the beginning of the week following.*"[9] This report in the *Impartial Protestant Mercury* goes on to the real point of the article, how two apprentices were accosted by a surgeon at one in the morning after they had put up notices for the controversial *Right of the Kingdom, or Customs of our Ancestors*, printed by Richard Baldwin. The surgeon was offended, and the encounter became newsworthy when a fistfight ensued and the combatants were brought before a magistrate.

That title pages often served this double duty – as advertisement, as well as part of a book's preliminary matter – sometimes encouraged the booksellers to use more extravagant language and include more details about the book's contents. This was a natural selling strategy, for the title page advertisement, especially when separated from its text, had to give the buyer enough information to make purchase seem an attractive option. So one finds, for example, the beguiling language of the Shakespearean title page ("*The most excellent Historie of the* Merchant of Venice"). This led to what H.S. Bennet calls "the wildest filling up of the title-page with overemphatic statements, calculated to catch the eye of the passer by,"[10] and then to title pages that could practically have doubled as comprehensive tables of contents. Booksellers were never bound to follow any one method of course, and title pages were also styled according to other traditions relating to genre, format, and intended readership: title pages for the classics and verse, for example, were usually the simplest in design.

The distribution of title page advertisements must have been effective, for the custom was still going strong in the eighteenth century. The bookseller Charles Rivington, writing to the Secretary for the Society for the Encouragement of Learning in 1740, advised that "If the Society order 2 or 300 single titles of every Book they publish, to be printed in order to disperse thro' the Town and in the Country; It will be of advantage to the sale, and is what I always do in my own Books."[11] The practice remained a familiar part of the literary tradition too, with, for example, Pope's description of "Curl's chaste press, and Lintot's rubric posts" in the *Dunciad* (I. 40). Many examples of the production of title pages for separate distribution are recorded in the ledger of the eighteenth-century printer, Charles Ackers.[12]

There were, of course, other advertising strategies available to the bookseller and his customers. Word of mouth was important, from the earliest times to this day. Hawkers still cried broadsides, pamphlets, and books in the streets, and book fairs attracted book buyers of all kinds. Later on, printed prospectuses joined title pages and posters to advertise the publication of new works, or at least the intention to publish them. Auction catalogues invited ordinary customers to consider purchases from whole libraries of second-hand books, trade-sale catalogues encouraged colleagues in the book trade to acquire shares in copyrights or remaindered stock, and catalogues advertised books available at the Frankfurt book fairs.[13] Individual readers were targeted by lists of books inserted at the end of the volume they had just purchased. But, beginning in the seventeenth century, advertising – in particular the advertising of books – was to become an important function of the new serial publications.

The natural links that were being forged between the English book trade and the owners of the periodicals that began to spring up early in the seventeenth century are evident to anyone who looks through many imprints. The people printing, publishing, and selling the books were quite logically the very ones who saw that there were opportunities in publishing news and essays on a periodical basis. Among those who took advantage of the opportunities offered by the new media was Edward Allde, who printed ballads and later the works of Thomas Dekker and Christopher Marlow; he also printed the periodical *Newes from Turkie and Poland* – among others.[14] Nathaniel Butter and Nicholas Bourne were the publishers satirized in Ben Jonson's *Staple of News* in 1626 for their provision of "pamphlets of *Newes*, set out euery Saturday, but made all at home, & no syllable of truth in them";[15] Butter regularly entered books in the Stationers' Company registers (most notably as the publisher of the 1608 edition of *King Lear*), and we know Bourne was assigned the copyrights in a number of theological books that his former master, Cuthbert Burby, had owned. Bernard Alsop is another: he is associated with a number of news serials, but, like Allde, also printed dramatic works. Diversified interests in books, periodicals, job-printing, and perhaps medicines, kept many businesses afloat.

It took the book trade a while to discover the full potential of the periodicals they had invested in, but they were quick to see that periodicals offered advantages. Not everyone who passed a bookseller's stall could read. But nearly everyone who bought a printed paper could, so here was a chance to appeal to a better defined market. Targeting the market like this was an advance on the simple posted broadside, and so was using a vehicle that appeared with such regularity. Clustering advertisements for the same book or books was one new strategy offered by the periodicals. As early as 1657 the proprietors of a new periodical for "The Offices of Public Advice newly set up in Several Places in London and Westminster" offered rates for numbers of advertisements for the same item: The fee would be "to print each advice so entered four weekes together in the same book," the "book" being the periodical itself.[16] Repeating the same advertisement several times for a set fee had obvious marketing advantages, in that the product could be brought to the attention of an irregular readership, and at the same time become more familiar to a regular one. There were certain practical advantages too, for the printer could set up the type for an advertisement and leave it standing for as long as it was current. Repetitive advertising in newspapers, magazines, and journals is still with us.

More accurate market targeting and more efficient use of the periodical advertisement clearly were refinements. Yet for the most part the book advertisements in the early English periodicals were not in themselves any more sophisticated than their hand-written posted predecessors. Examples can be found throughout the seventeenth century. For the earliest, one need only read through Joseph Frank's *The Beginnings of the English Newspaper*, or Folke Dahl's *Bibliography of English Corantos and Periodical Newsbooks*: in September 1624, Butter and Bourne, in their *Continuation of the Weekly News*, suggest that a map of Breda would be available within the week – no price is mentioned, but presumably it was to be available for purchase then with the newsbook.[17] This seems to be the first recorded advertisement for printed material. There are other examples in the same periodical. It is not surprising to find that they are usually for books produced by Butter and Bourne. In the 1640s, the *Perfect Diurnall* became the leading advertiser, carrying more than any other weekly, for a fee to the booksellers of 6d. each. It ran the first medical advertisement, one that suggested apples and frankincense as a remedy, and up to three book notices an issue.

Joad Raymond has reproduced a number of the more unusual advertisements in his anthology of newsbooks, but only one of those is for a book, which appeared in 1649. It is a one-liner of great simplicity: "At the brazen Serpent in *Pauls* Church-yard, is to be sold a new book, of the beauty of Providence, very usefull to support the hart of Gods people these trying times."[18] That's it. It is true that the language of this advertisement has an almost modern transcendent quality about it, for it seems to look beyond the book itself to what owning the book can do for its readers: it promises to support and lift up its readers in those regicidal times. But in doing so, it neglects some practical marketing information. The author is unidentified, and even the exact title is uncertain. It is impossible, without examining the item in question, to know if this was a little book or a big one, a cheap or an expensive one. The publisher of the book is unnamed too, although one might have expected that to be either John Clowes or Robert Ibbitson, the booksellers named in the imprint of the *Perfect Occurrences*, the periodical in which this advertisement appeared. Instead, the only clue is that the book is to be sold at the Brazen Serpent in St Paul's (just enough information for a reader to place an order), not an address ever connected with Clowes or Ibbitson. Rather the tenants there in the 1640s were Robert Dawlman and Samuel Gellibrand, who specialized in theological books, and it was almost certainly they who were selling this priceless and heartwarming publication.[19] Gellibrand incidentally was associated with other periodical publications, but evidently not with *Perfect Occurrences*. This suggests that Clowes and Ibbitson, if nothing else, were branching out to advertise books for other booksellers. This must be a cautious suggestion, for the exact ownership of seventeenth- and eighteenth-century serials is never transparent and often complicated.

Within a few decades of this example the booksellers were using printed trade periodicals to advertise amongst themselves. This was a new development, but one aimed more at the wholesale than the retail trade. Robert Clavell proposed taking in his bookseller colleagues' announcements for the *Term Catalogues* in 1669, suggesting payment in kind ("for every Book inserted in my Catalogue of above 8 shillings, one Book in Quires").[20] As Graham Pollard has noted, the *Term Catalogues* quote the prices for almost all the books listed for their first few years (to 1671), but thereafter books with prices were in proportional decline, to less than half after 1682 – a curious phenomenon that goes counter to the trend to include the prices in other book advertising.[21] There were even two rival trade advertising serials in 1680, both of them called the *City Mercury* in a marketing strategy that is difficult to fathom now.

By 1688 something like twenty-two periodicals circulated, including ten newspapers, a quarto newsbook called *Modern History*, two trade papers (if *Bibliotheca Universalis*, which seems to exist in one number only, is counted), and official publications like the *Bills of Mortality*.[22] There were advertisements for books in both the authorized newspapers, the *London Gazette* and *Publick Occurrences*, but only three of the other eight 1688 newspapers – the *English Currant*, *London Mercury*, and *Universal Intelligence* – carried any book advertising. *Poor Robin's Publick & Private Occurrences* evidently invited advertisements, but failed to elicit anything serious.[23] Typical of *Poor Robin*, is one for "Pillulae Morbiferae," an antidote for fleas that was supposed to be forced down their little throats. Perhaps it lacked appeal for the booksellers, but the notice for these pills suggests the extravagant language that was to become standard for medical claims in the eighteenth and nineteenth centuries.

Book advertising in the early newspapers was a more serious, prosaic business, limited as much by the demands of finite column space as by anything else. Most provided rather more information than the mid-seventeenth-century example cited. Indeed, the basic text was usually lifted straight from title pages, that is from a form the booksellers and their customers had come to know well. A title page outside a bookseller's shop could readily appeal to his local retail customers, who were always able to stop in to discover further information about price, binding, and date of publication. But a title page's minimal marketing information (even though couched in language that was effusive and alluring) was not always enough to convince far-flung newspaper readers and potential book customers. More information was added, enough to allow readers to place an order from a distance: the price, the format, style of type, binding options, and the date of publication became increasingly important elements of the book advertisement. Curious as it may seem now, the author's name was often less significant than the subject matter.

This advertisement, with some slight adjustments, appeared in both the *London Gazette* and *Publick Occurrences* 1688: "To Morrw [*sic*] being *Friday* the 2d of *March*, will be published a Book, Entituled, The Legality of the Court held by His Majesties Ecclesiastical Commissioners Defended. Their Proceedings no Argument against taking off Penal Laws and Tests. Sold by Richard Janeway in Queen's-Head-Alley in Pater Noster Row. Price 6d."[24] The main selling points here must be topicality and timeliness. The bookseller does not think it important for readers to know that the author is the controversial Henry Care (indeed, even Care would have seen that that information might reduce the book's chances), nor that the volume is published in quarto format. The title here is more or less the same as that found on the book's actual title page, but the imprint in the advertisement contains only the directions necessary for sales. The title page gives Janeway credit for printing the book too, but that is information irrelevant to this newspaper notice. The amount of information additional to that on most title pages varied from advertisement to advertisement, although obviously for ordering at a distance it was always important to include the names and addresses of the booksellers from whom the book could be purchased – whether or not the title page gave them. The rhetoric of such advertising remained a fairly simple one.

The conventions of another book-advertising medium, the prospectus, were more sophisticated, for they were constructed to persuade readers to invest in a publication that had not yet seen the light of day. The Bodleian Library's John Johnson collection preserves a number of seventeenth-century prospectuses. This one for a folio volume of Thomas Manton's sermons is not untypical:[25] "PROPOSALS *Concerning the Printing a*

Volume of Elaborate SERMONS upon the One hundred and nineteenth Psalm. *Preached in his life-time by that eminently Learned and Judicious Divine*, Thomas Manton, *D.D. and now from his own Manuscripts carefully perused by Dr.* William Bates, *&c. for the Press.*" The volume's backers – booksellers Thomas Parkhurst, Jonathan Robinson, Brabazon Aylmer, and Benjamin Alsop – go on to outline seven engaging points. (1) The volume will be printed on more than 300 sheets of the same quality and in the same style of type as the prospectus itself. (2) The publishers *"rationally hope* to finish the Work by *Midsummer-Term* next; In order to which, *Four Presses* shall be constantly employed in the Service." (3) The volume, complete and in quires, will be delivered for only 10*s*. down, 14*s*. on delivery. (4) Those who buy six copies can have the seventh free. (5) Money back if the subscription fails. (6) The project can be completed on schedule only if funds allow it: the publishers are depending on the subscribers. (7) As a final inducement: "That it may not appear we design the Publick benefit, we must signifie to all persons, That though for the invitation of Subscribers, we require no more than Four and twenty shillings; yet others must not expect it at less than Twenty seven shillings and six pence in quires." Everything any sensible reader could want is here: the text is by a distinguished and popular Presbyterian preacher, carefully edited by William Bates, himself called the "silver-tongued" divine. It was an investment that came with a significantly lower price and certain money-back guarantees for subscribers, and one that would most likely (*rationally*) meet its schedule.

It was not long before the language of the prospectus, with its greater attention to detail and persuasive strategies, became an element of many periodical advertisements for books. More in this developing spirit is an advertisement in the *London Gazette* on 28 May 1688 for the second edition of Edward Bulstrode's *Reports*.[26] The book's "undertakers" – booksellers Thomas Basset, Thomas Dring, Charles Harper, Samuel Keble, Matthew Wotton, William Crooke, Thomas Sawbridge, John Place, and J. Harrison – offer compelling reasons for embarking on this new edition: the first edition is difficult to find, and even if copies could be found they are expensive at 50*s*. Readers willing to subscribe to the new undertaking by 7 July 1688 can reserve a copy in quires for 10*s*. down, 10*s*. on receipt. Those slower off the mark can have their copies for 10*s*. more, although that sum will also buy a binding for the *Reports*. Or Virgil's *Opera*, advertised in the *Gazette* of 13 February 1688: it is "Newly Reprinted from the best Edition ... the Text being printed on a Fair Roman Character ... the most Useful and Compleat Edition ever yet published." Thomas Dring and Abel Swalle offered all this for only 7*s*. By the end of the seventeenth century there is certainly evidence of a greater degree of subtlety and complexity both in newspaper advertisements for books aimed at the reading public and in the trade publications. The serials trade was also beginning to see that it was worth finding the space for longer advertisements.

By the beginning of the eighteenth century probably the most important lesson the book and newspaper trade had learned was that periodical advertisements of any kind were profitable. This concern underlines the interdependence of books and periodicals: it is probably fair to say that the success of a periodical came to depend more and more on how much advertising income it was able to generate, while the sales of books (and, it follows, of other products and services) often came to depend on how well and how extensively their proprietors made use of the advertising media, especially periodicals. Documentary accounts of seventeenth-century periodicals are relatively rare, but advertising always figures in those still extant. Various papers setting out the *London Gazette*'s income for Lord Middleton, Secretary of State, in 1684, for example, suggested that if 1,800 copies were printed and sold each day, the newspaper would bring in £780 annually. On top of that, "Suppose þᵉ Advertisements be six each day it is 6*l* a week and in 52 weeks is 312:0:0."[27] That gives a total of £1,092, which would still leave a sizeable profit after expenses.

The sheer volume of periodical advertisements at the turn of the century is suggested in the printer Daniel Pratt's patriotic petition to suppress certain periodicals. His justification is that "there are now Several printers, who print, Ten or twelve thousand farthing papers and others Daily and Weekly and in Every of them take in and insert Advertisements, to the Great Detriment of his Majestys Revenue and to the fair Traders."[28] The accelerating rise of the book advertisement in three periodicals during the last few years of the seventeenth century has been charted by R.B. Walker: in 1696, just after the lapse of the Printing Act, the *London Gazette* carried 56 advertisements for books, against a total of 203 (28 per cent); in 1700 the total was 79 of 240 (33 per cent). The *Post Boy* more than doubled its book ads in the same years, from 98 of a total 187 (52 per cent) to 200 of 360 (56 per cent), while the *Flying Post* went from 50 book ads of a total 126 (40 per cent) to 178 of 375 (47 per cent).[29]

Periodical advertising of all kinds continued to increase from those relatively high levels at the end of the seventeenth through most of the eighteenth century, despite the introduction of a hefty advertising duty of 1*s*. in 1712 (10 Anne c. 18) that was increased in 1757 and 1780.[30] Moving to the youthful provincial newspaper press, advertisements in one paper, the *Salisbury Journal*, started with a first annual total in 1737 of just over 200 advertisements, of which more than half were for books; by the 1750s there were more than 1,000 advertisements printed in the paper each year; the figure topped 3,000 in 1768; and there were nearly 3,400 in 1770.[31]

No serious book marketing exercise could afford to ignore the periodicals. There is some evidence in surviving records of the value placed on the link between the book and newspaper trades. One good example comes from the minute books of an SPCK meeting to decide how their publications might best be marketed. A committee meeting on 24 May 1716 discussed Ostervald's *Arguments and Observations on the Old Testament* in the wake of an earlier meeting that had found weaknesses in the advertising campaign:

> It was reported from the Committee that Mr. Downing had inform'd them that Mr. Ostervald's *Arguments* had been twice advertis'd in the Evening Post, twice in the St. James's Evening Post, and twice in the Post Boy; and that as soon as the Holydays are over he will advertise in the Post Man, but that he had not put it in the Gazzete [*sic*] because it could not be done under 11. Shillings which will publish 3. advertisements in other papers.[32]

The economic success of advertisements was an incentive for publishers to develop a fuller range of strategies to exploit the periodical media. They experimented with typography and language, placement and format. Differentiated segments of the reading markets were approached, and book sales were aimed at more specific audiences defined by expertise, sex, occupation, or wealth. Possibly the most innovative development in eighteenth-century advertising was in the marriage of the weekly periodical press with books issued in inexpensive weekly parts.

Although periodical book advertisements were not illustrated in any conventional sense in the seventeenth and eighteenth centuries – that was to come later with the development of technology for cheap picture production and printing – newspaper printers showed real genius in their use of type, not just for books, but for all kinds of notices. Caps and small caps, italic, and roman type in various sizes were all employed. So were little pointing hands, asterisks, and daggers. Type rules were used to separate columns as well as advertisements from the news itself (although sometimes they were intermingled). These ingenious decorations were so much evident that Sir Richard Steele's *Guardian* could confidently poke fun at the practice. "Nestor Ironside" wrote in with some helpful suggestions:

To the PRINTER.

SIR,

I Have frequently taken great Satisfaction in hearing the Composures of *Nicolino Haym*, a Man of great Merit and Skill in his Profession, accompanied with so much Modesty, that he loses the Force which our Affectation of Foreigners might have towards his

Advancement, and is, by his Deference and Respect to us, under the same Disadvantage as if he were born among us; therefore I direct you to insert his *Advertisement* with all the Stars, Daggers, Hands, Turn'd Comma's and *Nota Bene's* which you have in the House, and to omit no Variation of Letter, by way of Capital, Small Capital, Italick, or any other recommendatory Artifice in Printing, which I have privately ordered you to use from time to time to set off my own Writings.

NESTOR IRONSIDE.[33]

The letter was published on 16 April 1713. The next day's *Guardian* brought more suggestions: for decoration with *"Two Line Great Primmer, Two Line English, Double Pica, Paragon, Great Primmer, English, Pica, Small Pica, Long Primmer, Brevier, Nonpareil* and *Pearl* Letters," all to be placed "in an Island of *Stars, Daggers, Double Daggers, Crosses,* &c." Related practical measures included reduction in type sizes to accommodate the growing number of income-earning advertisements, and increases in the number of columns per page from two to three to four to assist readers with the smaller type. These adjustments were always presented as improvements.

Subterfuge was employed in other tactics to turn the reader's tentative wish into a well-defined need. Advertisements were sometimes hidden in the news, or casually linked to a topical event. For example, a report of the attack and conquest of Oczakow in the *Salisbury Journal* news section of 5 September 1737 was followed by the observation that "An exact Account is printing." Thomas Bowles's *Compendious and Rational Institution of the Latin Tongue* a few years later was announced with a disingenuous "We hear from Oxford, that there is just published ..." Benjamin Collins, the *Journal*'s proprietor, knew what he was doing here, for he was one of the provincial booksellers from whom Bowles's book could be purchased. The little six-penny book, *The Hampshire Wonder; or the Groaning Tree*, followed some time after the groaning tree had figured in its own news story. Separate printed accounts of more interesting trials, gallows confessions, or the libretti to locally staged musical events were often offered for sale immediately after reports of them appeared in the newspapers. This was as close as the eighteenth century got to the subliminal marketing message.

Occasionally, though, the advertisement was in startlingly full view, as if the idea were to surprise consumers into the knowledge that, after all, they really did need to own a particular book. Readers could not help but notice the advertisements placed in the normally empty margins of a newspaper, especially when they were printed at right-angles to the rest of the text. Printing outside the margins meant extra work for the printer though, and was a rarely used device.

The language of book advertisements had the same general aim, to create the right conditions for buying. In the eighteenth century, considerable effort went into finding the words to make products irresistible, particularly in the medical world, where something like name-brand recognition was clearly developing in nationally advertised products like Daffy's Elixir, Hooper's Female Pills, Dr James's Fever Powders, and Friar's Balsam. The book world was not above trying to make capital from better known names in the trade too – authors and publishers both – and book marketing campaigns were frequently national in scope. But the language that went with books was generally less exuberant than that used to market quack medicines and was varied constantly in more sophisticated attempts to appeal to different sensibilities. For example:

1. To those who would not want to miss an important cultural trend: "near One Thousand having already been disposed of" (*Authentic Account of the Strange Affair of Squires and Canning*, 29 July 1754); "the first two Numbers of this Work are reprinted ... near two Thousand Subscribers" (*Travels of the Late Charles Thompson*, 18 October 1743); "more than 5000 having been sold off in a few months" (Sarah Jackson's *Director; or, Young Woman's Best Companion*, 10 February 1755); "Above 30,000 of the said Book have been sold" (*Introduction to Geography*, 1 January 1739); "to satisfy the earnest Demand of the Publick" the work will be printed at four presses (reminiscent of the proposals for Thomas Martin's *Sermons* – Henry Fielding's *Amelia*, 23 December 1751); "N.B. The first Impression of this Book was printed and sold off since the first of January ..." (the second edition of *Myrtle*, a collection of songs, 12 May 1755).[34]

2. To those who were looking for a bargain: "the largest, cheapest, and best Collection ever publish'd" (*The Lark, The Nightingale*, and *The Syren* collected together to make 1,300 songs, 15 July 1740); "more in Quantity and greater Variety than any Book of the Kind and Price" (*The Gentleman's Magazine*, 14 May 1745).

3. To those who were interested in quality or authenticity: "This work will not be patched up by obscure hackney writers" (*The Critical Review,* 1 March 1756); "As this Work will consist of Original Pieces, every Number will be entered in the Hall Book of the Company of Stationers" (Mark Akenside's *Museum, or Literary and Historical Register*, 14 April 1746); "to prevent the Public being impos'd on by spurious and trifling Accounts" (*The Authentic Tryals of the Several Rebel Officers Who Were Executed for High Treason*, 11 August 1746); "such Noblemen and Gentlemen as have subscribed to the Author" (*Don Quixote*, printed on Royal paper, 7 April 1755).

4. To those who wanted to be up-to-date: "to all who have Lands overflowed by the late Inundations" (a new letter by John Stevenson, to be supplied free with the next issue of the *Salisbury Journal*, 23 February 1756); *"Just imported"* (Rousseau's *Nouvelle Heloise*, 5 January 1761); the countless advertisements that begin "Just published" or "This day is published."

5. To those who could be defined by age, sex, or station: "for all good Boys and Girls" (*Nurse Truelove's Christmas Box*, 16 April 1750), "entertaining Books with Cuts for the Instruction and Amusement of the Youth of both Sexes" (*New History of England*, 2 March 1747); *"for Amusement of Children Three foot high"* (*Collection of Pretty Poems*, by T. Tagg, 24 May 1756); *"for the Use and Improvment of ... Those who have not had the Benefit of a Learned Education"* (*New, Comprehensive and Universal English Dictionary* compiled by Daniel Bellamy, 16 April 1764).

6. To those who wanted to be part of the book: "having engaged several Ingenious and Learned Gentlemen to settle the Geography ... of GREAT-BRITAIN and IRELAND, ... begs the Favour of his Friends to transmit him an Account of the several Towns and Places in the Neighbourhood where they reside" (12 January 1756).

Wiles notes publication in fascicules (also called numbers or parts) from as early as 1678, when Joseph Moxon's *Mechanick Exercises* began to be issued in monthly numbers.[35] Yet it was not until the 1730s that booksellers designed advertising campaigns that were perfectly in tune with the periodical press – especially the weekly provincial press. They produced books in inexpensive parts that could be delivered by the very newsmen who were making the weekly newspaper rounds. This was an effective technique for the country, where potential customers were more scattered than their London counterparts, but had access to the relatively sophisticated networks established by the weekly newspaper trade. The readers got a (usually) free delivery service in return for purchasing fascicules as they were issued. The booksellers were quite explicit about what they had in mind: a notice in the *Penny London Post* for the *Circle of the Sciences*, a series published for children by John Newbery and Benjamin Collins, points out that "This work is in great Forwardness, and for the Sake of those who can't afford to lay out much Money at a Time will be published in little Volumes, bound, at Six-pence each."[36] The theory was that readers would commit themselves to the system, would not notice the mounting cost, and would always find it less trouble to continue than to turn back. These same principles are the basis of today's Book of the Month Club.

It is clear that book advertising was profitable, at least for the periodical trade, but it is difficult to gauge how persuasive it was. Figures for surviving titles compiled from the *English Short-Title Catalogue* are suggestive, especially in the lists of current holdings recorded for each title, but they say little about how many copies of each may have been bought by contemporaries.[37] There is no question that book production increased from the seventeenth to the eighteenth century, and corroborating studies have shown that book ownership was gaining ground at the same time. In one study Lorna Weatherill recorded that from 1675 to 1725 the appearance of books in probate records increased from 17 to 56 per cent in London, from 23 to 30 per cent in her "Major Town" category, from 18 to 42 per cent in "Other Towns", but decreased from 18 to 13 per cent in the "Rural/Village" category. These figures suggest an average rise overall from 18 to 35 per cent.[38] Of course, one can only surmise what role advertising played in that increase. Relating advertising to real production figures is a surer way of calculating how effective an advertising campaign might have been, but unfortunately almost all of the eighteenth-century documentation is missing. The comparisons can seldom be made, but good examples of production runs can be found in ledgers of the printers Charles Ackers, William Bowyer, and William Strahan, and these can be combined with a survey of advertisements in the *Salisbury Journal*. The Ackers ledger also provides evidence of advertising by title page.

The first documentary evidence of John Green's compilation, *A New General Collection of Voyages and Travels: Consisting of the Most Esteemed Relations, Which Have Been Hitherto Published in Any Language*, is an entry in the Ackers ledger of 27 September 1743 for printing 1,000 copies of a proposal. Several more editions of the proposal were printed: 7,500 copies to be stitched into the *London Magazine* of 1 October 1743 (7,500 was the normal edition size at this time for the *London Magazine*); editions of 1,000 and 2,000 on 4 and 7 October; 12,000 regular proposals and 250 to be pasted on boards on 27 October; and so on to 35,000 proposals with another 250 for pasting on boards on 25 November 1743.[39] The link here between the *London Magazine* and the *Voyages and Travels* was a perfectly practical one, for Thomas Astley published both. Clearly he felt that a large investment in advertising would help protect and develop his investment in the part-book.

The *Salisbury Journal* campaign began on 1 November 1743, about a month after the first proposals were issued. The date of this first newspaper advertisement is interesting in itself, for it pre-dates by a month or two the earliest advertising (in the *Scots Magazine* of December 1743) noted by R.M. Wiles.[40] The timing probably had something to do with the close relationship between the proprietor of the *Salisbury Journal*, Benjamin Collins, and his colleague, the said Thomas Astley. The provincial newspaper advertisement was clearly pre-publication, for it was in fact an invitation to subscribe through Collins or his former apprentice, Richard Baldwin. The compilation was planned for four volumes quarto, to be issued in 164 weekly numbers of either three sheets each, or two sheets and a map, to be sold for 6*d.* each. A copy of the Royal Privilege and Licence to publish by subscription was included. Two weeks later (15 November 1743), most of the last page of the *Salisbury Journal* was given over to proposals for the project; this was followed by an announcement that the first number would be published on Saturday 3 December. Thereafter, notices of different numbers appeared fairly regularly through mid-1744 and then with less and less frequency until the beginning of 1746. This was a serious marketing venture, incorporating proposals printed in vast numbers, poster boards, and a periodical advertising campaign, backed up by a network to deliver the parts of the book on a regular basis.

How did the *Voyages and Travels* fare? Astley had calculated a relatively modest edition, for the Ackers ledger records printing 1,750 copies of the first sheet (signature B) of the first number. This evidently did not meet demand, and this first sheet was reprinted twice, once to produce another 350 copies, and then another 1,000, for a total of 3,100. Two thousand copies of the next two sheets (signatures C and D, that is the remainder of the first number) were printed at first; they were reprinted in 1,100 copies to make up the full edition of 3,100. With numbers 2 and 3 the edition size slipped to 3,000, and then to 2,500 for numbers 4 to 33 (that is to the end of Volume One). By the time the last parts of Volume Three were printed, the edition size was 1,500, where it remained to the completion of Volume Four with number 162, suggesting that something like 1,500 subscribers held on until the last fascicule. In addition to the normal print runs, the ledgers record that 500 extra copies of the first two sheets of number 26 had to be printed, as well as 2,250 copies of a cancelled leaf in number 58.[41] An edition of 1,500 might seem modest in light of the investment in advertising, but in fact that could have produced a sizeable return for the publisher.

The *Voyages and Travels* was completed in four volumes. There were a total of 162 quarto numbers to be purchased to make up the set – not counting a separately printed index and the prelims to each volume. Six pence a week might not seem like much at the outset (that was part of the strategy of course), but that amounted to £4.12*s.* by the time all the numbers had been paid for. This was definitely at the upper end of the scale for travel books, and of course the owner had to pay for binding on top of that. Although larger editions of the first numbers were selling initially, the final production figures settled at 1,500, and it seems reasonable to use that figure to calculate Astley's returns. They were very good: £6,900 for 1,500 162-number sets. Against that can be set what information about costs we have from the Ackers ledger. Astley paid Ackers £24.16s. for printing advertising material and £753.10s.6d. for printing the numbers themselves. This does not include paper costs (part of which seems to have been absorbed in Astley's *London Magazine* accounts with Ackers), nor the costs of an advertising campaign in the periodicals, neither of which can now be ascertained. Nevertheless, these figures suggest that a number-book strategy could easily pay dividends. Figures for the *Salisbury Journal* bear this out: in the 1740s, for example, more than ten per cent (62 of 549) of the titles separately advertised were for number-books.

There can be little doubt that advertising books in periodicals assisted the reading public to develop the desire for more books. (Connected with that were, of course, the numerous eighteenth-century advertisements for educational establishments, where the reading public might be formed, but that is outside the scope of this discussion.) Book advertisements in the early periodicals were relatively unsophisticated, and naturally borrowed from the long-established advertising traditions, in particular from the simple posted notice. But the strategies became more refined as advertising campaigns were linked to successful book marketing, the language of the new prospectuses was taken on, and, most important, the periodical trade realized how profitable advertisements could be. Selling by the weekly number was one of the most innovative devices the book trade employed to create demand for books: it offered books that appeared to be perfectly affordable to even the very poor, and it offered a regular means of delivering them.

Book advertisements were familiar enough to be satirized in the late seventeenth century. By the mid-eighteenth century book advertisements were so familiar a part of the public consciousness that they could be incorporated into family entertainment. One parlour game involved listing, as if in an advertisement, mock book titles. The language is borrowed from periodicals, although the titles would have been tailored to those present. A list of nineteen "books" recording a family game at Tredegar Park begins:

New Books – July 6 1771 – in the Press and speedily to be published.

1. A Treatise on sociability, hospitality and generosity, by Charles Treago, NB this bound in very small compass. Birmingham type.
2. Johnny St Peera's Rhetorick, penned by the dumb young man.
3. Charles Lanwern's new cyder act, and philosophy, with his epitomes, in folio, of each of his explanations of them. Also his treatise on honesty and good neighbourhood, a very imperfect edition. Apply to Whitson for the explanatory supplement.
4. Priory Charles activity, a very surprising and new performance.

5. A trip to France designed, but unluckily postponed, or Trevethin Johnny not knowing which side his bread was buttered, and quarreling with it. NB Johnny was in danger by his mistake of loosing after the next breaking up of school, a present of upwards of two hundred plumbs, which has for a long time been given him and his father at each return to school.[42]

The ease with which book advertising was accepted into the family here, is perhaps one measure of the success of the cooperative book and newspaper trade in the eighteenth century.

NOTES

I am grateful for the help of Rosamund McGuinness, whose work on music advertising has generally informed this paper.

1. Horace, *Satires*, I. iv: 71–2.
2. Martial, *Epigrams*, I. cxvii: 11–13.
3. Armando Petrucci, *Public Lettering: Script, Power, and Culture*, trans. Linda Lappin (Chicago, IL, and London: University of Chicago Press, 1993), 1.
4. Colin H. Roberts and T.C. Skeat, *The Birth of the Codex* (London: printed for the British Academy by Oxford University Press, 1983).
5. See Rudolph Pfeiffer, *History of Classical Scholarship from the Beginnings to the End of the Hellenistic Age* (Oxford: Clarendon Press, 1968; special edn. for Sandpiper Books, 1998), 28–9.
6. *The Works of Thomas Nashe*, vol.1, ed. Ronald B. McKerrow (London: Sidgwick & Jackson, 1910), 343.
7. Ronald B. McKerrow, *An Introduction to Bibliography for Literary Students* (Oxford: Clarendon Press, 1927), 90 n. 2.
8. C.H. Herford, Percy Simpson, and Evelyn Simpson (eds.), *Ben Jonson*, vol.8 (Oxford: Clarendon Press, 1965), 27–8.
9. *Impartial Protestant Mercury* (10 Jan. 1682).
10. H.S. Bennet, *English Books and Readers, 1558–1603: Being a Study in the History of the Book Trade in the Reign of Elizabeth I* (Cambridge: Cambridge University Press, 1965), 260–61.
11. Letter of 5 Feb. 1740, British Library, Add. MS. 6190, fo. 106.
12. D.F. McKenzie and J.C. Ross (eds.), *A Ledger of Charles Ackers, Printer of* The London Magazine (Oxford: Oxford University Press for the Oxford Bibliographical Society, 1968).
13. Graham Pollard and Albert Ehrmann, *The Distribution of Books by Catalogue from the Invention of Printing to A.D. 1800* (Cambridge: Roxburghe Club, 1965).
14. H.G. Aldis *et al.*, *A Dictionary of Printers and Booksellers in England, Scotland and Ireland, and of Foreign Printers of English Books 1557–1640* (London: Bibliographical Society, 1910), 5–6.
15. *The Staple of Newes*, in *The Workes of Benjamin Jonson: The Second Volume* (London: printed for Richard Meighen, 1640), Prologue, Act iii.
16. Advertised in *Mercurius Publicus* (14 May 1657), *Publick Intelligencer* (18 May 1657). Cited in J.B. Williams, *A History of English Journalism to the Foundations of the* Gazette (London: Longmans, Green, and Co., 1908), 167.
17. Joseph Frank, *The Beginnings of the English Newspaper 1620–1660* (Cambridge, MA: Harvard University Press, 1961), 11; quoted in full, with facsimile reproduction, in Folke Dahl, *A Bibliography of English Corantos and Periodical Newsbooks 1620–1642* (London: Bibliographical Society, 1952), 125 and fig. 4.

18. Joad Raymond (ed.), *Making the News: An Anthology of the Newsbooks of Revolutionary England 1641–1660* (Moreton-in-Marsh: Windrush Press, 1993), 237.

19. Peter M. Blayney, *The Bookshops in Paul's Cross Churchyard* (Bibliographical Society Occasional Papers 5; London: Bibliographical Society, 1990), 21–3.

20. See the discussion of trade advertising in D.F. McKenzie, "Trading Places? England 1689–France 1789," in Haydn T. Mason (ed.), *The Darnton Debate: Books and Revolution in the Eighteenth-Century* (Oxford: Voltaire Foundation, 1998), 14–16.

21. Graham Pollard, Bodleian Library Oxford, MS. Pollard 280, fo. 184.

22. This count is constructed from Carolyn Nelson and Matthew Seccombe (comps.), *British Newspapers and Periodicals 1641–1700: A Short-Title Catalogue of Serials printed in England, Scotland, Ireland, and British America* (New York: Modern Language Association of America, 1987).

23. "Advertisments. *If any person require it, will upon reasonable Terms, be incerted in this paper to be published Weekly, &c. which will be received at the* Brittains *Coffee-house* in Goat-Court, *near* Fleet-Bridge" (26 May 1688).

24. This appeared in the *London Gazette*, 1 March 1688, and in *Publick Occurrences*, with the first phrase omitted, more than a month later (3 April). The book is recorded in Donald Wing (comp.), *Short-Title Catalogue of Books Printed in England, Scotland, Ireland, Wales, and British America and of English Books Printed in Other Countries 1641–1700* (New York: Modern Language Association, 2nd edn. 1994), C527.

25. The prospectus itself is Wing M533, while the book seems to have been published with the title *One Hundred and Ninety Sermons* in 1681 (Wing M526). See John Feather, *Book Prospectuses before 1801 in the John Johnson Collection: A List with Microfiche* (Oxford: Bodleian Library, 1976).

26. Wing B5445.

27. All Souls Oxford, MS 204, fo. 81c.

28. British Library, Add. MSS. 33054 (Newcastle Papers), fo. 189.

29. R.B. Walker, "Advertising in London Newspapers, 1650–1750," *Business History* (1973): 117.

30. The duty on advertising was raised at intervals until 1833, when it was reduced from 3*s*. 6*d* to 1*s*. 6*d*. The tax was abolished in 1853 (16 & 17 Victoria c. 63).

31. C.Y. Ferdinand, "Selling It to the Provinces: News and Commerce round Eighteenth-Century Salisbury," in John Brewer and Roy Porter (eds.), *Consumption and the World of Goods* (London: Routledge, 1993), 393–411.

32. SPCK Minutes, 24 May 1716. The SPCK Archives are currently (October 1998) in transit from SPCK headquarters, Marylebone Road, London to their new home in the Cambridge University Library.

33. John Calhoun Stephens (ed.), *The Guardian* (Lexington, KY: University of Kentucky Press, 1982), 134.

34. All these advertisements appeared in the *Salisbury Journal*; the date of first appearance is given.

35. R.M. Wiles, *Serial Publication in England before 1750* (Cambridge: Cambridge University Press, 1965), Appendix B: "Short-Title Catalogue of Books Published in Fascicules before 1750." An earlier example is the part-publication in 1668 of *Catechetical-Preaching-Exercises* (see D.F. McKenzie, "The London Book Trade in 1668," *Words: Wai-Te-Ata Studies in Literature*, 4 (1974): 86).

36. Quoted in S. Roscoe, *John Newbery and His Successors 1740–1814: A Bibliography* (Wormley, Herts: Five Owls Press, 1973), 73.

37. The most current form of the *English Short-Title Catalogue* (*ESTC*) is the on-line version available through the Research Libraries Information Network (RLIN). This incorporates imprints from 1475 to 1800, including the *Eighteenth-Century Short-Title Catalogue* (also known as the *ESTC*). A CD version of the combined database (London: British Library) is forthcoming.

38. Lorna Weatherill, "The Meaning of Consumer Behaviour in Late Seventeenth- and Early Eighteenth-Century England," in Brewer and Porter (eds.), *Consumption and the World of Goods*, 220, Tables 10.4 and 10.5 .

39. McKenzie and Ross (eds), *Ledger of Charles Ackers*, 168, 180, 231.
40. Wiles, *Serial Publication in England before 1750*, 334–5.
41. McKenzie and Ross (eds.), *Ledger of Charles Ackers*, 245–6.
42. The first refers to Charles Morgan of Tredegar; the second to John Lewis of St Pierre; the third to Charles Van of Llanwern; the fourth to Charles Milborne of Wonastow; and the last to John Hanbury (see Richard Hanbury Tenison, *The Hanburys of Monmouthshire* (1995), 183). Satirical catalogues have a longer history: see, for example, those in *Poems on Affairs of State*, vol. 3 (1704), 432–7.

"Stung into action ...": Medicine, Professionalism, and the News

G.S. ROUSSEAU

> There is no other Method of fixing those Thoughts which arise and
> disappear in the Mind of Man, and transmitting them to the last
> Periods of Time; no other Method of giving permanency to our Ideas,
> and preserving the Knowledge of any particular Person ... Books are
> the legacies that a great Genius leaves to mankind, which are
> delivered down from Generation to Generation.
>
> (Addison on "publication," *Spectator* 166, 10 Sept. 1711)

Just before Christmas 1997 this headline flashed up on the CNN internet as
emerging from New York: "defining what's news is a pricey proposition."
The context was TV news and the tabloids, but the claims in the controversy
brewing were rather more interesting. The headline read: "'The fact that we
package and present the news a little differently than your counterparts does
not alter the fact that we deliver *the* professional news,' said Arthur King
whose King World Productions puts out 'inside Edition' and American
News Media." We deliver *the* news. The lead paragraph continued: "Just
what constitutes news programs has been thrown up for grabs in a prelude
to a TV ratings system of news programs resembling the movie industry
through ranking of seventeen news programs." The squabble amounted to
issues of packaging professionalism. Could serious news be presented in
alternative ways? How alternative could it be? What is serious news as
distinct from the ephemeral or trivial?

The flash-up may serve to remind academic historians of one persuasion
or another that news and controversy continue to be allied even today. But
the news has also had a long history of involvement with the progress of
knowledge – knowledge especially as truth claims. And in this relation
controversy has been no less contested. The recent history of knowledge,
especially in its scientific realms where fact and fiction, probability and
prediction, play such principal roles, has been dependent upon the news;
and, as the CNN report says, especially upon serious news conveyed in

G.S. Rousseau, De Montfort University

reliable forms. This essay wishes merely to consider the development of scientific news in one narrow category: the birth of a medical press. Other sciences, organic and inorganic, could have been considered. But medicine is perhaps the most fitting of all the sciences for our purposes because it touches so directly on human life: it always has and continues to today. It was also born in our historical era under the most ideological socioeconomic conditions. And, still more emphatically, it developed hand in hand with the rise of newspapers because those who passed its pills and potions owned shares and parts of the early newspapers in which they advertised their panaceas. Indeed, it is hardly going too far to claim that during the eighteenth century daily news and diuretics, politics and pharmacology, especially the economic dimensions of the monopoly on the secret recipe, went hand in hand, adjacent columns in the same broadsides and gazettes.

The signpost or trope in the title – "stung into action" – contains the germ of the author's four-part thesis about (1) news and the developing professions; (2) the crucial role of the history of the infrastructure of professions and the politics of professionalisation; (3) the complex function of eighteenth-century newspapers as agents in, and for, the dissemination of allegedly curative, and usually, "secret" recipes and panaceas; and (4) the creation of a suitable socio-historical context to understand what medical news *was* and how it then developed.[1]

All four points assume *publication* as the essential ingredient of news. That is, that "news" must be "published" for it to become news. More crudely put, in the formulation of Marshall McLuhan, that in some fundamental way the medium *is* the message in the case of news and that information not put into print, or publication, is of another order of news. The philosophical complexity of this requirement has been addressed by other scholars in this volume, and it may be that the history of news studies is not yet sufficiently far advanced to tackle the matter with any degree of certainty. Nevertheless, and in full view of the state of current scholarship, the role of publication as a precondition for news appears – somewhat schematically – in these ways for the four points.

1. All scientific news (including medical news) of which this author is aware in the early modern period thrives on a notion of *publication*. That is, what is contained in memoirs, diaries, letters, travel notes, and so forth may or may not be of interest to readers; however, a scientific press, and certainly a medical press, assumes that publication is the basis of the progress of knowledge leading to truth, and that only the published record of this truth – however small these fragments of truth may be – constitutes the developing science or that which can be known with certainty about the area.

2. If the medical news is construed as some type of truth leading to progress in cure, then the obstacles to this news in the historical period 1650–1800 exceeded its triumphs, as we shall aim to show for a few specific cases.

3. The plan here isolates and identifies three moments when challenge to the obstacles permitted progress to triumph. The price paid for such challenges to authority differed in each case and the penalty itself varied, but in each case the obstacle paved the way to the so-called worthy news that followed, thereby permitting these tentative conclusions.

4. First to ask what medical news was and what obstacles it faced; secondly, what influenced and altered it in the early modern period.[2]

II

The matter about publication is far more complex in relation to the news than it appears. It may be an issue too mundane to be included in Habermas' abstract systems, even when he discusses the print culture of Addison and Steele in *The Public Sphere*. This was a new "Republic of Letters," in Addison's coinage, which thrived on print.

Yet a broad group of early modern historians have good reason to dwell on the word and concept *"publication"* and its nuances.[3] The long eighteenth century seems to have been the pivotal moment. Before then, something need not be "printed" to be "published"; it *could* be printed but need not. This is the basic use of the word "publication" throughout the period of William Cowper and the Gothic novelists, and the sense in which news can be, and indeed is, "published," that is, the sense of being made known and shown abroad, but not necessarily *printed*. Afterwards – in the Victorian period and into our century – there is a counterpoint pattern in which "publication" as something made known does not require print. For example, if someone claimed in Edwardian Edinburgh in 1904 that Mrs Smith has died, one hardly asks for printed confirmation; either her death is true and therefore in the public domain, or false. Public knowledge since the eighteenth century has resided in many domains beyond the printed one; more crucially for the moment, the social construction of the category *publication* impinges everywhere on the case study, below, of the emergence of a medical press, or medical news, despite the unrefined means currently at our disposal to configure publication as a meaningful eighteenth-century category.

Concurrent with this new energy focusing on publication was the growing sense (certainly from the seventeenth century forward) that publication *requires* print. Thus a wide range of dictionary definitions of publication attach to this one when claiming that publication is always "the issuing, or offering to the public, of a book, map ... or other work of which copies are multiplied by writing, printing, or any other process."[4] For Johnson in the *Dictionary* publication is an "act": as he writes, "the act of notifying the world; proclamation."[5] Notification did not require print, as in Johnson's example, selected from religious thought in which the truth of God is "published" to mankind. But for Addison and his *Spectator* ephebes – Steele and the Whig wits – publication *was* print, not merely great books but increasingly ephemeral journalism, and this is the tradition of print as publication that becomes the dominant eighteenth-century mode despite its increasingly controversial associations with trade and profit. "Hearkee / Mr. Sir Robert," a character ironically claims in Samuel Foote's comical play *The Bankrupt* of 1776; "if I understand your meaning at / all, it is, that provided people could be prevented / from publishing, you are willing the press should / be free"[6] – pithily exposing the flaw, even the impossibility, of such a thing.

One can therefore postulate that increasingly down through the eighteenth century print constitutes one of the most solid reference points from which certain knowledge (in the spectrum from probability to likelihood and certainty) and truth claims measure their legitimacy. Michael Warner, the historian of the colonial American period, claims as much in a well-justified metacritique on Habermas:

> At least in the British American colonies, a state of thinking about print appeared in the culture of republicanism according to which it was possible to consume printed goods with an awareness that the same printed goods were being consumed by an indefinite number of others. This awareness came to be built into the meaning of the printed object, to the point that we now consider it simply definitional to speak of printing as "publication." In print, understood this way, one surrendered one's utterance to an audience that was by definition indefinite. Earlier writers might have responded with some anxiety to such mediation or might simply have thought of the speaker-audience relation in different terms. In the eighteenth century the consciousness of an abstract audience became a badge of distinction, a way of claiming a public opinion.[7]

Warner accounts for this transformation as part and parcel of the development of Anglo-American republicanism, claiming that the language of republicanism "was extended to print contexts as a structuring metalanguage."[8] The claim may be true, but it is not republicanism's incursion into language that concerns us here so much as notions of publication in relation to print itself; especially the idea of decoding the view, now taken for granted as almost transhistorical, that print has always been tantamount to publication and publication to print: a simple tautology historically universal. It was not, however, always so in the early modern period, as will be shown.[9]

It may be that this transformative historical moment represented by the long eighteenth century depended on the writer's dramatic conception of herself/himself with or without publication; that is, within or without printed medium. This position seems to be the thrust of the famous Addisonian passage about "the personated Character" viewed in Habermasian contexts. The basis of the Habermasian argument is the homology of print and publication and knowledge. If a developing profession – for example, medicine – wished to gather status, it *had* to publish.[10] Otherwise, it would remain a private rather than public enterprise, an activity for private persons writing unpublished letters to each other no matter how dire the need for medical diagnosis and cure. The historical issue for medical news may then be not so much its publication as its professionalization in the eighteenth century, with print culture as living proof that it was indeed professionalizing. Warner again iterates the general version of this theory in the context of Habermas' defects:

> From the eighteenth century we in the modern West have inherited an understanding of printing as publication, but we now understand a vast range of everyday life as having the reference of publicity. The medium of print is now only a small part of our relation to what we understand as the public, and the fictitious abstraction of the *Spectator* [Addison's] would seem conspicuously out of place in the modern discourse of public icons.[11]

Perhaps so, but we would still have to explain the role publication played in the developing professionalization of medicine then. As historians we might continue to marshal these moments to demonstrate that prior to the development of a medical press, in which certain standards and truth claims could be assumed, much depended on the reader and his or her self-interest. Therefore, the reader of the early medical press must be understood both as a social creature and intellectual mindset. And in this sense the situation *vis-à-vis* the medical press was different from assumptions we take for granted today about habits of reading in relation to knowledge in the public sphere. Some of us who read, for example, the *New York Times* or *Wall Street Journal* think we are reading a world-class newspaper, and in so doing make all sorts of assumptions about the nature of its information and its truth claims despite lingering scepticism. Yet the fundamental mindset we bring to the act of such reading has barely been discussed, even by the major theorists of the public sphere, especially Habermas and his commentators. The riddle of this story, as some medical historians know all too well, is that you could not assume much in, or about, truth and certainty in medicine before the nineteenth century, least of all about the dissemination of its information.[12]

There were obstacles to every group participating in the medical encounter. First was the barbarism of medicine itself. No one needs to be a medical historian to recognize that medicine before approximately 1800 was not merely primitive but that there was little agreement about its diagnoses and therapies. A few internationally known professors in each country defined the norms and rules (Boerhaave in Holland, Richard Mead in England, the Monro brothers in Scotland), and the others followed suit.[13] Squabbles and fracas exploded daily, often comically, but these were the equivalents of our media debates among lawyers and doctors, not the forum where medical knowledge was played out. Closer to the economic heart of these newspapers was the tribe of vendors and apothecaries touting their secret recipes and chemical concoctions.[14] This connection endures as the unresearched dark side of early Georgian papers; and a killing in research would be made, so to speak, by a scholar who could discover ledgers or bank accounts that actually documented these fiscal arrangements. For everywhere in those early papers there was mention of secret pills and potions and their costs of preparation and sale. But their chemical recipes could lawfully be protected in silence just as various stories we consider to be "news" in our time are withheld from the press despite the fiercest efforts of determined journalists. This tension introduced a dynamic that has barely been understood, let alone studied much by historians, because so few of the recipes, or bank accounts, have ever been found: that is, the newspaper's awareness of the source of the recipe and its interest in protecting that secret.[15]

III

All these economic, fiscal, and legal arrangements must be considered in relation to the new health for sale in Georgian Britain and its widespread commodization. As important was the developing role of publication, which lies at the heart of the thesis presented here. The medical news in the unstable public sphere before the end of the eighteenth century was almost entirely dependent on who you were and what your economic interest was. If you were, for example, a quack empiric doctor rather than a licensed physician or surgeon in the 1660s, the first appearance of the *Philosophical Transactions* was hardly news to you, nor were you about to read it. A few years later, when this new publishing organ printed its announcement that blood had been transfused into the veins of a dog, that was not news either. The speculation a few years later, in the 1670s, that the brains of animals and humans might some day be removed and transplanted might have struck the anomalous quack as "news worthy," but not many others.[16] These early readers, and non-readers, of medical news already possessed a sense of what was worthy of publication.

The launching in 1682 of the periodically published *Medicina Curiosa* was news to those doctors looking for medicine's new "truth," as it claimed to offer "a variety of new communications in physick, chirurgery and anatomy," but not to uncertified quacks who made their living by discovering and then writing up, for publication, various panaceas.[17] The many plague remedies advertised in the Restoration press (crude though that press was) make the point in another key, as would Sydenham's scant medical papers of the 1680s, which few unlicensed doctors read.[18]

This state of affairs continued throughout the Restoration more or less unabated and ameliorated by the remarkable culture of toleration fostered in the London coffee-houses, especially in the approximately half-dozen so-called "medical coffee-houses."[19] These were precincts where different points of view could be thrashed out openly; free zones for the open discussion of conflicting ideas about disease and therapy as well as the status of the physician, surgeon, apothecary, and quack. Such proliferating fora for criticism inevitably played a part, however indirectly, in eventually shaping a medical press, although it would be practically impossible to demonstrate rigorous cause and effect in this public Restoration sphere. All aspects of the medical enterprise were thrashed out in the coffee-houses where doctors received their letters and replied to them, as well as conducted business with lower medical orders and met their patient clients. Then, as new medical journals slowly began to appear, the medical events of significance (such as Sydenham's unique attempt to demythologize the mythologies about gout and establish gout once and for all on firm clinical medical footing) were those considered important to (what we would call) research scientists. But such medical events were not "news" to the quacks, apothecaries, and herbalists who prescribed and treated patients, and for whom the disclosure of an authentic chemical recipe was worth much more than any transfusion of blood into human veins or even the transplantation of organs.

But when John Hill (1714–75), for example, an apothecary and collector of natural objects for aristocrats, published his scathing satire on the Royal Society, entitled *Lucina sine concubitu* – Lucina gives birth to a baby without a man – this was considered "news" by all manner of readers.[20] Some part of the novelty resided in Hill's reputation as an uneducated opportunist and parvenu. As much was owing to the public's outrage that he – a young man without credentials – would take on this learned body. Couched as a prose satire in the lineage of Swift and his contemporaries, this work traces the birth of the virgin Lucina without any known father in an attempt to ridicule eighteenth-century biologists known as preformationists. Their belief, satirized widely by experimentalist fiction writer Laurence Sterne in *The Adventures of Tristram Shandy*, was that a "preformed homunculus" or little gentleman exists who is the perfect adult in miniature. Complete in his biological structure and anatomic parts from the time of conception, the homunculus was contained in the mother's womb and barely required the father's fluid to give it life. A sizeable portion of the Fellows of the Royal Society at mid-century gave credence to this preformational biological view – hence the power of Hill's satire to bite them, as well as those who took the opportunity to join in the fray and disparage their opponents, the preformationists. Hill's satire eventually played an important part in "stinging the Society into action." Its trustees, shortly afterwards in the 1750s, tightened up their requirements for the publication of papers in their transactions.[21]

The aftermath of the hilarious Lucina affair made Hill's name a household word, and he thereby continued to create "medical news" throughout the 1750s, generating scandal upon scandal, some disturbing enough to the medical profession to provoke them each time into retaliation. His movements and motives were reported in the dailies and weeklies (which were not medical, of course). And when Hill was publicly caned at Ranelagh in June 1753 by Mountefort Browne, a young town buck who thought Hill had insulted him, the caning was "news" that captured the front page of the London dailies and weeklies because it was the notorious *Hill*.[22] If another, it may have gone unreported. Public canings were routine in Georgian London, but Hill was often reckless: a phenomenon *sui generis*, a "*lusus naturae*" in the creation of one cartoonist, Hill had transgressed all the social boundaries. Unlicensed, unqualified, he nevertheless called himself "the doctor," and through patronage had crossed over class borders. He would have been just as much a candidate for front page coverage in the *medical* press of the day had there been one.

We are still taking stock of diverse contexts for the matter about publication and a developing medical press. In this sense Hill's fifty-plus books and tracts provide just the type of information needed to understand why he had to validate himself so direly in his print culture.[23] Another example makes the case about context (for the medical press) in still another light. In the decade 1756–66 Tobias Smollett's (1721–71) *Critical Review* commented on many of the medical books then published in English.[24] The proliferation of tracts among wrangling physicians was statistically new but did not constitute "news" to the quacks necessarily barred from the College of Physicians. Conversely, monthlies such as the *Gentleman's Magazine* continued to publish medical letters and bizarre case histories ranging from anatomical deformity to wombless women, but these were usually so irate in their reportage that doctors took no notice of them. Yet to the doctors whose books were reviewed, as well as for trained brethren within the medical fraternity, a review in the *Critical Review* was "news," especially depending upon whether it endorsed or damned the work.

To medical writers like Hill and Smollett, "news" was made in Grub Street when, for example, Smollett hired or fired reviewers, as the identity of these writers, however anonymous their writing, became known. By the 1760s a new book reviewer hired by the *Monthly Review* was "news," especially if the writer had previously been writing medical reports and book reviews anonymously for the *Critical Review* or another competitor.[25] For both these periodicals – main outlets for medical writing at mid-century – the editor's original copies containing signed initials after each review survive.[26] The relative merits of anonymous reviews versus signed ones remained a vexed issue in the medical news through the century. A stable press with checks and balances about identity and anonymity might have avoided these pitfalls, but it did not arise until the nineteenth century.

Authentication and verification of medical content represented irrelevant criteria as a basis for "news" if profits and sales were the goal. By mid-century most newspapers ran medical adverts purely on a pay and share in the profits basis. Hence, many medical men who read in 1757 of the launching of *Medical Observations and Inquiries*, which would contain case histories by major medical figures, did not consider the announcement "news." To physicians who beefed up their medical practices by claiming they were on the cutting edge of medical research – here too, not to all – the announcement was news indeed, especially because so many of the "histories" were to be written by recognized authorities. Bishop Berkeley, the philosopher of idealism, had concocted a tar water remedy in the 1740s that sold widely and drove out most competitors within a year.[27] Apothecaries and empirics far and wide remarked on its success in profits. Yet to physicians who construed Berkeley's "universal remedy" in a long line of quack panaceas ranging from Dover's pills and potions to the glut of assafoetida tablets and other tinctures, it hardly constituted "news." The role of print and "publication" in these successes and failures has fallen victim to the chemical ingredients and financial profits garnered.[28]

Andrew Duncan, a Scottish apothecary and vendor, thought he would stir the pot of "medical news" in 1786 (thirty years after the case study below) when launching an Edinburgh-based annual called, familiarly, *Medical Observations*, which cost less than its rivals and claimed to offer better news.[29] He defined the improvement as the diversity of information and speed with which he could assemble it. The volumes appeared annually, which Duncan discovered to be too little time to assemble each issue. In such a short period he thought he could not authenticate the reliability of his information. He wondered whether the case histories had been tampered with and whether the patients were telling the truth. To quacks interested in pushing pills and potions, Duncan's annuals constituted no "news." The secret recipes commanded centre-stage, even to affluent desperate patients willing to try anything. In hindsight, one of the coups of the long eighteenth century was that so many of the financial successes – Ward's pill and drop, James's famed fever powders, Hill's tinctures – never were. This fact had no bearing on their efficacy or therapeutic value, yet everything to do with preservation of the secret for profit.[30]

Few pills or potions made their discoverer more profit than Robert James's fever powders, based on a recipe so secretly guarded that not even the closest relation knew what it contained. This was the Robert James who was a qualified certified doctor who hobnobbed with the cream of his medical brethren despite the quackish nature of his panacea: a universal remedy claiming benefit for every condition. After his death, a battle for the secret lingered for a generation, fought out in Grub Street among the pamphleteers and in the courts. Thus entered publication yet again: first at the time of dispersion of James's original panacea, now to pry open the secret of its chemistry. Public celebrities such as Oliver Goldsmith, John Wesley, and others joined in the scribbling fracas.[31] Widows and children were especially involved in these wrangles and gave testimony about what they had heard or seen. To the physicians in the College the fray hardly constituted "news," although its turns continued to be chronicled in the daily press. The point here pertains especially to the "publication dimension" – the phrase to be emphasized – of these developments.

IV

Eclectically, therefore, we have been marshalling different types of evidence to demonstrate that publication played a major share in defining what constituted "medical news" then. It remains now to summon the role played by obstacle – especially the obstacles to publish and print. For if publication was then the validating card, those who did *not* break into print, like those protecting secret chemical components, were suspect. One body of periodical publications constituting the news explicitly makes this point so plainly that their claim to have been "stung into action" literally highlights this standard about publication and its obstacles.

This was the 1757 launching of *Medical Observations and Inquiries*, a quondam publication of a group of London physicians: young, Scottish, not yet established, mostly in agreement that the College of Physicians had given up on medical research as it had not yet published its own annals.[32] The underlying assumption, again, was that "news" in anything could only

be news if printed. Therefore, if the College was not yet printing its
discoveries, it *had none*. The College's silence, the argument went, was
proof of a backward-looking medical establishment of staid physicians.
Hence the need for this radical medical press of 1757.

Yet what did the new *Observations* amount to? Its early volumes sold
few copies and the print-run was small. Contributors were paid by
publicizing their names rather than in guineas. A modern-style print-cost
analysis is necessary to understand what was at stake in this dissemination
of "medical news" by a rival group and the responses it elicited; responses
that can demonstrate how it laid the foundations in the late eighteenth
century for the *British Medical Journal* (first volume 1799) and the gradual
formation of a controlled British medical news.

The nine-page preface of the first volume of *Medical Observations*
proclaims its rationale: the paradigm itself about "news" and publication. To
render its rhetoric more persuasive, the authors chronicle their progress
from initial assembly to final publication:

> A few years ago, some physicians in London, agreed to meet together
> for their mutual improvement in the practice of their profession. The
> reigning diseases of the season, with the methods of cure that were
> most effectual; new discoveries in physick, either here or abroad, and
> more especially such as they themselves had either made or examined,
> were intended to be the principal topicks of conversation. (iii–iv)

Now enter the public sphere and the route from observation to
proclamation:

> When these meetings had continued a considerable time, some of the
> members became desirous of making the publick partakers of the
> advantages that might be derived from such an association;
> accordingly they, with some other physicians, formed themselves into
> a Society, for collecting and publishing Medical *Observations* and
> *Inquiries*. (iv–v)

The preface's justification includes philosophical and narrative basis but
publication remains the *sine qua non* of the programme:

> The reader will easily comprehend, from this first volume, the nature
> of our plan; which is indeed no other than that recommended by the
> great Lord Bacon; who advises us to revive the Hippocratic method of
> composing narratives of particular cases, in which the nature of the
> disease, the manner of treating it, and the consequences, are to be
> specified: to attempt the cure of those diseases, which, in his opinion,
> have been too boldly pronounced incurable: and lastly to extend our
> inquiries after the powers of particular medicines in the cure of

particular diseases. Agreeable to this rational plan, the Society will proceed to collect and publish such facts and observations as occur to them, and appear conducive to the advancement of medical science. (ix–x)

The plan requires control and selection but novelty – as in "the news" – forms its most solid requirement:

> It is by no means their [the plan of the authors] intention to publish indiscriminately, whatever papers they receive; but to select, for this purpose, such as shall appear of use and importance. All new and useful observations, described with clearness and candour, will be thankfully received, and published when a sufficient number are collected to make a volume: as also, such single cases as tend to confirm or explain, what was before imperfectly known or understood, or from which some new truth may be clearly deduced. (x–xii)

The assumption is that "publication" exists in a particular relation to "useful information"; freezing that information, so to speak, in a printed form into which it should not be placed unless useful by virtue of its truth. Hence:

> those facts and cases, that are either doubtful, or from which it is difficult to derive any useful information, will be reserved till a number of others, sufficient to give them weight and value, shall be collected. Relations of unsuccessful attempts, or even errors in the cure of diseases, often furnish matter of instruction; for which reason, such accounts will be acceptable, and the relator treated with the candour due to a person ingenuous enough to acknowledge a mistake; and his name, if it be desired, shall be concealed. (xi–xii)

But every measure in this regimen of new control, it was said, will be taken to squash private egos: "Hypothetical disquisitions, points of controversy, numerous and needless quotations; in short, whatever has rather a tendency to shew the parts and erudition of the writer, than to advance medical knowledge, will be suppressed" (xi–xii).

Primary in this notion of "news" is the *recording of acts* in medicine and science rather than the idea that the news solidifies activities, that is, that the publishing of "news" is a much lesser act than the worthy one it "publishes." Moreover, the "society" does not state its perceived sense of the longevity of these "case histories." Nor its sense of durability: that is, how long the material will continue to be "news." The style of the articles (see below) is crude: as if they are here today, to be supplanted by others tomorrow. No sense appears of publication as enduring for its own value as literature. The notion is rather that case histories will be published as long as there are patients, each replacing the prior.

This then were the "society's" 1757 ideology and agenda, especially as each touched on method (Baconian empiricism) and purpose: to suppress every form of personal intervention. The latter impinged on form and content, style and presentation, and is more problematic than the editors of the society imagined in 1757. They saw every reason to explain themselves in their prefaces, but none to provide an index. They signed their articles, but protected their patients' confidentiality. And they wrote in a cultivated simplicity in accordance with their edict about vanity and puffery of the self. But their *raison d'etre* – to "sting the College into action" – was the fundamental agenda and was accomplished entirely through publication. The aim was successful and produced results almost thirty years later (1785), again in published form.

V

These aims and tensions of 1757, later on of 1762, 1769 and so forth up to 1784 when volume 6 appeared, produced printed results (direct or indirect) in the form of *Medical Transactions published by the College of Physicians in London*; yet *another* group from either the young turks of 1757 (named in the Appendix), or – as we shall see – the Royal College of Physicians in London in 1785.[33] Some of these different ideologies are glimpsed, although in procrustean fashion, by the analysis of the contents of the first 1757 *Medical Observations*. The first volume contained twenty-nine articles consisting entirely of case histories written by doctors who signed their names and who, despite their nationalities, were mainly resident in London. Approximately a third were Scots without established reputations: a fact not to be ignored.[34] The patients' names were protected: that is, invented names such as Smith or Clark replacing the real ones. Pharmacy, general medicine, and anatomy formed the three main areas of interest in descending order; public health, obstetrics, and a miscellaneous grab-bag the three least, again in descending order. Articles average five to six pages of rather larger type, there being only one or two articles over thirty pages in any volume. The style consists of simple sentences unembellished by rhetoric or simile, and with a minimum of technical language. The readership of these volumes is clearly not limited to physicians or surgeons and the editors have practised what they preached about "the parts and erudition of the writer." The volume bears no trace of individual editors' names.

If the six volumes of *Medical Observations and Inquiries* published between the appearance of the first in 1757 and the last in 1784, when the series ended as the result of the College's response, are analysed, important patterns arise informing the point about publication in relation to "medical news." For example, it is significant that 145 of the 207 articles have no proper noun (name) whatever. Proper names most frequently cited (in descending order) are Hippocrates, Sydenham, Mead, Morgagni, and Galen, indicating that this homage to the Ancients was merely a gesture made by the contributors to gain credibility; rather that the collective group aimed to persuade readers by its knowledge of ancient wisdom (whether they had read what they cited is another matter). Sydenham and Hippocrates are mentioned with almost equal regularity; however, Hippocrates' name crops up in the widest range of articles in terms of subject matter. Sydenham, ranked next, is mentioned in connection with specific subjects (for example, diseases, fevers, conditions, and maladies such as measles). The professional aim of such persuasion – the act of naming as a coded sign language – is transparent. An unknown "society of medicine" whose members had never been admitted to the College, and whose professional interests were for blatant professional reform, could win more adherents by parading its medical education than its pedantry.

Style here verges on the simple, *sans* flourish, allusion, or quotation. Even compared to the least complex of first-person autobiographical narratives of the period (1730–50), the style here lacks even the slightest conscious flourish, as the statistics in the Appendix show. Sentences are short to middling, the language simple enough that anyone educated could understand the patient's case history. Terms are not defined, nor are assumptions interrogated: the implied audience is also professionally medical. Otherwise, these patterns would not have been followed.

The cadre of writers employed is as important for penetrating how the *Medical Observations* then constituted "news through publication." Who were they and how were they recruited? What controls were placed, if any, on the "news" they submitted in these case histories? The 207 articles published over 27 years were written by 119 different male authors. Not one was female and no comment about a gender gap figures anywhere in the six volumes. Of these 119 men, the majority was young, under 40. Only two (John Andre and William Rutty) are known to have been over 50, and three in their forties (George Cleghorn, John Fothergill, and Gowin Knight). The rest were under 40, and many were under 20, several writing as young as the age of 13 (William Watson), 16 (Thomas Cullum), and 17 (Thomas Percival). The largest age cluster by far is in the twenties: too young to have been established, let alone *bona fide* elected members of the College. The authors with the largest number of multiple entries (see the Appendix) are also those who generally became well-known doctors, six eventually elected to the College in London: Fothergill (22 papers), William Hunter (6), Brocklesby (3), Haygarth (3), Whytt (2), Maty (2), although a few never did: Thomas Dickson (7), Macaulay (4), Alexander Russel (6), Henry Thomson (4), a Scottish cousin of the poet-physician James Thomson.[35]

The Scots element is professionally revealing. The London College in the 1750s had few Scots among its members,[36] those who were members often practising in Edinburgh and Glasgow and also members of their local Scottish colleges. The fact in itself is without significance given that few Scots were elected. However, Scottish doctors had flocked to London in considerable numbers since the 1720s, and by the 1740s, when Smollett and James Douglas arrived,[37] they had formed a distinctive and supportive emigré community that remains to be studied in full and for which a massive but scattered annals of primary material survives. Competition between them and the English doctors was evident from the start: the more the Scots infiltrated, the fiercer attempts to bar them from the College became. One wonders whether it was the Scots who founded the original "society" that launched this publication. Could the society have begun as a support group of young emigrés in London who discovered their medical, or quasi-medical, background in common? For not all 119 authors were doctors; many were para-medical and some not at all (that is, not having had any medical training, even at the level of apprentice).

Even if the Scots were less instrumental than this hypothesis would claim, it is clear that the original authors shared professional exclusion from the College, as well as a desire for reform of the "medical news" in an era when a medical press had not yet emerged. This last matter is the one we must constantly disarm ourselves of lest we engage in anachronistic interpretation. The paradigm of "publication as the basis of news" had seeded itself; and in the 1750s the College had done nothing to substantiate its medical progress, nor would it had it not been stung into action by these proceedings. These unknown writers were probably unpaid for their submissions; remuneration coming from publicity alone. Nor are the inclusions of Fothergill, Brocklesby, Whytt, the Hunter brothers, and Haygarth difficult to fathom given their growing distinction at the time of publication, although only the Hunters were widely known in the 1750s.

The Scottish Fothergill (not to be confused with Anthony Fothergill, who was younger and never to become a celebrity in the medical realm) was by far the most prolific contributor, offering the society 22 articles dispersed through all six volumes, 1757–84.[38] Aged 45 in 1757, he was also the exception among these generally young and relatively unknown upstarts, destined to be elected to the College of Physicians. His original contribution to the first volume of 1757 had been three articles, increasing over the years and rising to nine in volume five appearing in 1776. Like Brocklesby, who also contributed to the first volume of 1757 and who likewise became one of the century's best-known medical practitioners, Fothergill was loyal to the enterprise of collecting "medical news." It may be that some part of his loyalty to subsequent volumes of the *Medical Observations* was based on his Scottish ancestry – for the series remained a Scottish enterprise printed in London throughout its duration to 1784 – and perhaps on an ancillary belief in the importance of news as a basis for progress in medicine.

VI

By 1784 the "society" had printed a total of 207 articles in six volumes containing stinging criticism of the College. Most of the volumes included self-reflective prefaces, as had volume one, conventionally offering apologies and gratitude, chronicling the death of members (as it did for John Fothergill, Daniel Solander, and William Hunter in the preface of volume six), noting topics of the greatest concern in the preceding years (the miraculous cure of cicuta or Persian Bark in volumes two, three, five, and six), describing exactly where "medical news" had been located since the last volume (as in the brief account of smallpox inoculation in the preface of volume three), and restating the editorial policy as well as the value of its reforms:

> Far from seeing this [sustained publication] with a jealous eye, the Society rejoices to find at length the spirit of inquiry and observation, which it has contributed to excite here, more universally diffused. Such from the beginning was there great object, and every institution, for making and preserving valuable improvements in physic, must coincide with their views in promoting the good of mankind. (3: viii)

In 1785 the College of Physicians of London replied with its own *Medical Transactions*, patterned entirely on the earlier volumes.[39] Each of the features described above was imitated, ranging from signed articles to similar stylistic features and an almost identical flat rhetorical style. In a sense this was news as imitation; mimetic action capturing the earlier "news as publication." The volumes in the *earlier* series had continued to appear every few years – 1757, 1762, 1769, 1772, up to 1784 – but with one difference in the later volumes: the original turks among those who were still contributing in 1785 were older, more established, admitted more English figures into their ranks, and a certain number had themselves now been elected members of the College, such as Brocklesby, Fothergill, both Hunter brothers, and Maty.[40]

But what was the substantive relation of this series started in 1785 to its predecessor begun in 1767 and continued in 1772? This is the question that has not yet been addressed, nor have we turned to it here except in passing. Some of the authors of 1767 reappear in 1785, others do not. A case can also be made that the Royal College's 1785 response is in some meaningful sense a hack compilation excerpted from the volumes published in 1767 and 1772. But it would be perfidious to generalize about the two series without a thorough comparison of the two versions (1767 and 1785); or to hazard a guess whether the claim of being "stung into action" in 1785 was a mere repetition of 1767 or some genuine renewal of the aggravated condition into which the College believed it had now been placed. For example, the authors of the 49 articles of volumes one (1767) and three (1785) respectively in the earlier series (that is, 1767) included poet-physician Mark Akenside, naturalist George Baker, physician Edward Barry, doctor-writer Erasmus Darwin, physician William Heberden, the great John Hunter, and botanist Richard Pulteney. But not all of these remained in the 1785 publication. By 1785 some were dead (Akenside), others no longer interested. In the version of 1767 several were in their sixties, and William Heberden, who took the lead with nine article entries, was in his fifties. The point is that the "medical news" changed in just one decade as the sense of progression in scientific knowledge accelerated. Pharmacy and general medicine remained at the top of the list, as did the number of articles without any proper names or stylistic features other than unadorned English sentences. This pattern became the model for further imitations that appeared afterwards with regularity in the 1780s and 90s, as in the nine volumes of *Medical Commentaries: exhibiting a concise view of the latest and most important discoveries in medicine and medical philosophy.*[41] Crucial in this formula was "the latest" and "most important," each resting on publication rather than discovery for its status as "news" and the sense of being up-to-the-minute. Or reverse the grammar: no publication, no news.

Nevertheless, in 1785 – three decades later – the College was still claiming it had been "stung into action" in its recycled *Medical Transactions Published by the Royal College of Physicians*, not to be confused with the earlier series called *Medical Observations and Inquiries* (1757), or – as significantly – the earlier compendious work of the same name, *Medical Transactions* (1767). The matter of elapsed time between 1767 and 1785 therefore looms again now in a new key: that is, is the response of 1767 similar to the later exasperation of 1785 or are these two different events with different contexts? Sir George Clark, the twentieth-century historian of the London Royal College of Physicians, hits the mark when he asks *why they waited so long*. Why did the College delay, even until 1767? In fairness to Clark, he may not have been interested in the history of news and overlooked the degree of discomfort eventually felt by the members who were "stung into action" in 1785.[42] Why else would they reissue the old compendium of 1767–72 or commission a new series in 1785 based on it?

Print history does not offer certainty. The College's preface claimed it would be publishing at regular intervals: to announce its own "news" and to counter the claims of priority of others (and, in its view, unauthorized groups such as these medical turks). This it did, but not without raising a host of issues about the news that had been exacerbated in the generation between the 1750s and 1780s. These included authorship (especially the composition of the articles), authenticity (verification of the information), confidentiality (especially of patients, as this was medicine), and identity (where remedies were implicated, as they were usually secret and protected).

Licensing acts had come and gone, especially the final lapsing of the Act of 1662 in 1695, as had stamp acts down through the eighteenth century, placing stress on what could be said, as in 1737, and at precisely what stage. But not even stamp acts had solved any of the four issues listed at the start as they touched on the developing news. Hill's *Lucina* had been anonymously printed, but its authorship was instantly recognized; hence the Royal Society could retaliate swiftly and appropriately, which it did. In the case of secret preparations, in which there were few checks and balances, the feuds were fought out, in pamphlet wars that were often acrimonious and anonymous, as in the hundreds of medical tracts collection in the British Library published in the eighteenth century. Authentic medical case histories, however, superimposed the supposed confidentiality of the patient without whose suffering these reports would not have been written. All this in an epoch in which the patient's identity was still unprotected, and when it was protected, it was so for reasons of social class or rank.

The four components of the medical news – *anonymity* (especially of the articles), *authenticity* (verification of the information), *confidentiality* (especially of patients, as this was medicine), and *identity* – were increasingly regulated as the eighteenth century ploughed on. Everywhere in the production of all this information was a growing reading public whose needs were altering.

VII

Without appearing Whiggish at large or facilely offering Whig views of history, it must finally be said that it would be hard to define what constituted medical news then apart from its conditions in publication as the crucial validating force. This is not merely a sceptical conclusion, but aims to be fiercely historical without reducing complexity to neat reductive patterns. The obstacles the news faced – including professional interests as well as anonymity, confidentiality, and professional advancement – afflicted the medical world then as much as any other realm. This analysis may not seem to extend far enough, but it does suggest that there was no such monolithic thing as "medical news" before the establishment of a medical press – there were many versions of news. The most predictable ingredient was the fact of publication as constitutive of something novel and worth recording.

To the reader – the imbiber – of this news, much depended on who you were and what benefit you could expect the "news" to bring you. At least this was the state of affairs for a developing medical news in the late Restoration and eighteenth century. One would surmise it applied as well to other professional types – in guilds, among lawyers, divines, clerks, and so on. Whether it applied universally is unlikely; that is, whether publication was as vital to a sense of novelty as it was in the medical domain. Only further study of the news in *many* professional camps in the long eighteenth century will tell. But there can be no doubt about the homology of publication and print, and of print as the best, and perhaps only, legitimate proof of professionalization. To claim that remnants of this paradigm – the remains of that Georgian period – survive in our world, especially in academia, would be an understatement. Addison was prescient after all in 1711, requiring only the slight alteration of his "Books" to our "Electronic Books."

APPENDIX

This appendix provides facts and data about the six-volume *Medical Observations* (1757–84), which must not be confused with *Medical Transactions published by the College of Physicians in London*, which produced at least three volumes in its series (1767, 1772, 1785, see below); the *Medical Transactions Published by the Royal College of Physicians*, which began annual publication in London in 1785; or the *Medical Commentaries*, which began publication in Edinburgh a year later in 1786. By the late 1780s medical news was appearing annually both in England and Scotland.

Title: MEDICAL OBSERVATIONS AND INQUIRIES. BY A SOCIETY OF PHYSICIANS IN LONDON. LONDON.

Dates of the six volumes:

vol.1 1757
vol.2 1762
vol.3 1769
vol.4 1772
vol.5 1776
vol 6 1784

Number of Articles in each of the volumes:

Vol.1 = 29 [the Contents claims 30 but no no. 1]
Vol.2 = 36
Vol.3 = 37
Vol.4 = 37
Vol.5 = 37
Vol.6 = 31

Total number of articles = 207

Authors of the 1757 series alphabetically listed and by age:

The number after the author's name is the age. Authors with few contributions have no age given and some of the ages are unknown. Hence Samuel Pye does not have age given although his age is known.

Anon. ***
"a physician in the country"
Alanson, Edward
Andree, John = 58
Antrobus, Thomas
Armiger, Thomas
Badenoch, James
Baine, Bernard
Balfour, [no forename]
Bard, John
Bird, William
Bond, Thomas
Brady, Terence
Brumwell, [no forename]
Burchall, [no forename]
Bayford, [no forename given]
Brocklesby, Richard = 35
Campbell, D.
Chalmers, Lionel
Cheston, Richard Brown
Cleghorn, George = 41
Clephane, John
Colde, Cadwallader
Cooper, William
Cullum, Thomas Gery = 16
Dickson, Thomas
Dobson, Mathew
Doubleday [no forename]
Douglas, [Andrew ?] = 21
Douglas, Archibald
Else, Joseph
Evans, Cadwallader
Farr, William
Ford, [Edward] = 11
Fordyce, John
Fordyce, William = 33
Fothergill, [Anthony?] = 25
Fothergill, John = 45
Fraser, Thomas

French, James Bogle
Garthshore, M. Maxwell = 25
Gibson, Henry
Gordon, Abraham
Graham, James
Hall, John
Hay, William
Hey, [William] = 21
Haygarth, John = 17
Hewson, William = 18
Hooper, Joseph
Hunter, William = 39
Hunter, John = 29
Ingham, Samuel
Jacquin, J
Joannis, [no forename known]
Johnstone, [no forename known]
Pelham, James
Kelly, Christopher
Kerr, James
King, [no forename known]
Kirkland, Thomas = 35
Knight, Gowin = 44
Knox, [no forename known]
Lambert, [no forename known]
Landford, John
Leake, William
Loftie, [no forename known]
Lloyd [no forename known]
Ludlow,[no forename known]
Lucas, James
Lynn, John
Maty, M. = 39
Macaulay, George
Macbride, David = 31
Mackenzie, Murdock
Mackenzie, Alexander
Mason, John
Mitchell, G.
Morris, Michael
Nicholson, Arthur
Oliphant, [no forename known
Owen, [no forename]
Pearson, [George?]
Pearson, John
Percival, Thomas = 17
Perkins, Lee
Pugh, [no forename known]
Pulteney, R. = 27
Pye, Samuel
Ramsay, James = 24
Rush, Benjamin
Russel, Alexander
Rutty, John = 59
Sandiford, William
Saunders, Richard Huck = 37

Sequira, J.H.
Sharp, W. [only Samuel 1700–1778]
Skene, G.
Silvester, J.
Smith, John
Swieten, Baron Van
Symonds, [no forename known]
Thomson, Henry
Thomson, William
Teckel, John
Travis, John
Triquet, P.
Turner, Mathew
Vage, [no forename known]
Vaughan, [no forename known]
Wade, [no foremame known]
Wall, Martin
Wathen, Jonathan
Watson, William = 13
Watson, Henry
Whateley, Willliam
White, Charles = 29
White, Thomas
White, W.
Whytt, Robert
Wilmer, B.
Wright, Jen.
Wright, William = 22

Number of different authors of articles = 119

Number of women = 0

Authors with multiple entries in the six volumes:

Badenoch, James = 2
Bond, Thomas = 2
Brocklesby, Richard = 3
    Vol. 3 = 1 Vol. 4 = 2
Cleghorn, George = 2
Clephane, John = 2
Cooper, William = 2
Dickson, Thomas = 7
Else, Joseph = 4
Fothergill, John = 22
    Vol.1 = 3 Vol.2 = 0 Vol. 3 = 2
    Vol.4 = 5 Vol.5 = 9 Vol. 6 = 3

Garthshore, M. = 2
Hay, William = 2
Haygarth, John = 3
Hooper, Joseph = 2
Huck, Richard (see Saunders below)
Hunter, William = 7

Vol. 1 (1), Vol. 2 (3), Vol. 6 (3), plus appendices to articles in Vols. 2, 4 (2), and 5.
Kerr, James = 2
Lucas, James = 3
Macaulay, George = 4
Macbride, David = 2
Mackenzie, Murdock = 2
Mackenzie, Alexander = 2
Maty, Matthew = 2
Morris, Michael = 4
Percival, Thomas = 2
Pye, Samuel = 5
Rush, Benjamin = 3
    Vol. 4 = 1, Vol. 5 = 2
Russel, Alexander = 6
Saunders, Richard Huck = 2
Silvester, J. = 2
Thomson, Henry = 4
Thomson, William = 2
Travis, John = 2
Watson, William = 5
White, Charles = 3
White, W. = 2
Whytt, Robert = 2

Articles listed by medical categories:

General Medicine = 45*
Surgery = 31
Anatomy = 40
Public Health = 15
Obstetrics = 12
Pharmacy = 52
Miscellaneous = 10
Medical History = 0

*Note: General medicine combines cases exclusive of surgery or the extensive use of drugs – for example, cases of diseases such as smallpox or of an accidentally swallowed feather.

Length of individual articles:

no. of pages	no. of articles in each of the six volumes						total figure in this category
1-3	2	3	1	1	5	0	12
4-6	7	12	8	8	7	11	53
6-9	3	6	12	13	13	6	53
9-12	3	5	3	4	4	5	24
13-15	3	1	4	1	2	0	11
16-18	1	3	5	5	1	2	17
19-21	3	4	1	2	2	1	13
22-24	1	1	0	2	0	2	6
25-27	1	1	1	0	2	1	6
28-30	0	0	0	0	2	1	3
31-40	3	0	1	1	0	1	3
41-50	1	0	0	0	0	0	1

51-60	0	1	0	0	0	0	1
61-70	0	0	0	0	0	1	1

Longest articles:

Gordon, Abraham. "The Cure of the Lues Venerea by the Mercurius Corrosivus Sublimatus" Vol.1, 1757. 47 pages.

Hunter, William. "The History of an Emphysema" Vol.II, 1762. 57 pages.

Various Authors. "A Sketch of the Epidmic Disease which appeared in London towards the end of the year 1775. Vol.6, 1784. 65 pages.
[the combined authors of this essay are Pringle, Heberden, Baker, Reynolds, Cuming, Glass, Ash, White, Haygarth, Pulteney, Thomsom, Skene, Campbell]

Proper Names

no. of proper names	no. of articles containing this feature
0	145
1	21
2	17
3	10
4	5
5	1
6	3
7	0
8	1
9	2
10	0
11	1
12	0
13	0
14	1

Proper names most frequently mentioned:

Mead, Hippocrates, Sydenham:
Of these three Sydenham and Hippocrates are mentioned with equal regularity. However Hippocrates' name crops up in a wider range of articles if correlated to their range of subjects. Sydenham is mentioned more than the other two in relation to specific subjects eg. measles.

Use of recognizable literary features such as metaphor, analogy, simile:

No. of features per article no of articles with combined features always totals 207

0	94
1-2	76
3-4	25
5-6	6
7-8	5
9-10	1

Vocabulary:

SIMPLE = Intelligible to the lay reader. Little use of Latin or technical terms.

INTERMEDIATE = Greater employment of technical language but essence still comprehensible to lay reader.

COMPLEX = Extensive use of technical language. Specialist knowledge required in order to understand adequately.

SIMPLE	113
INTERMEDIATE	71
COMPLEX	23

Sentence structure:

SHORT = average sentence 1-3 lines.
MEDIUM = average sentence 4-7 lines.
LONG = average sentence length 8 lines and above.

articles classified in terms of their sentence structure:

SHORT =	22
MEDIUM =	136
LONG =	49

Quotation count by article:

This is a count of the number of quotations (literary, medical, other) used in each of the 207 articles

No. of quotations	No. of articles
0	166
1	30
2	4
3	6
4	0
5	0
6-10	1

MEDICAL TRANSACTIONS PUBLISHED BY THE COLLEGE OF PHYSICIANS IN LONDON. 1767, 1772, 1785.

Dates of three known volumes:

vol.1 1767 (title page reads 1768)
vol.2 1772
vol.3 1785

Age of the authors ten years earlier in 1757, the year when rival *Medical Observations* published its first volume

No age is known in cases where no number appears. Leading contributors of the 1767–1785 series included Mark Akenside, George Baker, John Haygarth, William Heberden, John Power, Henry Revell Reynolds. The average age is considerably older than the group who published in 1757.

Akenside, Mark = 36
Baker, George = 35
Barry, Edward = 61
Coyte, [William Beeston?] = 16
Darwin, Erasmus = 26
Dawson, John = 23
Haygarth, [John?] = 17
Heberden, Thomas
Heberden, William = 47
Hunter, John = 29
Knight, Francis
Lane, T.
Munckley, N.
Pearson, George = 6
Percival, Thomas = 17
Power, John
Pulteney, [Richard] = 27
Reynolds, Henry Revell = 12
Spence, James
Walker, John
Wall, John
Warren, R. = 26
Watson, William = 13
Wood, Thomas

Multiple entries listed by subject matter

Akenside, Mark = 3
    1. "Cancers" 2. "Use of Ipecacoanha in Asthmas" 3. "Swelling of joints"

Baker, George = 9
    1. "the endemial colic of Devonshire" 2. Lead Poisoning 3. "colic of Poitou" – a history ; 4. "colic of Poitou" – causes of its efficacy; 5. "Flos Cardamines – an anti-spasmodic remedy" 6. "an account of a singular disease that prevailed among some poor children, maintained by the parish of St.James." 7. Peruvian Bark 8. Appendix to Darwin's paper 9. "colic of Poitou"

Darwin, Erasmus = 2

    1. "Use of Foxglove, in some dropsies and in the Pulmonary Consumption." 2. Postscript to preceding paper.

Heberden, William = 9
    1. water purity 2. ascarides 3. night blindness 4. chicken-pox 5. "the epidemical cold" 6. angina pectoris 7. "the method of preparing the Ginseng root in China" 8. measles 9. queries

Hunter, John = 3

1. rum – a cause of Colic in Jamaica 2. "an uncommon disease in the Omentum" and "a double of kidney on one side of the body with none on the other" 3. jail/hospital fever

Pearson, George = 2
　　1. "a division of the liver, occasioned by a fall" 2. dropsy

Several of the articles in this rival series are anonymous[43]

NOTES

1.　A vast literature on the printing history of medicine of the eighteenth century now exists, and to a lesser degree of the professionalization of medical arrangements then. Authoritative works include: Roy Porter, *In Sickness and in Health, The British Experience, 1650–1850* (London: Fourth Estate, 1988); idem, *The Greatest Benefit to Mankind: A Medical History of Humanity from Antiquity to the Present* (London: Harper Collins, 1997); idem (ed.), *The Popularization of Medicine 1650–1850* (New York: Routledge, 1992); idem, *Health for Sale: Quackery in England* (Manchester: Manchester University Press, 1989); Roy and Dorothy Porter, *Patient's Progress: Doctors and Doctoring in Eighteenth Century England* (Cambridge: Polity Press, 1989). For the profession of medicine, see P.J. Corfield, *Power and the Professions in Britain 1700–1850* (London: Routledge, 1995), and W.F. Bynum and Roy Porter (eds.), *William Hunter and the Eighteenth-Century Medical World* (Cambridge: Cambridge University Press, 1985).

2.　I draw on the work of scholars from Joseph Frank forward who have written about the early development of the news (1961) and construct my argument with specific focus on an emerging medical press in the eighteenth century. However, my exploration could not have been undertaken without the previous study of Roy Porter, "The Rise of Medical Journalism in Britain to 1800," in W.F. Bynum *et al.* (eds.), *Medical Journals and Medical Knowledge – Historical Essays* (London and New York: Routledge, 1993), 6–28, which excavated this material before I did and lucidly presented its results within the context of medical history; or without Habermas' pioneering work on the public sphere. See especially Porter, p.22, which provides a list of secondary works dealing with the rise of a medical press in the eighteenth century. The notes below barely begin to do justice to my indebtedness to both scholars.

3.　Often they do so under the aegis of constructing the histories of print culture; see especially E. Eisenstein, *The Printing Press as an Agent of Change: Communications and Cultural Transformations in Early Modern Europe* (Cambridge: Cambridge University Press, 1979), II: 637–705; idem, *Grub Street Abroad: Aspects of the French Cosmopolitan Press from the Age of Louis XIV to the French Revolution* (Oxford: Clarendon Press, 1992).

4.　R. Burchfield *et al.*, *New Oxford English Dictionary* (Oxford: Oxford University Press, 1988) sub "publication," entry 2A. A note on the semantics of the word publication would be helpful here if there were space. Suffice it to say that its early history remains unwritten and is more complex than appears. Already, for example, in the early eighteenth century is the notion that reproduction or multiplication of the thing published is a requirement – hence approaching Habermas' sense in the social public sphere. By the mid-eighteenth century all manner of apothecaries claim they will "publish their medicine" – what exactly do they mean? As early as 1768 William Wilkie, a scribbler, complained that "publishing has become a trade," in his *Fables*. Johnson (Samuel Johnson, *A Dictionary of the English Language* [London, 1757], sub "publication") wrote much about the "open publication of heavenly mysteries" in relation to the world of Hooker, but it is unclear what the nuances of such "publication" are. Many more examples could be reproduced to demonstrate a wide spate of meanings and shades. The point is that we think of "publication" in monolithic, almost flat, terms in face of a diverse and curved concept.

5.　Johnson, *Dictionary*.

6.　Samuel Foote, *The Bankrupt* (London: G. Kearsy and T. Evans, 1776), III: 471.

7.　Michael Warner, *Letters of the Republic: Publication and the Public Sphere in Eighteenth-*

        Century America (Cambridge, MA: Harvard University Press, 1990), 67.

8. Ibid., 63.

9. The below case does not prove in itself that the universal is true but does demonstrate the degree to which publication had become the precondition of novelty in the world. Another range of questions would arise if the (below) case were an exception to the pattern.

10. Corfield, *Power and the Professions*, makes a similar point in her chapter on the profession of medicine.

11. Warner, *Letters of the Republic*, 66.

12. Porter, *The Greatest Benefit*.

13. For these arrangements, see L. King, *The Road to Medical Enlightenment, 1660–1695* (London: Macdonald, 1970).

14. Porter, *Health for Sale*.

15. A connection between newspaper advertising and the trade in pills studied as early as the 1920s; see. S. Thompson, *The Quacks of Old London* (London: Brentanos, 1928); more recently, see the discussion of medical recipes and newspaper adverts in G.A. Cranfield, *The Press and Society* (London: Macmillan, 1978), 54–6. For case studies, see (for a murderous feud over the secret of the anodyne necklace) F. Doherty, *A Study in Eighteenth-Century Advertising Methods: The Anodyne Necklace* (Lewiston, NY: Edwin Mellen Press, 1992); idem, "The Anodyne Necklace: A Quack Remedy and its Promotion," *Medical History* 34 (1990); for James Ward, see M.H. Nicolson, "Ward's 'Pill and Drop' and Men of Letters," *Journal of the History of Ideas* 29 (1968): 177–96. Eighteenth-century comic drama abounds with comments about quacks advertising their medicaments in newspapers; see Owen MacSwiny, *The Quacks: Or, Love's the Physician. A Farce* (1745).

16. *Philosophical Transactions of the Royal Society of London* (1678).

17. *Medicina Curiosa* began life in June 1684 but only survived one summer. Roy Porter is right to notice the ephemerality of these early attempts at a medical press.

18. For Sydenham in relation to plague and its potions, see Roy Porter and G.S. Rousseau, *Gout: The Patrician Malady* (New Haven, CT: Yale University Press, 1998), chap. 6, *passim*, 41–8, 391.

19. See the standard work by Bryant Lillywhite, *London Coffee Houses: A Reference Book of Coffee Houses of the Seventeenth, Eighteenth and Nineteenth Centuries* (London: Routledge and Kegan Paul, 1963). The role of toleration within Restoration coffee-house culture has not been historically studied, either medically or in other professional and intellectual spheres; and the standard institutional histories of colleges of physicians and surgeons overlook them altogether, always to the author's detriment. By the era of Pope and Addison their original function as free zones for controversy and toleration had been atrophied to the point of non-recognition, a further reason they have been underestimated for the earlier period of the Restoration. Few institutions, however, are more germane to Habermas' notion of the public sphere than the Restoration coffee-house.

20. For Hill as self-puffer and promoter of himself in the news at mid-century, see primarily the testimony of his contemporaries: [anonymous], *Short Account of the Life, Writing, and Character of the Late Sir John Hill* (1790); idem, *Whipping Rods, For Trifling, Scurrhill, Scribblers, i.e. sic; As Mr. F—t on Taste ... with Other of his Principal Performancess* (London, 1752). Christopher Smart, who took the bait about puffery in newspaper culture seriously, composed an entire mock-epic about Hill, *The Hilliad* (London, 1753). Lady Hill, his wife, denied that Dr Hill courted the press merely "to make news" in *An Address to the Public: by the Hon'ble Lady Hill; Setting Forth the Consequences of the Late Sir John Hill's Acquaintance with the Earl of Bute* (London, 1788).

21. Matthew Maty, the Dutch polymath resident in London during these years, wrote *An History of Instances of Exclusion from the Royal Society* (London: 1784), where Hill figures prominently. But see also Hill's version of the exclusion in his *Review of the Works of the Royal Society of London* (London: R. Griffiths, 1751).

22. See G.S. Rousseau, *The Letters and Private Papers of Sir John Hill* (New York: AMS Press, 1981).

23. For press coverage of the scandal, see G.S. Rousseau, *The Renaissance Man in the Eighteenth Century* (Los Angeles, CA: William Andrews Clark Memorial Library, 1978), 52–67.

24. For the evidence, see J.G. Basker, *Tobias Smollett: Critic and Journalist* (Newark, NJ: University of Delaware Press, 1988), especially the sections on attribution; P.J. Klukoff, "New Smollett Attributions in the *Critical Review*," *Notes and Queries* (Nov. 1967): 418–19.
25. Benjamin Christie Nangle, *The Monthly Review ... first series, 1749-1789: Indexes of Contributors and Articles* (Oxford: Oxford University Press, 1934) documents the point with individual cases; see Nangle's Biographical Appendix.
26. See Basker, *Tobias Smollett.*
27. M.H. Nicolson and G.S. Rousseau, "Berkeley's Tar Water and the Men of Letters," in H.K. Miller *et al.* (eds.), *The Augustan Milieu: Essays Presented to Louis A. Landa* (Oxford: Clarendon Press, 1970), 111–23.
28. A point repeatedly made by R. Porter in *Health for Sale.*
29. See the discussion of Andrew Duncan's activities in Porter, "Medical Journalism in Britain to 1800," 16–17.
30. Late eighteenth-century newspapers were permeated with assurances that often followed their own advertisements: "Mr W. assures us that he will publish his medicine as soon as its efficacy be established," *The Medical Journal* (1803), ix: 287.
31. See G.S. Rousseau, "The Great Fever-Powder Fraud: Drug Disuse and Media Explosion in Eighteenth-Century London," *Papers of the Clark Library Seminars* (1989), talk of 24 Feb. 1988.
32. Bibliographically it is important to distinguish the *Medical Observations and Inquiries* from all these series which are often similarly named: *Medical Transactions* (Edinburgh, 1768–1820); *Medical and Philosophical Commentaries* (London, 1774–86), 6 vols.; *Medical Commentaries: exhibiting a concise view of the latest and most important discoveries in medicine and medical philosophy* (Edinburgh: C. Elliot, 1786–95), 9 vols.; and certainly different from the Royal College's *Medical Transactions Published by the Royal College of Physicians of London* (London, 1785). Several are discussed in Porter, "Medical Journalism in Britain," notes 49–71.
33. Therefore two *different* series were appearing in 1785: (1) the third volume of the old series begun in 1767–68 and (2) the first volume of the new series begun in 1785. Internal analysis shows these were different compilations with different articles and different authors but another study would be required to perform this analysis for the second series beginning in 1767. Porter appears not to have consulted both series or taken account of them in his analysis (Porter, "Medical Journalism in Britain", 22).
34. For the expatriate community of Scottish physicians in London at mid-century and their socio-economic dilemmas see G.S. Rousseau, "Beef and Bouillon: A Voice for Tobias Smollett, With Comments on his Life, Works, and Modern Critics," in idem, *Tobias Smollett: Essays of Two Decades* (Edinburgh: T.T. Clark and New York: Seabury Press, 1982), 80–123.
35. The contribution of these figures to the medical progress of the day is discussed by L.S. King, *The Medical World of the 18th Century* (Chicago, IL: University of Chicago Press, 1958).
36. For the evidence, see G.N. Clark, *A History of the Royal College of Physicians of London* (Oxford: Clarendon Press, 1964–72, 2 vols.), II: 542–5.
37. L.M. Knapp, *Tobias Smollett: Doctor of Men and Manners* (New York: Russell and Russell, 1963), 27, 47–8.
38. In the absence of a modern biography of John Fothergill as an elite practitioner and scientist, see King, *The Medical World of the 18th Century.*
39. That is, on the series beginning in 1757 as well as 1767; see the titles distinguished in n.32.
40. Both Hunter brothers, John and William, contributed, William the more prolifically, producing a total of seven articles; see the Appendix.
41. (Edinburgh: C. Elliot, 1786–95). Porter claims ("Medical Journalism in Britain," 17) that "Duncan clearly saw himself not just as printing cases but as providing an interesting miscellany and as dealing in news." Duncan apparently did, as his third section each year was titled "Medical News," but this section was a farrago of listings culled from all types of medical societies and groups without the sense that evidence or authority counted for anything. Clearly one category of "news" by this time, the 1780s, was the "breadth of

coverage" (Porter's phrase, ibid., p.17) and, perhaps more importantly, the sense that his annual digest was reaching the largest possible audience of readers.

42. Clark, *History of the Royal College*, II, Chap. 28, "The Licentiates, 1752–91," 552–73.

43. When Porter notes ("Medical Journalism in Britain," 15) that "all papers in *Medical Transactions* were signed, being the work of members of the College," he presumably refers to the 1785 series, not the earlier one started in 1767.

Tropes of Promotion and Wellbeing: Advertisement and the Eighteenth-Century Scottish Periodical Press

HAMISH MATHISON

> The prints – newspapers an' reviews,
> Frae time to time may aft you rouse.[1]

Three observations provide the basis for the following work. First, advertisements for medicinal products changed in style and method over the course of the century. Second, those advertisements were related to and reflected political and governmental issues. Third, the Scottish eighteenth century witnessed the development of a complex and more or less discreet discourse of promotion informed by philosophical and national issues of the right governance of communities.[2] These observations demand explanation, and prompt their own questions: questions of how the advertisement of literary texts came to share a language of promotion with the advertisement of patent medicines and physicians; questions of what forces propelled the everyday advertisement of those products rather than others; questions of the status or authority of branded medical products and branded literary products.

In order to answer some of those questions, this paper turns to two Edinburgh newspapers. It is grounded in a study of the *Caledonian Mercury* between the years 1729 and 1787, whilst it takes its concluding example from the *Edinburgh Chronicle* of 1759. Other Edinburgh newspapers could perhaps have been chosen, for example Alexander Donaldson's *Edinburgh Advertiser* or the *Edinburgh Evening Courant*. The *Mercury*, however, presents itself for two simple reasons. Firstly, the *Mercury* carried advertisements consistently throughout the eighteenth century, and was published regularly with compositional habits that may be compared and contrasted year on year. Secondly, the *Mercury* was involved in the problems that beset the Edinburgh periodical press when the Jacobite army entered the capital in 1745, at which time the son of Thomas Ruddiman, one of its publishers, was gaoled and subsequently died as a consequence of his incarceration.[3] Meanwhile, the *Edinburgh Chronicle* represents the changes

Hamish Mathison, University of Aberdeen

and opportunities which the Edinburgh trade in newspapers experienced in the second half of the century, being a shorter lived speculative venture that attracted occasional verse.

To begin with some generalizations: the kinds of advertisement that appeared in the Edinburgh periodical press changed between the 1720s and the 1780s. As with English provincial newspapers, the number and frequency of advertisements increased, and became more sophisticated. Not only did Edinburgh newspapers advertise more kinds of products, commodities, and events, but those that were advertised invoked a sophisticated language of nationhood, necessity, and well-being.

At first glance, the ontology of the Edinburgh newspaper press may appear to be that of its English provincial counterpart: news was taken from London, and there was a gradual growth in the advertisement of consumer products. That growth was led, of course, by the now well recorded advertisement of patent medicines.[4] However, the Edinburgh newspaper press must be read in a rather more nuanced fashion. A different set of political circumstances from those in England influenced the development of the Scottish newspaper. That led, as will be seen, to a distinctive advertising practice. It is that practice and the tropes to which it gave rise that lie at the heart of this study. On the basis of the evidence available, there appears to be a direct correlation between political, economic, and social changes in Edinburgh at the time, particularly following the Jacobite rising of 1745, and the kind of advertisements that the Edinburgh newspaper press carried. These changes cannot be fully accounted for by the alterations in the city's demography that undoubtedly took place and which are well recorded elsewhere.[5] Rather, emergent ideas of the kinds of nationhood which Scots perceived as beneficial to society at large gave rise to a specific discourse. That discourse was peculiar to the realm of advertisement within the periodical press and is most clearly revealed in the kinds of advertisement that medical products and practitioners underwent and initiated.

The first principle to establish is the evolution that the advertisement of products, services, and events underwent in the course of the eighteenth century. The folio *Caledonian Mercury* appeared thrice weekly, and during its first full decade of existence, the 1720s, the space dedicated to advertisements was sited at the back of the paper. Foreign news abstracted from the London papers was usually carried on its first two pages, Court and Scottish news on the third, advertisements on the fourth. At this time, some two-thirds of the final page, that is a column and a half, was given over to advertisement. The occasional edition would appear with no advertisements whatsoever, and sometimes an edition would project advertisements onto the previous page where the Court and Scottish news usually ran. The section dedicated to advertisements was clearly labelled as such, setting it apart from the body of the paper with a horizontal rule, sometimes two, and the heading "ADVERTISEMENTS" in large type across the column which began the commercial portion of the newspaper.

An analysis of the edition of 24 January 1729 reveals that at this time the paper was published by William Rolland, and only printed by Thomas Ruddiman. The Ruddimans' business was a subsidiary of Rolland's before they came to wholly own it. Thomas Ruddiman's brother, Walter, really ran the business, the polymath Thomas being Librarian for the Faculty of Advocates in Edinburgh and deeply involved in the projects of Scoto-Latinity. Of the eight advertisements on the page, five advertise the sale of land or property, two are legal notices that concern the estates of debtors, and only one is for a product: the "best PANTYLES made in this Kingdom" from the Prestonpans "Tyle-work." It is important to note that only one advertisement was for a commercially available product (the pantiles) and even that is of interest to trade customers, rather than individual consumers. The page is thus generated by local concerns and economic affairs: it contains no nationally advertised products, no products for personal consumption, no advertisement of personal services or entertainment. There are no branded or authored products available here and this is reflected in the style of the advertisements: factual information is presented with little attempt to market, sell, or promote goods or services. The key point is that before the events of 1745 the periodical or newspaper press in Edinburgh was not involved, in any significant degree, with the promotion of consumption, nor did it particularly allow for the figure of the consumer in promotion of goods, services, and events.

In contrast, by 1786, the only page of the *Mercury* which never carried advertisements was the inside front page. The example of the edition of 5 April 1786 offers three columns of advertisement instead of the two seen in the 1720s, whilst vertical and horizontal rules and a much more complicated use of type have been introduced. By 1789 there was no longer a heading to denote the start of the advertisement section. As a consequence, the promotional text follows on from the "news" itself, in this instance for Speediman's "STOMACH PILLS":

> Although the good effects of the STOMACH PILLS are well known to the very many who have used them, yet, in this advertising age, it is almost necessary to point out to the public in general, and more especially to those who may not be so happy as to know of so valuable a medicine, that these pills are the best remedy yet found out, in all complaints of the Stomach and Bowels.[6]

What is immediately obvious is the advertiser's awareness of "this advertising age," as if people had become somehow inured to the effects of promotional texts, and that it is "necessary" to educate or at least to inform an afflicted public of the efficacy of stomach pills. There is a possible further implication of the wording of this particular advertisement. It seems to imply that if one knows of these pills, and if one has a friend who is suffering from "head-aches, cramps, wind, and other obstructions," then it is one's duty (for it is "necessary") to point out the benefits of Speediman's remedy.

This advertisement displays several kinds of change when compared to the type of advertisement found in the earlier *Mercury*. It is for a branded product, it is a national product, manufactured in London and distributed around the country, whereas Prestonpans was the most distant manufactory represented in the 1729 *Mercury*. It employs a more or less complicated kind of advertising language, characterized by a self-awareness of the medium of promotional texts and an appeal to a consuming public that is aware of advertising media and, perhaps, resistant to it.

The media of periodical advertisements, then, changes over the course of sixty or so years in the middle of the eighteenth century. Advertisements became more sophisticated, there were more of them, and they advertised a greater range of goods and services. Whilst public auctions, land sales, and legal notices still made up much of the advertising in the Scottish periodical press, after 1745 a new kind of advertisement came about amidst the advertisements for the disposal of forfeited Jacobite estates. It was aimed at a previously unconstituted consuming public that was prepared to purchase for its well-being or enjoyment nationally available products that were centrally produced and nationally distributed. These products were branded and appealed from their metropolitan origin to a national and, increasingly, rural consuming public. For the Scottish newspaper, this came about more slowly than in the English provincial press, and that was one consequence of the events of 1715 and, later, 1745.

What were the detailed conditions of possibility for the changes attendant upon the political history of the Scottish newspaper? The answer lies in what could be called the "poetics" of such advertising, in the kind of tropes that adverts employed as they worked on behalf of their products, in the interconnections between manufacturers, products, and their consumers.

It was not until 16 June 1746 that the *Caledonian Mercury* carried the first example of what was to become a common trait in the periodical advertisement of patent medicines, that is, advertisement by royal patent. Advertisements were still carried at the rear of the newspaper, and apart from the advertisement for branded medicines, advertisements for public auctions of commodities (on 16 June 1746 those were for coal and hay) and legal notices remain. However, sixty per cent of the advertising space was now given over to the kind of medicine we saw in the 1786 *Mercury*:

products that were branded, centrally produced, and nationally distributed. These could in addition claim to be international products, retailed abroad (Holland was a favourite claim) as well as in England and Scotland. Only after the defeat of the Jacobite army could the national promotion of what can be labelled and promoted as a "British" medicine make a serious impact in the Scottish press. Not just British, of course, but also sold under the guarantee of the Monarch, "By the King's Royal Letters Patent." Not content with securing the health and constitution of the realm, George now guarantees the constitution of the individuals under his governance. Several different brands of medicine were advertised in the edition of 16 June 1746. Six kinds of remedy were on offer, with the patent held by J. Newbery. As different people have different ailments, so the marketing of products responded to the division and special needs of increasingly complex consumers, and gendered consumers at that, as evinced by the advertisement of the hugely successful "Dr. Hooper's FEMALE PILLS."

This trait, the promotion of a medicine or medicines under the guarantee of royal patents, accompanied the more frequent illustration of advertisements with wood cuts. For example, in the *Mercury* of 10 November 1759 "Dr. Bateman's Pectoral Drops" were promoted not only by the textual guarantee but also by a woodcut representing the monarch's seal.

The complexity of this strategy extends beyond the reference to the King, for such woodcuts not untypically accompanied reports of legal actions brought for infringement of patent, thus blurring the boundary between advertisement and news, a boundary which the *Mercury* in the earlier part of the century maintained with strong, typographic, emphasis. The reporting of trials was a staple of most provincial newspapers during the eighteenth century. In Scotland, criminal proceedings were commonly lifted from the London papers, although Scottish trials received widespread coverage. What we witness in the years following 1745 in Scotland is the incorporation of not only monarchic patronage into advertising discourse, but the inclusion of a British judicial guarantee as well. This can be seen if we consider another advertisement for "Dr. Bateman's Pectoral Drops," this time from Wednesday 14 November 1759. It too was accompanied by a woodcut bearing the legend "BY THE KING'S PATENT" and it offered two items of judicial news. First, that "Cluer Dicey and Company, of Bow Church Yard, London, original proprietors of DR. BATEMAN'S PECTORAL DROPS" had won their case against "Thomas Jackson, who was originally a Clog or Patten-maker" for counterfeiting the product and claiming that some of the published reports of cures effected by the medicine had been Jackson's, not Cluer Dicey's. Secondly, Cluer Dicey published further oaths taken before the Lord Mayor of London as to the effectiveness of their Drops. The package of assurance is impressive: majesty and judiciary combine in the promotion of the product: the "advertising age" would seem to have arrived. The proprietor of "Jesuits Drops," Robert Walker, published the complete copy of the fourteen-year patent which had been assigned to him. Walker embellishes the story, and we see George II taking a keen interest in the venereal well-being of his subjects:

> The incomparable WALKER'S JESUITS DROPS, having performed such great and surprising cures on all stages of the venereal Disease in both sexes, as well as in old stubborn gleets and weaknesses of the Reins and kidneys, whether occasioned by the venereal disorder or otherwise, his Majesty, that his Subjects in Scotland should have the said medicine genuine, and for preventing any impositions upon them with spurious medicines, under the name or title, to the prejudice of their health, as well as endangering their lives, was also graciously pleased to father honour the said Robert Walker with his Royal Letters patent, for that Kingdom for fourteen years.[7]

The monarch's influence on advertisement in the Scottish periodical press bears emphasis. Not only was the Crown, its government, and its judiciary invoked in the retail of advertised products, but of course it quite literally stamped its authority upon every newspaper. The promotional inclusion of royal patent seals went hand in hand with the stamping of every newspaper issued for the purposes of stamp duty. This duty rose consistently throughout the century, from a halfpenny at the start of our period to a penny and a half in the reign of George the Third. The duty on advertisements rose in a similar way, from the one shilling duty raised on every advertisement by Queen Anne in 1712 to two shillings in 1757.[8] By the start of the nineteenth century the stamp duty alone on newspapers added 130 per cent to the cost of their production. This led some commentators to criticize the government for making newspapers economically unviable, or at least forcing them to accept advertisements from dubious sources just to get by:

> a license is given to quacks and mountebanks political and medical; authors and authoresses, dull, poor, stale, or in their dotage; auctioneers, Jews, jobbers, and gamblers, ad infinitum, – to praise themselves, their works, their commodities, their terms, their honour, and their honesty, at so much per line, king's duty included.[9]

The increasingly pervasive presence of monarch and government in the advertisements that the *Mercury* carried in the eighteenth century is important, for advertisers employed the figure of the monarch to invoke a kind of corporeal Britishness, a manner of public and private constitutional health that was previously unavailable in Scotland, and certainly without stability between 1715 and 1745.

The open letter represents a clear development in the poetics of advertisement: having had the guarantee of the royal seal, the guarantee of the printed patent, and the verities of reported criminal proceedings, there was a move towards another pole, this time that of the individual guarantee and the invitation to partake in a community of well-being where trust in a product was not bestowed from above but from amidst one's peers. For example, "Spilsbury's Antiscorbutic Drops" were advertised heavily in the *Mercury* throughout the 1780s, and an example drawn from 19 November 1781 contains two declarations of the cure's efficacy. The first was a simple report of the cure's efficacy witnessed by a Mr James Sexton. The second was apparently a letter from William Tesseyman, a bookseller in York. The attestation of efficacy by a signed witness was a not uncommon practice: what this advert does in particular though is to introduce the open letter, for one of the first times in the *Mercury*, as an advertising tool. Not just any signatory, of course, but a bookseller's, with a shop where he can be contacted for "Further particulars, with a reference to the person." At the same shop could be had Spilsbury's own "Treatise on the Scurvy, Gout, Diet, and Remedy, of which the reviews are lavish in the praise therof." The open letter appears to offer an honest publication of the experiences or opinion of a private individual or individuals. The power of an open letter lies in that publication of private experience. The worth of the product *seems* to be credited from the private, not the public, realm. That realm is of course much closer to the experiences of the consumer than that of Royal patent, whilst seeming to bypass commercial consideration in a way reminiscent of the appeal to duty noted above with reference to Speediman's advertisement of 5 April 1786.

The relationship is perhaps better understood in terms of the appeals which are shared between advertising discourses, and here the paper turns to a consideration of the way in which medical advertisements in the Scottish newspaper press may be usefully compared with the promotion of literary texts: specifically the second edition of Robert Burns' *Poems, Chiefly in the Scottish Dialect*. Two letters which appeared on the 11 November 1786 front page of the *Caledonian Mercury* sought to move the public to some kind of action or "benevolence." The value of comparison lies in the observation of how the letters are obliged to freight the notion of benevolence with a commercial meaning in order to perform in a social sphere whilst quieting the commercial resonance of their texts in order to be seen as legitimate social productions.

One of the two items is an open letter to a Dr. Degravers, thanking him for his "benevolent attention." The other is a letter which refers to a "common farmer" in Ayrshire named Burns. The letter to Degravers is at the foot of the left-hand column and is signed by six grateful patients relieved of their suffering, whilst the other letter sits at the foot of the right hand column and is signed "Allan Ramsay," and identified as having come from Dumbartonshire, 7 November 1786.

The letter addressed to Degravers is a study in epistolary artifice which reveals the vitality of demotic "sentimental" language. It appears beneath two similar advertisements for professional services, one placed by a teacher of French, Alexander D'Asti, and the other by Robert Nicol, a teacher of Arithmetic and Book-Keeping. The open letter to Degravers, immediately below these two pieces, is substantially different. Placed in the same column as Nicol's and D'Asti's, although it appears to be a letter, it is in fact an advertisement. It was the practice of the paper to gather similar material together if possible. Shipping news and trade sales were two examples of this common compositional habit. The compositional habits of the newspaper suggest that the open letter to Degravers is in fact an advert, and an analysis of what it goes on to say confirms this.[10] It opens:

> WE think it our duty to return you these public thanks for your benevolent attendance, when we were afflicted with the most distressing disorders, and we jointly wish that the relief that we have humanely received from your superior skill and knowledge of the human Eye and Ear, may be the occasion of a proper encouragement in this country; for, indeed, we want such a Gentleman as you in this place.[11]

The "occasion of a proper encouragement" is a troublesome phrase. The "relief" that the patients who have submitted the letter have felt is the occasion of a proper encouragement in this country, but the encouragement of whom? The phrase claims to thank Degravers, for its "encouragement" is an expression of gratitude ("please be encouraged by our thanks") yet at the same time the "encouragement" is an exhortation to other sufferers to "reward" Degravers with their business, to "encourage" him to stay lest he leave "this place." People are "encouraged" to go and visit him for the letter is headed "TO DOCTOR DEGRAVERS, / WEST OF CANAL STREET, EDINBURGH": thus it contains all the information necessary to allow an ill reader to go and "encourage" Degravers to stay by paying him a visit. There is no material in the letter which does not further the Doctor's cause. The kinds of operation which he may be expected to perform with success are listed in the series of signatures which appear at the foot of the letter, being a series of personal testaments to the singular skill of the Doctor and the concomitant inability of others to cure the likes of:

Jane Waugh, at Mr Smith's, wright and trunk-maker, Nether Bow, opposite the Linen Hall, cured of a *Fistula Lachrymalis,* after having been cut twice in the Infirmary, without any relief.

James Walker, wright, middle of Old Assembly close, in the quill manufactory house, the top of the left-hand stair, cured of a tumour on my right Eye, which had baffled the Infirmary's assistance.[12]

The letter therefore *performs* as an advertisement, it provides a reason to go to Degravers, a reason to purchase his services before those of others, a list of specific diseases he specializes in, a list of contented customers, the place where the treatment may be purchased.[13] Above all, the form of the open letter not only attests *in itself* to the satisfaction of the customer arguing for a degree of satisfaction which prompts the patient into print and expense, but also preserves the sense of Degravers' kindly motives and economic innocence. He himself is not seen to be advertising, not seen to require patrons, but to be himself a patron through his benevolent attendance.

"Benevolence" is a key word for this advert, favouring Degravers' humane medical attention over the economic patronage of his clients. "Benevolence" obscures the movements of an economic patronage here through that patronage's inclusion within a lexical item freighted with the sentimental meanings which Carol McGuirk identifies as present in the Edinburgh of 1786–87.[14] To preserve an image of himself as benevolent attendant, in order to advertise without being seen to advertise, required an open letter. Had Degravers advertised in any other way he would have undermined the nature of the service he claimed to offer, that of a "benevolent attention" which knows only its medical efficacy and not its dependence on patrons for economic survival.

A published letter could function as an advertisement. Sophisticated advertising modes were available to promoters in the Scottish press by the 1780s. The effect of such changes on the promotion of literary texts is complex. A letter such as Ramsay's can be read as an item the purpose of which lies not so much in its voiced content as in the unvoiced strategy and aims of the text. The presence of Degravers' letter on the same page as Ramsay's denies the latter its innocence precisely because Degravers' piece teaches that letters can dissemble, that their material goal may be at variance with their cultural seeming. The letter claims to be that which it is not (a simple letter of thanks) in order to enact the requirements placed upon it as an advertisement. Degravers' text responds to both its audience and that audience's "sentimental" discourse of benevolence by upholding the image of the doctor as one who operates without concern for finance, the doctor as practitioner of a humane profession.[15] By advancing an image of the doctor, it acknowledges that the advertisement of Degravers was the only way to guarantee revenue whilst participating in a non-economic rationale of eighteenth-century "sentimental" thought.

If such a letter encodes a knowledge of economic concern in the process of marketing a product (here that product is Degravers' medical skill), then the letter from Ramsay might be expected similarly to involve itself with a representation of the economic when it seeks to advance or draw to attention the product (a collection of poems in the Scottish dialect) offered by Burns. The medical profession employed the "authoring" of its products in its advertisements: *Degravers'* skill, *Dr Smith's* Restorative Medicine or *Spilsbury's* Antiscorbutic Drops. The letter from Ramsay similarly participates in the creation of an image of authority in order to promote a product: Burns' poems.

The letter from Allan Ramsay has two important implications. Firstly, given the literary resonance of its signatory (most probably a pseudonym), it is important to grasp that espousing the work of a common farmer can function like the letter which thanks Degravers: it performs as an advertisement. The letter from Allan Ramsay acts as a "puff"[16] for the 1787 edition of Robert Burns' *Poems, Chiefly in the Scottish Dialect*. Secondly, this form of patronage influenced the creation, reception, and interpretation of Robert Burns' work. This second point may appear a given, but in even the most recent and sophisticated full-length study of Burns' corpus, Carol McGuirk's *Robert Burns and the Sentimental Era*,[17] an essentially non-economic kind of patronage is argued for. Yet the study of how popular culture dealt with, supported, and fashioned the agendas of "sentiment" and "patronage" suggests that it is wrong to read the importance of "sentimental" thought as being a "high" cultural mode which trickled down towards a consumption and adoption by demotic voices and the communities which they inhabited. Bearing in mind the parallels which have been established between newspaper advertisements of "authored" products, it is possible to examine its performance as a letter which advertises Burns' work. This is because it calls attention to Burns' economic status whilst adapting that status to "legitimate" cultural ends. The claim being made for Ramsay's letter is twofold: first that it worked to promote Burns, taking its place in the publication history of Burns' texts, and second that its performance was a register of the concerns of Burns' readership and, indeed, of Burns' poetry.

Ramsay begins the letter with a form of speech-genre which provides Burns himself with one of his most powerful and recurrent textual strategies: the appeal to a sense of communal knowledge. Thus Ramsay begins his letter "It is an old saying ...," and just as he staked out the legitimacy of what follows through this appeal to communal, unattributable knowledge, the "common lore," of proverb rather than the specific nature of an authored writing, so the amount of detail at the foot of Degravers's letter served to diffuse its point of origination. Ramsay's proverbial introduction to his letter, "a prophet hath no honour in his own country," is introduced after its establishment as "an old saying." Ramsay's letter begins with a diffuse claim, an appeal to a widely held truth intended to be broadly irrefutable:

> It is an old saying "That a prophet hath no honour in his own country;" and I am of the opinion, that the same adage may be applied, in many instances, with equal propriety, to authors.
>
> Amongst the British Poets, Gay and Thomson, (whose writings do honour to themselves, to their country, and to human nature), are striking examples of the neglect which is but too frequently the attendant on modest merit. This part of the kingdom has not produced many poets; and therefore when a rarity of the kind appears, it becomes the business of those whose fortune and situation enable them to promote the cultivation of genius, to lend him assistance to such a laudable pursuit.
>
> Within these few weeks I have been highly gratified by perusing a collection of poems in the Scottish dialect, the production of a common farmer in Ayrshire, of the name of Burns. His language is nervous, and his sentiments would do honour to a much more enlightened scholar. In short, he appears to be not only a keen satirist, but a man of great feeling and sensibility.
>
> The county of Ayr is perhaps superior to any in Scotland, in the number of its Peers, Nabobs, and wealthy Commoners; and yet not one of them has, upon this occasion, stepped forth as a patron to this man, nor has any attempt been made to interest the public in his favour. His poems are read; his genius is applauded, and he is left to his fate. It is a reflection on the county, and a disgrace to humanity.
>
> To this self-taught poet I am an entire stranger; but his productions have afforded me so much pleasure, that if this hint should raise an emulation in that county, to rescue from penury a genius, which, if unprotected, will probably sink into obscurity, I will most chearfully contribute towards it, and I know many others who will follow the example.—Should my efforts to serve this man with the laity be ineffectual, I propose, as a dernier resort, to address the clergy of that county, many of whom he hath taken particular notice of in his poems,
>
> ALLAN RAMSAY *Dunbartonshire, November* 7. 1786.[18]

It is worth recalling the phrase used in Degravers' text which observed that he required proper encouragement in this country: "for, indeed, we want such a Gentleman as you in this place." The parallel is clear enough: the singular nature of what the poet, like the doctor, offers is such as to make an investment in their work an act of practical and national sponsorship: the coordinates of community and nation are invoked in order to further an individual's economic well-being. Of course, "Kingdom" is in itself a deeply ambiguous usage, for since 1603, certainly since 1707, Scotland's ability to figure its institutional self as a "Kingdom," to know itself as a coherent and unitary nation, had been under threat. Thus Ramsay's "Kingdom" flickers between signifying Ayrshire, and Scotland: two significations which are in turn subsumed within the "Kingdom" of Britain. Ramsay's usage lets the locus of patronage slide between political registers, now being an expression of regional loyalty, now being a call for the advancement of a Scottish poet by Scottish patrons. All the time, however, the universal presuppositions of sentimental discourse threaten to disallow the geographical privileges Ramsay seeks for a poet of "this Kingdom." The letter balances precariously between a straightforward appeal to an emergent patriotism on the one hand, and a sophisticated, universal, understanding of "human nature" on the other.

Ramsay goes on to attest to the efficacy of Burns' text, furthered with a guarantee of Burns' skill: "his productions have afforded me so much pleasure. I will most chearfully contribute towards [them]." Much as Degravers' "clients" established the seeming of their impartiality through the inclusion of their trade or place of residence, so Ramsay seeks to establish his own impartiality, writing that "To this self-taught poet I am an entire stranger," affirming the poet's universal appeal. Ramsay's letter rehearses the rhetorical movements of Degravers' letter: by so enacting these traits it functions as an advertisement not simply because it seeks benevolently to advance the poet to public notice, but because it is a letter which contains a performative potential founded on a similar act of financial denial to Degravers'.

To be sure, Ramsay's letter notices the economic motors which lie behind poetic production. As in the letter to Degravers, however, this invocation of economic necessity is heavily qualified by the "sentimental" agenda of a lexis which includes items such as "patron," "genius," and "unprotected" alongside phrases such as "a man of great feeling and sentiment." That lexis effectively subsumes the letter's articulation of economic concern on behalf of the poet. Ramsay teases apart Burns from his texts by claiming that Burns' texts are efficient in their presentation of an explicitly sentimental vision, and that patronage of the poet would be a rational act of sentimental patronage. That act of patronage would provide the moral theory of sentimental behaviour with its praxis of benevolent patronage. The letter positions Burns as a rural genius incapable of sustained poetic creation without the patronage of the "Peers, Nabobs, and wealthy Commoners" of Ayr and, now, Edinburgh. An appeal is made to a specific class of people to save a (sentimental) genius which would otherwise sink into obscurity whilst the (actual) farmer would find penury.

This representation of sentimental promotion, even patronage, so central to the development and promotion of a writer's fortunes, cannot be understood rightly outside the context of newspaper advertisements. What is more, some of the key themes available in "high" cultural contexts of the late eighteenth century are similarly available in the demotic forum of newspaper advertisements. Concerns about the relationship between public and private space, concerns over sexuality and health, concerns about nationhood and the individual within it are voiced by increasingly sophisticated promotional texts.

The way in which private and public interest commingle will be treated fully below, but for now it is well worth noting an advert for a steel truss that appeared in the *Mercury* of Saturday 8 April 1786, which in its visual representation of the product on offer clearly looked forward to the forms of advertisement that we are more used to today, with a picture and strapline. The text of the advertisement itself appealed once more to a sense of British medical skill, and the pan-national availability of the product:

> Encouraged by the approbation of several of the most eminent surgeons of both England and Scotland, who have unanimously pronounced this truss the most complete ever yet offered to the Public. – the proprietor now presumes to offer them to the afflicted, as the most certain and efficacious means of cure, and has appointed vendors in most of the principle towns of Great Britain.

The ubiquity of such advertisements has been noted, but this kind of advertising language was, on the empirical evidence of the Scottish newspaper press before 1745, available to advertisers in Scotland only after the Jacobite threat to the Crown and constitution had passed. In matters of health, England and Scotland are now clearly part of "Great Britain," occlusions of geography that stand comparison with the intellectually vigorous if equally troubled letter by "Allan Ramsay."

The final example is that of the arrival of John Taylor, the "Chevalier" Taylor, oculist, in Edinburgh in 1759. An itinerant surgeon of the eye, Taylor was born on 16 August 1703, and died, blind, in a Prague convent in 1772. He travelled extensively throughout Europe, working in virtually every court on the Continent. By all accounts a skilled surgeon, Dr Johnson remarked of his florid autobiography that it was "an instance of how far impudence will carry ignorance." His advertisements in the newspaper press of 1759 Edinburgh and the responses in print which they generated point to the connections between the advertisement of medical products (here Taylor's own skill), nationhood and the emerging discourses of efficacy and necessity in the eighteenth-century Scottish newspaper.

The first warning the citizens of Edinburgh had of the "Chevalier" Taylor's arrival was an advertisement placed in the *Edinburgh Chronicle* of Wednesday 17 October 1759. The *Edinburgh Chronicle* was an attempt by three powerful Edinburgh booksellers, Gavin Hamilton, John Balfour, and Patrick Neill, to establish a printed serial that incorporated not only news but also material of a literary nature. It retailed at two and a half pence a copy for the year of its existence, and in that time seemed to have enjoyed some success. Before turning to two rhymed responses to Taylor's work, it is worth taking a look at some of the tropes which were employed in his own advertisements. Taylor immediately made the well-established appeal to royal authority:

> The CHEVALIER **TAYLOR** OPHTHALMIATER to his present Majesty, and to the several other Crowned Heads, &c. Professor in optics in the university of Rome, &c. having given, in this capital, some specimens of his lectures on the art of cutting defects of the EYE, it has been requested, that he would give a regular course, as in all the courts abroad, and for so many years, in the most celebrated universities, and societies of the learned.

This was simply not an appeal that was available to advertisers in Scotland before the final defeat of the Jacobite cause in 1746. Taylor's claim is accurate: he was George II's personal eye surgeon, and held qualifications from Basle, Liege, and Cologne. Another appeal which has been noted above is that to the "general good": "A better argument cannot be offered to excite the Students of physic in this University, in example of so many other learned societies abroad, to endeavour to acquire knowledge in a profession, which so evidently tends, as well to private interest, as to a general good." Taylor, situating himself as mediator of private interest and public good simultaneously situated himself amidst the moral discourses of the Scottish Enlightenment. The very people to whom his advertisement appealed – the higher status readership of the *Edinburgh Chronicle*, literate and monied – are the people amongst whose communities both "high" and "popular" discourses of sentiment, the moral discourses of the Scottish Enlightenment, evolved. Taylor spoke the language of his market. In addition, Taylor provided two examples of the adoption by the medical practitioner of the means of the book trade: publication by subscription and the cross-marketing of texts. We notice that Taylor seeks payment by subscription, as his courses:

> Will begin on Friday, Nov. 9. at five o'clock in the evening; on condition of sixty subscribers, who are desired to send their names

immediately, and to whom tickets will be delivered. No money will be accepted, till the evening of the first lecture, so that the number may be completed, which there is no doubt will be effected, (as the names of the greatest part of this number are already given in), and consequently a certainty of their being continued every evening, at the same hour, till ended. – The same course will be given, after leaving this city, in London.

Taylor also offered all who attended a copy of his text on the "243 different defects of the EYE," the common incitement to purchase medical products through the offer of a free medical text, here repeated for the promotion of an individual's lectures. What we need to bear in mind, of course, is that Taylor was not just in Edinburgh to deliver a course of lectures. The lectures themselves were a form of advertisement for his private practice, a "front" in a way, as Taylor silently promoted his private surgical practice through the vociferous public promotion of his public lectures. In his promotional activity he can be seen to raise the categories of private interest and general good only to tease them apart in such a fashion as to maintain the seeming of his disinterested benevolence.

Taylor's advertisements elicited several responses. On 24 October 1759, one week after the appearance of Taylor's advertisement, a short pseudonymous poem entitled *"The* WONDERS *of* EDINBURGH" appeared, which is worth giving in full:

> Six pence we'll give th' Infirmary, no more,
> To see the LION, and to hear him roar.
> A CAMEL and a DROMEDARY too
> Now for as little are expos'd to view.
> But ere you go their properties to spy,
> Let Doctor TAYLOR regulate your eye
> For though it be afflicted with no ill,
> The Chevalier will make it better still.
> Whatever some may of these creatures say,
> He is a greater rarity than they.
> He can our eyes at pleasure ope or shut,
> As boys by turns blow candles in or out.
> What though some, envious of his growing fame,
> His deep incisions and bold slashes blame,
> If those who from him no relief receive,
> His matchless skill, when they his chambers leave,
> With half an eye, 'twas all he left, perceive.
> In ev'ry kingdom, dukedom, province, town,
> Has he rais'd contributions of renown.

> The frows of Holland erst who could but stare,
> He taught to ogle with a killing air;
> And, which ful well entitles him to rise,
> Made mighty monarchs see with their own eyes.
> Of wonders Edinburgh has such a store,
> The curious French will certainly come o'er.

Donations to the Royal Infirmary, Edinburgh's public hospital, are portrayed as falling, along with the takings of the entrepreneur who was at the time displaying a dromedary and camel at the head of the Royal Mile. To draw particular attention to the closing lines first, it is worth bearing in mind that the Edinburgh periodical press at the time was filled with reports of a possible invasion by French forces, and also carried in the autumn of 1759 a controversy surrounding the collection of subscriptions for the clothing of 362 French soldiers held prisoner in Edinburgh Castle. The French kept escaping, thus making the task of generating sympathy for their plight and collecting subscriptions rather more difficult than it might otherwise have been. Despite this scandal, the author notes that the French are more likely to arrive as tourists than conquerors. It is worthwhile drawing attention to both Taylor's and this pseudonymous author's European sensibilities: in a mocking revision of Taylor's European credentials and self-fashioned appellation of "Chevalier," sly attention is drawn to the "Frows of Holland," whose sexual nature has been refreshed by his attentions. It is not terribly far from the reference to the "Frows of Holland" to the problems of foreign kingship and usurpation so recently resolved, for he has "Made mighty monarchs," both in Britain and abroad, "see with their own eyes." The poem draws attention to the commercial resonances of Taylor's advertisements: the very field his advertising sought to suppress, by its comparison of Taylor's public performance to those of the camel, dromedary and lion which were then being exhibited. In a manner reminiscent of Taylor's own practice, the display of animals was itinerant, barnstorming a succession of Scottish towns and promoting itself in the periodical press as it went. Taylor's presence and advertisement in Edinburgh thus begins, quite inadvertently, to involve politics both national and local: Taylor has been able to "raise contributions" for his own work in "ev'ry kingdom, dukedom, province, town," as donations to the public hospital decline. On the one hand, this poem testifies to the excess of signification generated by Taylor's promotional method: an awkward profusion of locally generated meanings attached to his barnstorming presence. On the other, of course, such a poem records the success of Taylor's promotional method, and serves further to promote his singular skills. As we know, both the proprietors of newspapers and the advertisers therein sought ways throughout the eighteenth century to avoid the tax upon advertisements. The tone of this piece suggests that it is no "puff," that it is not an advertisement masquerading as occasional verse. Intention need not mask effect, however, as revealed by a second poem inspired by Taylor's visit to Edinburgh, entitled "CUPID A PATIENT: – Addressed to Dr TAYLOR, the celebrated oculist," which is a doggerel play upon Ovid's "Amor est medicabilis arte." The anonymous author, having noted Taylor's "establish'd vogue," questions his financial (and sexual) motives: "But don't despise the wicked elf, / Though he pretend he's poor; / For many a man besides myself / Will club to pay his cure."[19] The poet associates Taylor with Cupid on a straightforward level: both characters in the poem have the power to woo and win women who are unable to "see" their suitor's charms. What is more, though, Taylor is cast as he whose powers are so great as to assure Cupid, were cupid to be treated by him, of a correct aim very time: Taylor will guarantee that the course of Love's arrows will run straight. Taylor will ask no money for this service, although Cupid, upon treatment, may see some profit: "By which he ne'er will earn his bread, / While he's bereav'd of fight; / But by him money would be made, / Could he but aim aright."[20] The poet's lewd commentary on Taylor is all the more powerful for its presence on the same page as one of Taylor's own advertisements for his lectures, where subscribers are assured that "His magnificent apparatus is already arrived at York, so that, no doubt, it will be here in time." As the poet suggests in conclusion, perhaps there is in the end a financial motive behind Taylor's remarkable advertisements: "I languish for a heavenly fair, / Who's worth ten thousand pound; / Of which I'll give him two, if her / He will to purpose wound."[21] Attention is drawn then to the economic sphere, both in this poem and that of "*The* WONDERS *of* EDINBURGH," an attention that the advertisement of medical products, certainly Taylor's own advertisements, sought to mask in favour of a lexis of disinterested benevolence. The practice and content of advertisements are appropriated and recast by such satirical poetry, a field of moral promotion and rebuttal made possible and contained within the newspaper press.

To conclude, between 1729 and 1786, advertisements in the Scottish newspaper press changed. They grew more sophisticated and more widespread. There are clear links between governmental, executive, and judicial authorities and the advertisement of medical material. Further, these authorities were first supplemented and then effectively superseded by appeals to the dialogic authority inherent in published testimonies and, later, a community of debate such as that found in the *Edinburgh Chronicle*.

Crucially, there was some kind of watershed in the composition of advertisements in the Edinburgh periodical press that occurred around 1745. Much of the theoretical work that could accompany the conjunction of such themes has been omitted here, but there are a number of ways in which this kind of evidence may be significant. It would appear that in the period around 1745, though with a nascence before that time, there arose in Scotland a class of consumers who were interested in branded products which aligned themselves through their marketing with images of national, and for that we may read British, authority. That has implications for the consumption, marketing, creation, and meaning of literary texts too.

In a much broader way, the development of marketing techniques such as the open letter reflects a language of community and sociability that found its fullest eighteenth-century expression in the philosophical texts of Scottish Enlightenment. Taylor's text responded to its society by upholding the image of the doctor as one who operates without concern for finance, the doctor as practitioner of a humane profession. As instances of British nationhood were used to sell products, there simultaneously arose a discourse that looked elsewhere for its guarantees of economic (and moral) value, one that sought some sense of communal approbation and well-being. That in turn was rooted firmly in the moral discourses of the Scottish eighteenth century, particularly those concerning the necessity of "good agreement" advanced in Adam Smith's *The Theory of Moral Sentiments* (1759), where "good agreement" is a necessary if problematic precondition for the proper functioning and right governance of any society. It is a short step from the philosophical necessity of "good agreement" to the kinds of publicized "good agreement," the public and communal affirmation of benevolence, the invocation and discussion of private well-being and public good, that a phenomenon such as the Chevalier Taylor's represented. Let us recall the lexis of guarantee, authority, and duty within the nexus of Taylor's presence in Edinburgh, and the invocation of necessity in the earlier advertisement for Speediman's remedy, where advertisement was necessary for the health of the public, and where the text suggested that to inform the afflicted of the availability of the remedy was also a moment of duty. As advertisements in the newspaper press of eighteenth-century Scotland changed over the course of the century, then, it seems wise to attend to the political and cultural history that affected them: to do so is to do critical justice to a prose form (advertisements) and a newspaper press (the Scottish) that deserve continuing attention.

NOTES

Presented to "The News, 1600–1800: New Approaches to Newspaper History in the Seventeenth and Eighteenth Centuries", CES, London, Saturday 10 May 1998.

1. *"To Mr* ROBRET [*sic*] Burns, *Ayrshire,"* *The Edinburgh Evening Courant*, 12 April 1787.
2. This paper is in some ways a response to prevailing readings of the Scottish newspaper as a simple adjunct to the London press. See the useful essays collected in Robin Myers and Michael Harris (eds.), *Serials and their Readers, 1620–1914* (Winchester: St. Paul's Bibliographies, 1993).
3. See George Chalmers, *The Life of Thomas Ruddiman, A.M.* (London: John Stockdale and Edinburgh: William Laing, 1794), 206–7: "[Thomas Ruddiman] lost his only son, at the age of thirty-three. This son, who bore his own name, and was the hope of his years, was appointed the principal manager of *The Caledonian Mercury*, when James Grant, the active partner, rushed into rebellion, in November 1745. *The Caledonian Mercury* was regarded with particular jealousy, and its circulation was much impeded, by the ruling powers, in Scotland, even after the terrors of insurrection had ceased. For an unlucky paragraph, which had been copied into the *Mercury*, from an English news-paper, in significant Italics, was young Ruddiman imprisoned, in December 1746. The merit, and solicitude, of his father, obtained his discharge, at the end of six weeks imprisonment. But the prisoner had meanwhile contracted a disease, in the Tolbooth of Edinburgh, which brought him to his grave, on the 9th of September 1747."
4. See John Alden's "Pills and Publishing: Some Notes on the English Book Trade, 1660–1715," *The Library*, Fifth Series, vol. 7 (1952): 21–37, for a full discussion of the connection between bookselling and patent medicine, a connection which Alden draws out in terms of their shared networks of distribution. John Feather alludes to the connection in two works: *The Provincial Book Trade in Eighteenth Century Britain* (Cambridge: Cambridge University Press, 1985), 83–4, and the *History of British Publishing* (Beckenham: Croom Helm, 1988), *passim*.
5. Ian H. Adams, *The Making of Urban Scotland* (London: Croom Helm, 1978), 73. See also David Daiches, *Edinburgh* (London: Hamish Hamilton, 1978), 105–71; Douglas Young, *Edinburgh in the Age of Sir Walter Scott* (Norman, OK: University of Oklahoma Press, 1965), *passim.*; R.H. Campbell, *Scotland since 1707: The Rise of an Industrial Society* (Edinburgh: John Donald, 1985), 4–19 and *passim*.
6. *The Caledonian Mercury*, 5 April 1786.
7. *The Caledonian Mercury,* 14 Nov. 1759.
8. See G.A. Cranfield, *The Development of the Provincial Newspaper, 1700–1760* (Oxford: Clarendon Press, 1962), 226.
9. *The Periodical Press of Great Britain and Ireland: or An Inquiry Into the state of the public journals, chiefly as regards their moral and political influence* (London: Hurst, Robinson, & Co.; Edinburgh: A. Constable and Co., 1824), 62.
10. In addition, Degravers gave public lectures: see *The Caledonian Mercury*, 20 Jan. 1787. Admittance to his lectures on the eye and ear cost one shilling.
11. *The Caledonian Mercury*, 11 Nov. 1786.
12. Ibid.
13. The advertisement was repeated: see *The Edinburgh Evening Courant*, 28 Nov. 1786. There the name "James Walker" is replaced with "David Walker," although the detail of his tumour remains the same.
14. Carol McGuirk, *Robert Burns and the Sentimental Era* (Athens, GA: University of Georgia Press, 1985), 100: "The poet writes not so much of the movement of the transcendental feeling within himself as of its power in the world at large." Although McGuirk does not specify just where that "transcendental feeling" in "the world at large" is located, I argue that at least one locus is in the languages of the newspaper press, specifically the discourses of advertising and its necessary presuppositions of its consumer's values.
15. For a discussion of the performative aspects of "sentiment," see Robert Markley, "Sentimentality as Performance: Shaftesbury, Sterne, and the Theatrics of Virtue," in Felicity

Nussbaum and Laura Brown (eds.), *The New Eighteenth Century; Theory, Politics, English Literature* (London: Methuen & Co. Ltd, 1987), 210–30. See especially p.211, where Markley offers "the affective spectacle of benign generosity" as a working definition of "Sentimentality." See also R.F. Brissenden, *Virtue in Distress: Studies in the Novel of Sentiment from Richardson to Sade* (London: Macmillan, 1974), *passim*, but especially pp.11–55: "'Sentimentalism': An Attempt at Definition." Brissenden correctly highlights the philosophical context of the term "sentiment," suggesting that "'sentiment' ultimately comes to mean – a *reasonable feeling* – not merely in the language of ordinary educated people but also in the writings of philosophers," 54.

16. See R.B. Walker, "Advertising in London Newspapers, 1650–1750," *Business History*, XV, 2 (1973), 129: "One means increasingly used to outwit readers was the 'puff', here taken to mean the publication of an advertisement in such a way as to make it appear as news. Steele inserted in the *Spectator* puffs for actors, wine merchants, book sellers and quack doctors, and Samuel Foote made the plot of his play *The Bankrupt* hinge upon a false news item published for payment. Even the obituary of a doctor might contain a puff for the medicines that his widow would continue to sell. The office copy of the *General Advertiser* in 1744 shows how puffs were paid for at the usual advertising rates and, a signal advantage, the advertisement tax was evaded."

17. McGuirk, *Robert Burns and the Sentimental Era*.

18. The *Caledonian Mercury*, 11 Nov. 1786. The letter was reprinted in the *Edinburgh Evening Courant*, 13 Nov. 1786. There is no evidence available to establish whether the second appearance of the letter was the result of the author's having submitted it to the two newspapers, or if the *Edinburgh Evening Courant* had simply lifted some interesting copy from its rival in circulation and politics.

19. "To the EDINBURGH CHRONICLE. CUPID A PATIENT: Addressed to Dr TAYLOR, the celebrated oculist," *The Edinburgh Chronicle*, 31 Oct. 1759, st. 5.

20. Ibid., st. 9.

21. Ibid., st. 10.

Abstracts

The Decorum of News *by Fritz Levy*

The coming of the coranto, in the 1620s, marked a major shift in the process by which the dissemination of news moved from being slow, intermittent, and occasional to being relatively consistent and regular, and, as patterns of distribution were established, more rapid as well. Though the specific cause of the transformation was the need of the government to control the flow of news, such general factors as the growth of London as a political and intellectual centre, and a shift in social markers, such as those limiting access to news, also played their parts.

"The Itch Grown a Disease": Manuscript Transmission of News in the Seventeenth Century *by Ian Atherton*

Manuscript news – newsletters and separates – has been much neglected by historians, yet until the eighteenth century it was in many ways more important than printed news. Since many newsletters were written to a specific addressee, they allow the relationship between writer and reader to be studied, showing how attitudes to the news framed its writing and reception, and revealing hierarchies of news by source, genre, and gender. The later seventeenth century saw the form of manuscript news change to copy more nearly printed newspapers; nevertheless, the role of manuscript news in polarizing political debate has been overestimated by other historians.

Pamphlet Plays in the Civil War News Market: Genre, Politics, and "Context" *by S.J. Wiseman*

This article analyses the place of popular pamphlets, especially pamphlet plays in the political culture of the English civil war. It argues that these texts, with others, invite a reappraisal of the boundaries of the currently constituted canon of civil war political thought.

Women in the Business of Revolutionary News: Elizabeth Alkin, "Parliament Joan," and the Commonwealth Newsbook *by Marcus Nevitt*

This is an attempt to explore the relationship between gender, individual agency, and modes of news production in the middle decades of the seventeenth century. It foregrounds the collative and collective nature of the news trade in order to demonstrate the manner in which some women could deploy the collective material practices of newsbook publication to gain a space in the public sphere. Such practices are viewed as similar although less grandiloquent counterparts to the rhetorical strategies of self-effacement deployed by so many female pamphleteers to the same end at this time. In particular the article draws on extensive archival research to reveal the activities of Elizabeth Alkin (or "Parliament Joan" as she was dubbed by her male contemporaries) one of the most active "she-Intelligencers" of this period.

The Newspaper, Public Opinion, and the Public Sphere in the Seventeenth Century *by Joad Raymond*

The article discusses the model of a "public sphere" of rational critical debate formulated by Jürgen Habermas. It suggests that recent attempts to relocate the genesis of this public sphere in seventeenth-century Britain overlook the specific characteristics that Habermas attributes to it: reason, inclusiveness, and non-instrumentality. The reality of seventeenth-century debate, and the practicalities of the book trade ill fit this ideal type. The creation of an informed and critical public depended at least as much on commerce and polemical conflict as on open and reasoned exchange, and a fuller account of public opinion needs both more specific research and a model sensitive to these dichotomies.

Timely Notices: The Uses of Advertising and its Relationship to News during the Late Seventeenth Century *by Michael Harris*

Advertising developed in a variety of forms from the first invention of printing. With the new technology it became possible to produce and publish uniform texts in large quantities, and the material which fitted this new production capacity most effectively was the advertisement. One line of output, combining commercial interest and public benefit, was developed through an engagement with the printed serial. This article contains an analysis of some of the forms of advertising which were deployed during the later seventeenth century, suggests how they were related to news, and indicates the range of uses to which this specific form of printed information could be put. In particular, it shows how the producers of newspapers became agents in the information business, and uses the publications of John Houghton to illustrate the process.

Constructing the Frameworks of Desire: How Newspapers Sold Books in the Seventeenth and Eighteenth Centuries *by Christine Ferdinand*

This article briefly examines the history of book advertising from classical times, before turning to an investigation of the tactics seventeenth- and eighteenth-century booksellers used to create and sustain a market for their publications. The most ingenious were associated with the periodical press: in the first place periodicals provided a regular, reliable medium for advertising that became increasingly sophisticated, incorporating straightforward ads, invitations to subscribers, and even books sold in affordable weekly parts. Then, of course, the networks that supported the delivery of periodicals also provided the ideal mechanism for delivering books to distant customers.

"Stung into action …": Medicine, Professionalism, and the News *by G.S. Rousseau*

The development of a medical press in the English language occurred gradually rather than precipitously over the period 1660–1820, and was especially spurred by the professionalization of medicine into colleges and societies rather than medical methodologies or paradigms in crisis. Medical knowledge in this early modern period was diversely construed, even hotly contested; most routinely recognized as *certain knowledge* only when incorporated into printed form that encoded it into "publication." This step from print to publication constitutes the main thrust of the hypothesis. The author explains what publication amounted to, and under what specific conditions medical publication was occurring in this long eighteenth century. Habermas' theories about the public sphere are invoked, as are the views of several contemporary historians of early modern prose who have pondered the relations between knowledge and publication. *Group publication* among doctors is isolated here as a test case: first among a group of Scottish physicians, and then by established London physicians in the College of Physicians putatively attacked by the first group. The second established group can thus be said to have been "stung into publication" by the first, and the relation between medical knowledge, medical certainty, print culture and the requirement of publication brought into closer association in this early modern period than they have been before.

Tropes of Promotion and Wellbeing: Advertisement and the Eighteenth-Century Scottish Periodical Press *by Hamish Mathison*

The article examines the development of advertising language in the eighteenth-century Scottish newspaper press. It argues that the events of

1745 influenced advertising practice in Scotland, and that eighteenth-century philosophical and medical discourses were appropriated by advertisers in order to promote their goods and services. On the basis of these two observations, the paper examines a series of promotional campaigns from the mid and late eighteenth century: one on behalf of an Edinburgh surgeon; one on behalf of Robert Burns; one on behalf of the "Chevalier" Taylor, an itinerant surgeon of the eye. It concludes that emergent discourses of nationhood and virtue lie at the heart of advertising practice in the eighteenth century.

Notes on Contributors

Ian Atherton is Lecturer in History at Keele University, joint editor of *Norwich Cathedral: Church, City and Diocese, 1096–1996* (1996), and author of *Ambition and Failure in Stuart England: The Career of John, 1st Viscount Scudamore* (forthcoming).

Christine Ferdinand is Fellow Librarian at Magdalen College Oxford; she writes on the eighteenth-century book and newspaper trade. She is the author of *Benjamin Collins and the Provincial Newspaper Trade in the Eighteenth Century* (1997).

Michael Harris is Senior Lecturer in History in the Faculty of Continuing Education at Birbeck College. He has published extensively on the history of print and in particular the history of newspapers. He is author of *London Newspapers in the Age of Walpole* and is currently working on a full-scale history of news from 1660 to 1720.

Fritz Levy teaches at the University of Washington, where he has been since 1960. He has written on topics such as Tudor historiography, Philip Sidney, Francis Bacon, and the spread of ideas among the gentry.

Hamish Mathison is a Teaching Fellow at the University of Aberdeen, and has published on Robert Burns and on the eighteenth-century Scottish Book Trade. He is currently working on a history of the eighteenth-century newspaper in Scotland, and co-editing a volume on the relationship between newspapers in Ireland and Scotland in the "long" eighteenth century.

Marcus Nevitt is based at Sheffield University's Centre for Early Modern Studies where he is in the final stages of a Ph.D. on the relationship between female agency, prophecy, and polemic in revolutionary Britain.

Joad Raymond is a Lecturer in English at the University of Aberdeen. He is the editor of *Making the News: An Anthology of the Newsbooks of Revolutionary England* (1993), the author of *The Invention of the Newspaper: English Newsbooks 1641–1649* (1996), and of articles on seventeenth-century literature and politics.

George Rousseau is Research Professor of the Humanities at De Montfort University in Leicester. His primary interest lies in the interface of literature and medicine, a subject on which he has written several books, especially a trilogy published by the Manchester University Press (1991–92), *Perilous Enlightenment*. For this work on literature and medicine he was recently awarded a three-year Leverhulme Trust Fellowship in 1999–2001. His most recent book, written jointly with Roy Porter, is *Gout: The Patrician Malady* (1998).

S.J. Wiseman is a Lecturer in English at Warwick University; in April 1999 she takes up a post as Reader in Renaissance Literature at Birkbeck College. She is the author of *Aphra Behn* (1996) and of *Drama and Politics in the English Civil War* (1998).

Index

Abel Roper 149
Ackers, Charles, printer 159, 170–72
Addison, Joseph 128, 132, 176, 178, 179, 180
advertising 26, 128, 141–54 *passim*
  books 141–2, 153, 157–73, 215–8
  language of 167–8, 172–3, 206–23
  medical 145, 153, 160, 161, 168, 177, 181, 184–8, 206–23
  as a means of catching criminals 126, 147–8
Akenside, Mark 192
alcohol 115–16
alehouses and taverns 44, 54, 117
Alkin, Elizabeth 87–102
Allde, Edward 160
Alsop, Benjamin 164
Alsop, Bernard 160
Anderson, Benedict 130
Andrews, Alexander 4
Angel, Norman 6
Anglo-Dutch Wars 127, 146
  second 39, 109, 126, 153
Anne, Queen 211
anonymity 118, 121, 127, 184, 193
  pseudonymity 215, 220
Appadurai, Arjun 67, 79
Archer, Thomas 34
Arlington, Henry Bennet, Lord 49, 55
Arwaker, Edmund, poet 120
Astley, Thomas 170–72
Athenian Mercury, The (1691–) 117, 132
auctions 160
Aylmer, Brabazon 164

Bacon, Francis 15, 16, 51, 55–6, 58, 186, 188
Baker, George 192
Bakhtin, Mikhail 72
Baldwin, Richard, printer 159, 171
Balfour, John 219
Ball, Henry 121, 122
ballads 18–19, 26, 29, 39, 44
Bank of England 112
Barry, Edward 192
Bartholomew Fairing, A (1649) 76
Basset, Thomas 164
Bastwicke, John 4
Bates Francis, publisher 96
Bates, William 164
Battaile fought betweene Count Maurice of
Nassaw (1600) 24
Battle of Nieuport (1600) 31
Beaumont, Ursula, correspondent 49
Beecher, Sir William 41
Bennet, H.S. 159
Berkeley, Bishop George 184
Bible and scripture 14, 58
Bibliotheca Universalis (1688) 162
Bills of Mortality 51, 94, 97, 132, 151, 162
Birch, Thomas 1
Bird, Christopher 20
Bishops' Wars 42–3, 52
Blackbourne, Robert 102
Bodley, Thomas 58
Border, Daniel, journalist 87, 94–6, 98
Boston News-Letter 55
Bourne, Henry Richard Fox 4
Bourne, Nicholas 160, 161
Bowles, Thomas, *Compendious and Rational Institution* 167
Bowyer, William, printer 170
Bradford, Thomas 39
branded products 208–9
Brathait, Richard, *Whimzies* (1631) 51
Briefe discourse of the assault (1582) 24
Bristol 44, 58, 130
British Library/Museum 1, 193
British Medical Journal (1786–) 186
Brocklesby, Richard 190–91
Brown, Thomas 115–16
Browne, Montefort 183
Bruster, Douglas 33
Buc, Sir George, censor 29–30
Buckingham, George Villiers, Duke of 44, 57, 58
Bulstrode, Edward, *Reports* 164
Burby, Cuthbert, publisher 160
Burghe, John 50, 52
Burns, Robert 212–13, 215–18
Burton, Henry 4
Butler, Samuel, satirist 124
Butter, Nathaniel 160, 161

Cable News Network 176
Caledonian Mercury 1, 206–23
Cambridge 117
Campion, Thomas 23
Care, Henry 126, 163
Carleton, Dudley 20, 27, 29
Carlyle, Thomas 5
carriers 43

Books of Related Interest

The Intersections of the Public and Private Spheres in Early Modern England

Paul R. Backscheider and **Timothy Dykstal** (Eds)

Political revolutions often coincide with private upheavals. For some time cultural historians and theorists have debated the usefulness of the distinction between public and private spheres. This collection is a significant re-consideration of the usefulness of the public and private sphere model and offers important revisionary interpretations of many texts and of their contribution to modern thought and institutions.

280 pages 1996
0 7146 4275 4 paper

The Emergence of Quaker Writing

Dissenting Literature in Seventeenth-Century England

Thomas N. Corns and **David Loewenstein** (Eds)

This collection of essays by literary scholars and historians looks at the diversity of seventeenth-century Quaker writing, examining its rhetoric, its lemical strategies, its purposeful use of the print medium, and the heroism and vehemence of its world vision. Essays consider the writing of women prophets such as Margaret Fell and Mary Penington, the rather different voices of George Fox in the 1650s and that of his posthumous Journal, the politeness of William Penn, Joseph Besse's chronicle of Quaker suffering and the organization of early Quaker publishing.

148 pages 1996
0 7146 4246 0 paper

FRANK CASS PUBLISHERS
Newbury House, 900 Eastern Avenue, Ilford, Essex, IG2 7HH
Tel: +44 (0)181 599 8866 Fax: +44 (0)181 599 0984 E-mail: info@frankcass.com
NORTH AMERICA
5804 NE Hassalo Street, Portland, OR 97213 3644, USA
Tel: 800 944 6190 Fax: 503 280 8832 E-mail: cass@isbs.com
Website: www.frankcass.com

Telling People What To Think
Early Eighteenth-Century Periodicals from **The Review** *to* **The Rambler**
J.A. Downie and **Thomas N. Corns** (Eds)

'... the book reflects solid empirical research on a number of individual titles in a buoyant period in the history of the periodical press ...'
Review of English Studies

144 pages 1993
0 7146 4508 7 cloth

Pamphlet Wars
Prose in the English Revolution
James Holstun (Ed)

The English Revolution of 1642–60 produced an explosion of stylistically and ideologically diverse pamphlet literature. The essays collected here focus on the prose of this new revolutionary era, and the new public sphere it helped to create.

232 pages 1992
0 7146 3548 1 cloth

Coleridge and the Armoury of the Human Mind
Essays on his Prose Writings
Peter J. Kitson and **Thomas N. Corns** (Eds)

This book is a wide-ranging collection of writing by specialists in Coleridge and Romantic literature, on the subject of Coleridge's prose. Breaking new ground, these essays celebrate the richness and complexity of this highly influential prose writer.

128 pages 1991
0 7146 3426 3 cloth

FRANK CASS PUBLISHERS
Newbury House, 900 Eastern Avenue, Ilford, Essex, IG2 7HH
Tel: +44 (0)181 599 8866 Fax: +44 (0)181 599 0984 E-mail: info@frankcass.com
NORTH AMERICA
5804 NE Hassalo Street, Portland, OR 97213 3644, USA
Tel: 800 944 6190 Fax: 503 280 8832 E-mail: cass@isbs.com
Website: www.frankcass.com